Philip Sparrow Tells All

Philip Sparrow Tells All

Lost Essays by
Samuel Steward,
Writer, Professor,
Tattoo Artist

EDITED BY

Jeremy Mulderig

With a Foreword by
Justin Spring

The University of Chicago Press
Chicago and London

Samuel Steward taught at both Loyola University and DePaul University in Chicago and ran a famous tattoo parlor on the city's south side. His books include *Dear Sammy: Letters from Gertrude Stein and Alice B. Toklas*, *Bad Boys and Tough Tattoos*, and the Phil Andros series of erotic novels. **Jeremy Mulderig** is Vincent de Paul Associate Professor of English, Emeritus, at DePaul University in Chicago.

The University of Chicago Press, Chicago 60637
The University of Chicago Press, Ltd., London
© 2015 by The University of Chicago
Foreword © 2015 by Justin Spring
All rights reserved. Published 2015.
Printed in the United States of America

24 23 22 21 20 19 18 17 16 15   1 2 3 4 5

ISBN-13: 978-0-226-30454-0 (cloth)
ISBN-13: 978-0-226-30468-7 (paper)
ISBN-13: 978-0-226-30471-7 (e-book)
DOI: 10.7208/chicago/9780226304717.001.0001

Library of Congress Cataloging-in-Publication Data

Steward, Samuel M., author.
   [Works. Selections]
   Philip Sparrow tells all : lost essays by Samuel Steward, writer, professor, tattoo artist / edited by Jeremy Mulderig ; with a foreword by Justin Spring.
        pages ; cm
   Includes bibliographical references and index.
   Essays.
   ISBN 978-0-226-30454-0 (cloth : alk. paper) — ISBN 978-0-226-30468-7 (pbk. : alk. paper) — ISBN 978-0-226-30471-7 (ebook)
   I. Mulderig, Jeremy, editor. II. Spring, Justin, 1962– writer of foreword. III. Title.
   PS3537.T479A6 2015
   814'.54—dc23

                                    2015019943

♾ This paper meets the requirements of ANSI/NISO Z39.48-1992 (Permanence of Paper).

To Effie and Nell,
who made all things possible

CONTENTS

Foreword   ix

Acknowledgments   xiii

Sources Cited by Short Title   xv

Textual Note   xvii

Introduction: Reading Samuel Steward's Lost Essays, 1944–49   1

1   The Victim's Viewpoint: On Sublimated Sadism;
     or, the Dentist as Iago (January 1944)   17

2   On Cryptography (October 1944)   21

3   On Alcoholics Anonymous (November 1944)   27

4   On Fifteen Years of Lent (January 1945)   33

5   On Soldiers and Civilians (February 1945)   39

6   On How to Cook a Wolf (March 1945)   45

7   On How to Be a Spy (April 1945)   51

8   On Psychiatry (May 1945)   59

9   On Balletomania (June 1945)   65

10   On Books from Prison (September 1945)   73

11   On Cemeteries (October–November 1945)   81

12   On a Call to Paris (March 1946)   89

13   On the Importance of Dying Young (April 1946)   97

14   On Chicago (August 1946)   105

15   On Operas and Operating (December 1946)   113

16   On Men and Their Feathers (January 1947)   119

17   On Gertrude Stein (February 1947)   127

18 On Little White Ribbons (March 1947)   135

19 On Being Musclebound (April 1947)   141

20 On Teaching (November 1947)   149

21 On Fabulous, Fabulous Field's (January 1948)   155

22 On Fair, Fantastic Paris (April 1948)   161

23 On Ulysses, Grown Old (May 1948)   169

24 On the Comic Spirit (June 1948)   175

25 On Keepsakes, Gew-Gaws, and Baubles (September 1948)   181

26 [On Mohammed Zenouhin] (October 1948)   187

27 On the Dream, the Illusion (December 1948)   193

28 On Time-Saving Devices (February 1949)   199

29 On Getting to Be Forty (May 1949)   205

30 A Modest Proposal (July 1949)   211

Appendix 1: Essays in the *Illinois Dental Journal* by Philip Sparrow   217

Appendix 2: Book-Review Articles in the *Illinois Dental Journal* by Samuel Steward   221

Notes   223
Index   233

FOREWORD

I wish I could have included more of these essays in my 2010 biography, *Secret Historian: The Life and Times of Samuel Steward, Professor, Tattoo Artist, and Sexual Renegade*. They chronicle a substantial period in Steward's development, both as a writer and as a human being, and—just as importantly to a biographer—a period when he was writing little else.

The pieces were written during the 1940s, as Steward was passing through the most alcoholic period of his life. He seems to have undertaken them primarily in an effort to continue to write and publish. (Steward's really charming first novel, *Angels on the Bough*, had been published to fine reviews in 1936; as a younger man, he had also published a slim volume of poems; since then, there had only been several unpublished and unpublishable novels.) But these essays were also erotically inspired: composed as a favor to his dentist, Dr. William P. Schoen, who bore a striking resemblance to the actor Gregory Peck and who was looking for content to enhance the obscure professional journal he edited for the Illinois State Dental Society. Steward was infatuated with Schoen and called him "Dr. Pretty"—a play on words, for *schön* is German for the same. Thornton Wilder, one of Steward's many sex partners during the 1940s, had urged Steward to write essays and articles for magazines as a way of keeping himself engaged as a writer. But far from the New York magazine-publishing world, and never too sure of his talents, Steward didn't even approach the great popular magazines of the era, settling instead upon a little journal for Illinois dentists run by a man he wanted very much to seduce.

The essays are based in personal experience: reflecting, for example, upon how, during the war, Steward had briefly joined the navy, only to be ejected for food allergies; how he had taught cryptography to undergraduates as part of the war effort; how he had worked as a "super" at the Lyric Opera House; how he had adored Gertrude Stein; and even how he had come to loathe teaching. Steward had many personal ups and downs during the period he was writing these essays: having quit his teaching position at Loyola, he was unemployed and broke for a while. He disgraced himself among his friends with bad behavior brought on by heavy drinking—and one senses some of his anger and emotional instability in these essays, most notably the last of them. His private life during these years was similarly unstable: he was having sex in bathhouses, collecting dirty limericks and other graffiti, writing amateur pornography, hiring hustlers, picking up sailors in bars, and sometimes being beaten up or robbed by his tricks—experiences he came to savor even as they humiliated him. For several years he worked at rewriting the *World Book Encyclopedia*; and when the World Book gig came to an end, he took a make-ends-meet job in the book shop at Marshall Field's department store. Eventually, and after a good deal of drifting and soul-searching and worrying about poverty, he found his way back into teaching, this time at DePaul University.

As Steward's biographer, I found the years 1944–49 a near-blank so far as his archives and papers are concerned. Apart from the *Illinois Dental Journal* essays, I had only his amateur pornography (the "Toilet Correspondence," now housed in the Kinsey archive), a little book of dirty limericks, a collection of toilet graffiti, a few important letters, and his own later recollections of those years, as he had written them up into several memoirs, only one of which was ever published. And yet these were the years during which Steward's youthful hopes of literary celebrity and academic security came to an end. So too did his two most significant literary friendships, with Gertrude Stein (by her death) and Thornton Wilder (by mutual agreement). As a result, the *Illinois Dental Journal* articles were of key importance in charting his transition to a new way of living and thinking. By the end of it, in 1950, Steward had joined Alcoholics Anonymous and got himself sober. He had met Alfred Kinsey. He was well along in his study of tattooing. And he had committed himself ever more deeply to sexual recordkeeping—his own, highly personal form of sex research. In doing so, he had begun keeping not only the Stud File card catalog, but the remarkable journal—now in the Kinsey library—that would chronicle the next decade of his very active sex life, and, in a sense, replace the *Illinois Dental Journal* articles as the main testament of his everyday life experiences in Chicago, Paris, and San Francisco during the 1950s.

In my work as a biographer, I read Steward's *Illinois Dental Journal* essays with a mixture of emotions. I took great pleasure in reading them, of course. But who was this Philip Sparrow, so amusing and quirky and desperate to entertain—and why, given his obvious wit, his fine prose style, his erudition and intelligence, was he publishing such finely crafted essays in a so hopelessly obscure magazine? Why should a writer of such talent throw his efforts away in such a manner? Along with pleasure, I felt pathos for this pseudonymous author, who in so many ways seems just this side of a lost soul.

How wonderful then to have this selection of the best of his *Illinois Dental Journal* essays rescued from oblivion. Beautifully edited and annotated, they have been selected and arranged for the reader in a way that shows off the evolving Samuel Steward of the 1940s to best possible advantage. I can only hope that in the years to come, more of Steward's fine, lost writings—from his impassioned essays for *Der Kreis* to his whimsical pornography as Phil Andros—will similarly find their way back into print.

Justin Spring

ACKNOWLEDGMENTS

Everyone who writes on Samuel Steward owes a fundamental debt to Michael Williams, who rescued, sorted, and preserved eighty boxes of Steward's manuscripts, letters, journals, photographs, and miscellaneous documents after his death in 1993, and to Justin Spring, who later spent a decade of his life turning these materials into the biography that has established Steward as a major figure in twentieth-century gay history and literature. I am very grateful to Michael for generously permitting the use of documents and photographs from Steward's papers and to Justin for his interest in this project and his reading of the manuscript, which benefited greatly from his encyclopedic knowledge of Steward's life. This book would simply not have been possible without their support. Nor would it have achieved this form without the enthusiastic endorsement and editorial attention of Douglas Mitchell at the University of Chicago Press, with whom it has been my great good fortune to work.

I am deeply indebted to my DePaul University colleagues Bill Fahrenbach and Andrew Suozzo for their sustained interest in this project and their wise advice; they too played key roles in making this book a reality. My indefatigable friend John Marchese read the manuscript with care, insight, and an uncanny ability to identify the most obscure allusions in Steward's text; his contributions, for which these thanks are woefully inadequate, improved the presentation of every essay here. I am very grateful as well to Douglas Martin, who read and commented on the manuscript from the invaluable perspective of Steward's former student and friend. Thanks also go to Debra Moddelmog and Joe Ponce for their helpful notes on an earlier draft of the introduction. Many other friends and colleagues willingly allowed themselves to be drawn into the world of Steward's *Illinois Dental Journal* essays during the development of this book; I especially wish to thank Lesley Kordecki, Lucy Rinehart, Helen Marlborough, Miles Harvey, James Murphy, Jonathan Gross, James Fairhall, Bernadette Steinmeyer, Elizabeth Birmingham, and Mary Ann Maguire for their interest and assistance.

I am very grateful for the generous financial support for this project provided by the Vincent de Paul Professorship Fund at DePaul University. At the Kinsey Institute for Research in Sex, Gender, and Reproduction, Catherine Roehr-Johnson and Shawn Wilson welcomed me and made available the institute's collection of Steward's journals and letters. Thanks also go to Timothy Young of the Beinecke Library of Yale University, where it was my particular pleasure to be able to work with the papers of Steward and Gertrude Stein and where the reading-room staff may well be the most knowledgeable, helpful, patient, and relentlessly cheerful group of people I have ever met. Finally, this book benefitted in countless ways from the expertise of the editorial and production staff at the University of Chicago Press, among whom I particularly wish to thank Kyle Wagner, Jenni Fry, Amy Smith, Isaac Tobin, Joseph Claude, and Carrie Adams.

J. M.

SOURCES CITED BY SHORT TITLE

"Autobiography"   Steward, Samuel M. Clean typescript of unpublished
                   autobiography, untitled, 368 pages (revised version of
                   237-page typescript with holograph corrections dated
                   December 1, 1978). Yale Steward Papers, Box 19.

Bad Boys   Steward, Samuel M. *Bad Boys and Tough Tattoos: A
                   Social History of the Tattoo with Gangs, Sailors, and Street-
                   Corner Punks.* Binghamton: Harrington Park, 1990.

Chapters   Steward, Samuel M. *Chapters from an Autobiography.*
                   San Francisco: Grey Fox, 1981.

Dear Sammy   Steward, Samuel M., ed. *Dear Sammy: Letters from
                   Gertrude Stein and Alice B. Toklas.* Boston: Houghton
                   Mifflin, 1977.

IDJ   *Illinois Dental Journal.*

Kinsey Steward   Samuel Steward Collection, The Kinsey Institute for
Collection   Research in Sex, Gender, and Reproduction, Indiana
                   University.

OED   *Oxford English Dictionary.*

Spring   Spring, Justin. *Secret Historian: The Life and Times
                   of Samuel Steward, Professor, Tattoo Artist, and Sexual
                   Renegade.* New York: Farrar, Straus and Giroux, 2010.

Stein Letters   Gertrude Stein and Alice B. Toklas Papers, YCAL
MSS 77, Series II, Box 11. Yale Collection of American
Literature, Beinecke Rare Book and Manuscript
Library, Yale University.

Steward Letters   Gertrude Stein and Alice B. Toklas Papers, YCAL MSS
76, Series II, Box 126. Yale Collection of American
Literature, Beinecke Rare Book and Manuscript
Library, Yale University.

Yale Steward Papers   Samuel Steward Papers. General Collection, Beinecke
Rare Book and Manuscript Library, Yale University.

TEXTUAL NOTE

Only one of Steward's manuscripts for his *Illinois Dental Journal* essays exists—a photocopy he retained of the typescript of his essay intended for the October 1949 issue but never published, since his position with the journal was terminated after the July 1949 issue. But typographical errors in the published essays that Steward would certainly have corrected (for example, "Champs Elyssees") suggest that he did not have access to proofs of his essays before they appeared in print.

In the absence of other evidence, Steward's consistent stylistic preferences in his more carefully produced publications and in the unpublished typescript of his autobiography offer the best guidance for editing his *Illinois Dental Journal* essays. Steward's characteristic punctuation is often expressive rather than strictly correct (in all of his writing, for example, he favors commas between compound predicates, where modern usage would dictate no punctuation); it has been followed in all but a few cases where inconsistencies or obvious errors suggest a printing mistake rather than authorial intent. His idiosyncratic preference for British spellings (*lacklustre, meagre, litre, sombrely*) has also been preserved here, as has his consistent use of *coupla* for "couple of," a feature he seems to have borrowed from Gertrude Stein's spoken language. Steward's distinctive use of brackets and parentheses has also been retained: bracketed material is a comment on something immediately preceding; parentheses enclose material that is more properly parenthetical in nature.

In the course of more than five years of publication, wide variations in mechanics appeared in these essays as printed. In the interest of consistency and a readable text, open, closed, and hyphenated compounds have been brought into conformity with *Merriam-Webster's Collegiate Dictionary* and the *Chicago Manual of Style*, 16th edition, as have the presentation of book and film titles and the use of numerals versus written-out numbers. Diacritical marks in French terms and names—which Steward always includes in other publications—have been supplied where they were apparently dropped in the printing of these essays. Finally, obvious typographical errors (for example, "broadwalk at Atlantic City" for "boardwalk at Atlantic City," "not one noticed" for "no one noticed," and "Clare Booth Luce" for "Clare Boothe Luce") have been silently emended.

INTRODUCTION

Reading Samuel Steward's Lost Essays, 1944–49

Subscribers to the *Illinois Dental Journal* in January 1944 found something new among the publication's routine professional notices for dentists and its feature articles like "Sulfathiazole and Sulfadiazine Prophylaxis in Exodontia" and "Important Considerations in Porcelain Veneer Restoration": an essay by one Philip Sparrow, introduced by the journal's editor as a "nonprofessional writer" who, in a new monthly feature, would present a "'worm's-eye view' of the dentist, the dental office, dental methods, etc."[1] Such a bland introduction could hardly have prepared the dentist readers for an essay that began like this:

> There are some people of unjaundiced and unprejudiced eye who can admire in the digital dexterity of the dentist the same finger facility that marked a Rachmaninoff or a Paderewski; or who can perceive an aesthetic analogy between the delicate and torturing way a dentist plays on one's nerves and the smooth drawing of the bow across the strings that a Kreisler or a Heifetz is capable of; or profess to hear in the head-shuddering noise of a burr against an eye tooth the deep organ diapason of a Bach or a Pietro Yon. But we have never been able sufficiently to overcome our mundane emotions to appreciate such comparisons.[2]

Instead, Sparrow continued, he had concluded that dentists are less artists than sadists: like Shakespeare's villain Iago, he said, they seek a personal sense of superiority by making their patients suffer.

Philip Sparrow was actually Samuel M. Steward, and as the elaborate parallelism, clever analogies, and careful avoidance of a potential split infinitive in the passage above might suggest, he was in fact—among other things—a professional writer. Thanks to Justin Spring's recent biography—*Secret Historian: The Life and Times of Samuel Steward, Professor, Tattoo Artist, and Sexual Renegade* (New York: Farrar, Straus and Giroux, 2010)—today we have an extensive inventory of the many roles that Steward played during his life. Steward earned his PhD in English at The Ohio State University in 1934 and, at the time that he began writing as Philip Sparrow for the *Illinois Dental Journal*, was a professor in the English department at Loyola University Chicago. He had published scholarly articles and a novel that had won favorable reviews from the national press, and he counted Gertrude Stein and Thornton Wilder among his friends. In 1948, he began teaching English at DePaul University, a position from which he would be fired in 1956 when it became known that under the name of Phil Sparrow he was simultaneously operating a successful tattoo business on Chicago's Skid Row. Beginning in 1959, he became a regular contributor to *Der Kreis*, the pioneering gay magazine published in Switzerland from 1943 to 1967, and eventually wrote nearly a hundred articles and stories for *Der Kreis*, for the early Danish gay magazines *Eos* and *Amigo*, and in the 1980s for *The Advocate*.[3] A gay man who had discovered his sexuality as a boy in rural Ohio, he would have more than 4,500 sexual encounters during his life with eight hundred men, including all the members of his high-school basketball team, Rudolph Valentino, Lord Alfred Douglas, Roy Fitzgerald (later known to the world as Rock Hudson), a number of DePaul students, and very many sailors from the Great Lakes Naval Training Station north of Chicago[4]—all of which he meticulously documented in an alphabetical card file of his lifetime sexual contacts (labeled "Stud File") that would amaze the sex researcher Alfred Kinsey when they met in 1949.[5] After moving from Chicago to Berkeley, California, Steward became the tattoo artist of choice for the Hells Angels, while at the same time publishing distinctively literate gay erotic fiction under the name Phil Andros. His books late in life included an edition of Gertrude Stein's and Alice Toklas's letters to him, a memoir, a novel based on the life of the painter Sir Francis Rose, a book about the

Samuel Steward in the late 1940s. (Courtesy of the Estate of Samuel M. Steward)

tattoo business, and two murder mysteries featuring Stein and Toklas as sleuths.

This collection of Steward's contributions to the *Illinois Dental Journal* includes thirty of the fifty-six essays published between 1944 and 1949. After his first seven columns, the original plan for a monthly

Steward's card file of his lifetime sex partners. (Yale Steward Papers [author's photograph])

essay on dentistry from the patient's perspective was fortunately aban-
doned, and Steward began to write on a delightfully eclectic assortment
of topics—cryptography, psychiatry, espionage, opera, pet cemeteries,
bodybuilding, keepsakes, medieval recipes, Gertrude Stein, Chicago,
Paris, and the Women's Christian Temperance Union among them.
Available for the first time to a broad readership that Steward imagined
but never actually enjoyed, these engaging, richly allusive, often quirky,
and to date totally neglected essays not only demonstrate his stylistic
sophistication, breadth of knowledge, and mastery of the subjectivity
and informality associated with the familiar essay; they also present a
remarkably clear gay sensibility in an otherwise drab professional journal of the 1940s. As Steward's topics become increasingly autobiographical, his alter ego, Philip Sparrow, evolves into a multidimensional character whose experiences, personality, and wit become the focal point
of each essay—and whose homosexuality, though apparently beyond
the ken of most of his dentist readers, lies just beneath the surface of
the text.

Inventing Philip Sparrow

Steward's position as a monthly columnist in the *Illinois Dental Journal* arose out of pure coincidence: his personal dentist in Chicago, William P. Schoen, was at the time also the editor of the journal. "While I was at his mercy in the chair one day in 1943," Steward recalled later, "he talked me into starting a series of articles."[6] For Steward, whose writing career had stalled since the publication of his novel *Angels on the Bough* in 1936, the invitation provided his first extended opportunity to experiment with the genre of the familiar essay while at the same time pleasing Schoen, whom Steward found dashingly handsome and whom he referred to as "Dr. Pretty," a play on the German meaning of his name.[7] Steward and Schoen apparently agreed that his essays would appear under the heading "The Victim's Viewpoint" (a title perfectly suited to Steward's already well-defined masochistic inclinations) and that he would write using a pseudonym, for Steward had already begun contributing to the journal's annual book-review issue under his own name. Now he became Philip Sparrow, the name borrowed from the bird whose death is mourned in John Skelton's humorous sixteenth-century poem "The Book of Phillip Sparrow," a work that appealed to Steward as a "Rabelaisian hodge-podge of buffoonery and erotic hints."[8]

Neither Schoen nor Steward seems to have foreseen that the original plan for the Philip Sparrow essays was unsustainable, but after publishing just seven pieces about dentists and dentistry, Steward apparently realized that he had reached the limit of what could be done within such a confining rhetorical situation. At this point, therefore, the dentistry theme was discarded and the title of Steward's column was changed from "The Victim's Viewpoint" to simply "Philip Sparrow," complete with a sketch (almost certainly by Steward) of a newly hatched chick.[9] But the new focus on Sparrow as writer also presented a new rhetorical challenge: who was Philip Sparrow if not a dental patient, and what should he write about?

Steward's response to that question evidently evolved as the new series of essays progressed. He had brought wit and stylistic sophistication to the initial premise of the writer as dental patient, but in those first seven essays Sparrow had remained a largely abstract entity. In this

Philip Sparrow

On Cryptography

When Lysander of Sparta, who lived in 405 B.C., wanted to send to one of his generals a message not intended for prying eyes, he used one of two methods: if there were no great hurry, he shaved the head of a slave, wrote the communication on the fellow's pate, let the hair grow in, and started him on his way. Or if the message was urgent, he used a small round baton called a *scytale*, on which he wound in spiral fashion a soft leather belt, and then wrote his message along the length of the stick; when the belt was unwound it showed only a meaningless jumble of letters and fragments. But his generals had similar-sized batons, and it was simple for them by rewinding the belt to discover Lysander's orders. Suetonius, the Walter Winchell of ancient Rome, says that Julius Caesar used a secret cipher which consisted merely of shifting the alphabet by four spaces: thus, if Caesar wanted an *a*, he used an *e*, if a *b* an *f*, and so on. Francis Bacon, Lord Verulam, is said to have written a running story of his life into several of Shakespeare's plays by means of a cipher; and the whole wild argument over the authorship of the plays began with that crackpot idea.

Ciphers and codes—which are classed under the general term of cryptography, or secret writing intended for the purpose of conveying information to but a few chosen people—seem to be the particular joy and necessity of kings, diplomats, tramps, lovers, thieves, generals, and schoolboys. Especially in wartime is it imperative that communications be secret, because it would play hob with one side's plans if the enemy immediately knew what movements were contemplated, and acted to stop them. Ciphers in the last war had a tremendous role, and actually accounted in large measure for the defeat of Germany; in the present struggle, only one small story has leaked out about them; but that story told us that it was through the efforts of the cryptanalytic department in Washington that Axis messages sent to Germany from Argentina were broken down, resulting in Secretary Hull's stern denunciation of Argentina. It will be many years before the story is completely revealed, and perhaps it will never be.

In wartime, then, it is only natural that there be a renewed interest in this fascinating and complicated science. This enthusiasm is rather curiously handled; by a tacit and coy agreement, libraries in the Chicagoland area have withdrawn all books on cryptography from their shelves for the duration; yet for one dollar one may buy, over the counter in any bookstore, a reprint of one of the best books on codes and ciphers—Fletcher Pratt's "Secret and Urgent." One sometimes wonders just how a librarian's mind functions.*

In the layman's opinion, there is no distinction between the terms *code* and *cipher*, yet for the cryptographer they are miles apart. A *code* entails the use of a code-book, of which there must be many carefully guarded copies, on the field of battle, at the headquarters in the rear, and at the office of the general staff. Should a copy be lost, stolen, or photographed by the enemy, a whole new book must be composed, printed, and distributed. The code-books that the battleships of our navy carry are bound in lead, and are the first things to be thrown overboard in case of disaster. In a code-book, groups of five letters are arranged alphabetically, although the meanings of the groups are not close together. Thus, a message such as AWKLM AWKLN might when deciphered mean: "Am arriving at [AWKIM] five a.m." [AWKLN]. The advantages of a code-book are several: economy, because one

*No offense intended to the very capable Mrs. Josephine P. Hunt of the A.D.A.!

The first of Steward's *Illinois Dental Journal* essays published under the title "Philip Sparrow," October 1944.

passage from his first column, for example, the plural "we" not only sounds oddly impersonal but also leads to logical and grammatical complications that must have rankled Steward, always the careful writer:

> We have opened our mouth widely for many of these torturers, from Maine to Montana, and we are ready to swear that on more than one occasion—as we have been approached, lying there helpless and trembling—we have seen a diabolic gleam in their eyes as they reached for their tools. . . . Then they begin—but let us draw a curtain over this painful scene; even in thinking of it we have worked ourself into a cold dribble.[10]

In his attempts to define a more distinct voice for Sparrow in the newly conceived column, Steward seems to have chosen as one model the seventeenth-century essays of Francis Bacon (1561–1626). Like Bacon, he began several of his new essays with an aphoristic assertion that provides focus for the essay and predicts its development. Opening sentences like these by Bacon, for example—"Men in great places are thrice servants: servants of the sovereign or state, servants of fame, and servants of business"; "Studies serve for delight, for ornament, and for ability"[11]—apparently provided the model for these by Steward: "Ciphers and codes . . . seem to be the particular joy and necessity of kings, diplomats, tramps, lovers, thieves, generals, and schoolboys"; "Tradition hath it that there are six stages in getting drunk: jocose, amorous, bellicose, morose, lachrymose, and comatose."[12]

As the verbal play in this last example suggests, Steward also quickly outgrew the impersonal tone of the Baconian model, and after 1944 a major shift occurred as he began to make his essays about himself— more specifically, as Steward recalled later, about his "loves and prejudices, likes and dislikes, foibles and fripperies, reminiscences and tributes."[13] Sparrow's own identity thus increasingly becomes the major interest in the essays, which cumulatively give greater and greater definition to his persona. Already by January 1945, the anonymous "we" of the earlier essays has disappeared, replaced by an ever more distinct "I" who invites the reader into his world, where he now appears in a variety of new roles—as an extra in Chicago ballet and opera productions, a sufferer from a vast matrix of life-threatening food allergies, a friend of Gertrude Stein, a subscriber to bodybuilding magazines, a holiday-season salesperson in Marshall Field's department store, a writer ready with a literary allusion for any occasion, a self-described "keepsaker," a man turning forty, a cynical ex-professor ("Most classes are stupid," he observes, "so stupid that when you walk in and say 'Good morning,' they will all write it down in their notebooks"[14]).

At the same time, Steward constructed for himself a new implied audience of readers quite different from his actual audience of Illinois dentists. This new relationship between writer and reader and is already strikingly clear in Steward's February 1945 essay, "On Soldiers and Civilians," when he appeals to his readers to prepare for the stresses that will occur in society when soldiers begin to return from battle: "You and I—yes, *you*, sitting comfortably in your armchair, and I, pecking away at my typewriter—are going to be faced intimately and harshly, in a thousand now-unsuspected situations, with this conflict between those who went and those who stayed."[15] The dental office that defined the rhetorical situation of the earliest essays has vanished, replaced by easy chairs, a typewriter, and a new intimacy between Philip Sparrow and his imagined readers.

As he redefined his readers, Steward also embraced the task of shaping Sparrow into a multifaceted character who speaks in a variety of voices. Sometimes he casts Sparrow as a comically neurotic figure, beset by inconveniences, frustrations, accidents, and indignities of various sorts. Sparrow's first night as a "super," or extra, at a Chicago performance of the Ballet Russe, for example, turns out to be far from the glamorous experience he had envisioned:

> Into the little [dressing room] crowded twenty-four of us, undressing like sailors on shore leave in Panama, and fighting over clothes hooks instead of bags. . . . The weird and tacky costumes were evidently never laundered, but simply worn until they dropped off and embarrassed someone, after which they were replaced.
>
> A few quick strokes by the make-up man transformed us into bearded Arabs, and then we stumbled downstairs, holding our skirts high. My costume looked like a cross between a peppermint stick and a mint frappé, and I was achingly self-conscious.[16]

Similarly, a holiday stint as a salesperson in the book department—
that "domain of culture and knowledge"—of Marshall Field's department store turns into "a frenzied nightmare of females and squalling
brats, a time of aching feet and back, of muscles in the ankles and calves
that shrieked with pain, of complete nervous and mental and physical
exhaustion."[17] And Sparrow's hot-weather visits to Chicago's Foster Beach
result not in a leisurely summer of sand and surf but in a case of athlete's
foot, a camera accidentally dropped into Lake Michigan, a two-inch nail
extracted from his instep (with tetanus shots to follow), and a disfigur-
ing sunburn:

> Today, I look like something dreamed up by Hollywood for Boris Kar-
> lov. . . . Little children run screaming to their mother's skirts when they
> see me. Women try to stifle their gasps, and men turn pale beneath their
> tan. They all turn away shuddering, and try to keep from looking on my
> leprous face, the face that once belonged to a man. . . . I do not have
> enough sense to varnish a walnut, I guess, when it comes to beaches.[18]

In other essays, though, we encounter a more serious and reflective
Sparrow, one who muses soberly on issues that concerned Steward himself during the 1940s. In July 1949, Steward would turn forty, and his
sense of incompleteness at midlife is evident in several of his essays
published as that milestone approached. Commenting on the value of
keepsakes in September 1948, he repeats the anecdote of John Henry
Newman's refusal to give up his old blue cloak, even to the person who
had nursed him through illness in Malta in 1833, and continues with
words that seem intensely personal: "Newman's life had been unhappy,
broken, with lost friends, wrecked ambitions—cut up and disorganized.
Only the tangible things remained to be sure of. . . . So it is with all of
us."[19] In his December 1948 column, "On the Dream, the Illusion," he
reflects on the need to cling to one's dreams, however difficult that may
be, for "when the last dream is shattered and the last illusion destroyed,
there is little left to live for."[20] And as his fortieth birthday draws nearer,
he morbidly observes in his May 1949 essay that "more than half of the
sorrow of living lies in the obscure consciousness that we are slowly
dying."[21]

Still another voice is heard in what Steward called his tribute essays, several eloquent memoirs of people who had touched and changed his life. Typical of the obviously genuine feeling and the understated sense of loss that pervade these essays is the tone of his February 1947 column on Gertrude Stein. Steward had corresponded with Stein since 1933, when he was a graduate student at Ohio State, and had spent parts of two memorable summers with her and Alice Toklas at their summer home in the French countryside in 1937 and 1939. Her death following cancer surgery in July 1946 was a blow from which Steward was still reeling six months later as he wrote this essay, based on daily notes that he had taken during his visits with the two women. In paragraphs like this, Steward keeps the focus on Stein, with precise details and anecdotes that vividly depict everyday life in her presence, but by now it is clear that Philip Sparrow has become the controlling consciousness in the text:

> I think I understand her place in literature, but it was hard to be conscious of it while one was near her. I remember her as a great and human woman, an intricate yet human personality, tremendously alive. I think of her on a rainy day in a small garage, down on hands and knees on the oily floor discussing the axle of her car with a mechanic. I remember how we worked together in her little garden, both bent over hoes as we weeded the tomatoes. I see her walking along the dusty roadways, switching her dog leash at the ragweed as she talked, and now and then shouting to Pépé, the little Mexican chihuahua, to stop chasing chickens. I see her turn quickly away from the sight of a helpless calf with its legs tied for market, saying "Let us not look at that." I hear her hearty laugh as she showed me how, with one quick movement, she had mastered the French trick of catching a napkin under her arms.[22]

Identity Games

Having developed Philip Sparrow into a presiding presence in the essays, Steward seems to have delighted in the possibilities for spoofing his readers by simultaneously appearing in the journal in other guises as well. In the June 1947 issue is a two-page announcement that Philip Sparrow is taking the month off, and while the notice is putatively a message from the journal's editor, the writing is clearly Steward's. In it, the "editor" reveals that Philip Sparrow, "the bird who 'sees all, knows all' and tells it in the *Illinois Dental Journal*," is actually an experienced college teacher with a PhD in English and "a bright and searching eye in keeping with his name, a pert way of writing succinct statements, a mind full of vocabulary, vocabulary and more vocabulary in English and spilling over into Latin, French, Greek and a little German." He goes on to identify what he considers the best of the essays that have "enhanced the pages of our staid *Journal*" and to express the hope that Sparrow "will be with us for many issues to come."[23]

Much of the fun of this ruse for Steward must have been the opportunity to share it secretly with the handsome Dr. Schoen, still the actual journal editor, and the same can be said of his appearances in the journal's annual book-review issues as the distinctly academic writer Samuel M. Steward, identified (accurately) as assistant professor of English literature at Loyola University.[24] And Steward pushes the fun with his multiple identities further in a Philip Sparrow column on Basic English in which he stops himself in the middle of a Mark Twain–like rant on the German language by saying that he "has no right to encroach upon [this] field . . . , since languages and books seem to be the province of another contributor to the ILLINOIS DENTAL JOURNAL, one Doctor Steward of Loyola University, who alarms us in every September issue with his words on words and worms and this'n that."[25]

There is of course an element of risk in such role playing—the risk of going too far and being detected and exposed. But throughout his life, Steward found a thrill in taking risks—whether knocking on Rudolph Valentino's hotel-room door at the age of seventeen and leaving with an autograph, a swatch of pubic hair, and an entry for his future Stud File, or picking up partners for rough sex in the bars and alleys of Chicago, or operating a tattoo parlor on Chicago's Skid Row while teaching at one of the city's prominent Catholic universities. "I seem to have some fundamental urge to destroy myself," he wrote tellingly in his journal in 1956. "Why can't I lead a dull and happy and *carefree* life? The answer, I suppose, is that I'd rot; I have to have excitement, even at the price of ruin."[26] Taking risks as he wrote for the *Illinois Dental Journal* doubtless also increased the pleasure he found in this work, and one of his biggest risks was suggesting more and more explicitly that Sparrow is gay.

Homosexuality is in fact a pervasive trope in the essays, but Steward coded it in ways that most of his dentist readers were apparently unable to decipher, thereby making his gay references a kind of private game between himself and the presumably few knowing readers with whom they resonated. Many of Steward's allusions to gay writers, books, artists, and theorists probably passed over the heads of the majority of his readers; they would no doubt have recognized Oscar Wilde, but did they know anything of Gide's *Immoralist*, Mann's *Death in Venice*, and Cadmus's *Coney Island*, or of Verlaine and Rimbaud? Would they have understood Steward's essay on his period of "balletomania" in terms of the allure of the male body in tights? What would they have made of Sparrow's assertion that instead of a drab suit, what a man really wants to wear is a "pair of mauve pajamas edged with yellow"?[27] Had they any idea what was actually suggested by *Doppelgeschlechtlichkeiter*—Sparrow's made-up word presented to illustrate the clumsily consonant-heavy German language, but possibly translating as "a bisexual person"?[28]

As he inhabits the persona of Philip Sparrow with increasing confidence, Steward ratchets up the game of self-exposure with ever more explicit—even outrageous—gay suggestions. For example, in his March 1945 essay, "On How to Cook a Wolf"—a witty exploration of the vagueness of medieval recipes that draws its title from the popular 1942 book by M. F. K. Fisher—he concludes his examples with a recipe for cooking a wolf and then writes:

> For my part, I cannot rest until I find a wolf to try it. Unfortunately, there is in these parts a scarcity of the four-legged kind, so I have a notion to call up "Esquire Escorts" [Bonded Male and Female Escorts for All Occasions] and ask them to send me out an unbonded one, a tall, husky, grey-eyed blond of the two-legged variety. Then, clutching my trusty cudgel, I'll lay him flat as he enters the door, and set to work.[29]

Similarly, his August 1946 essay, "On Chicago," a celebration of the city he lived in for nearly thirty years, closes with a description of the city as a naked, hairy giant that adds an inescapable homoeroticism to Carl Sandburg's earlier poetic celebration of Chicago:

> I think of Chicago as a man-city, healthy, sweaty, and sensual. It is Gargantua with his head in Evanston, his feet in Gary, and he lies relaxed and smoldering along the lakefront. The trees of Lincoln Park are the curling man-hair of his chest, the trees of Jackson Park the foliage upon his legs, the tall buildings of the Loop his sturdy muscles, and the whole anatomy of the city his outstretched body.[30]

Sandburg's Chicago was a "half-naked" city of "the Big Shoulders."[31] Steward's is a completely naked, sweaty, smoldering one with curling man-hair, bearing a pronounced resemblance to the muscular, dominant sexual partners he preferred. As Steward pointed out in a 1983 interview, it was possible to write such passages in the 1930s and 1940s without attracting the notice of straight readers because of "the lovely protective umbrella of ignorance." "No one knew anything about homosexuality," he explained, "and if they did know anything about it, they thought it happened only in the wicked cities of Europe or maybe New York or somewhere, but certainly not in Chicago."[32]

Sparrow and His Successors

Steward's shift to autobiographical subjects in his essays after 1944, his modulations of Sparrow's voice, and his invention of an audience of general readers carried his *Illinois Dental Journal* columns far beyond the limitations inherent in the original plan for the series and placed them squarely in the tradition of the familiar essay. But because they appeared in a publication whose obscurity guaranteed that they would go unnoticed, the art of these essays—their sophistication and wit, their playful passages of double meaning—is tinged with pathos. As Justin Spring has observed, Steward wanted above all in life to be a serious writer,[33] so it should not be surprising that even to the project of writing for dentists in Illinois he brought all the professionalism he could muster, all the love of language that had buoyed him since his college days, all the learning, feeling, and humor at his disposal. Steward never expected these essays to find the readership that they deserved, but that fact did not keep him from throwing himself fully into the work of composing them.

And there are many indications that he was pleased with what he accomplished. After Stein's death in 1946, he sent most of his *Illinois Dental Journal* columns to Alice Toklas in Paris, who enjoyed what she called their "Sammish impishness."[34] Large pieces of the essays, moreover, turned up verbatim in Steward's later works: parts of his essays on Gertrude Stein and on Paris reappeared in the opening chapters of his 1984 novel, *Parisian Lives*; other sections of his Stein essay were reused in his 1981 memoir, *Chapters from an Autobiography*; and passages from more than a dozen other essays appeared in the 1978 unpublished manuscript of his autobiography.

Perhaps the most telling evidence for the importance that Steward attached to his *Illinois Dental Journal* essays is found in his second letter to Alfred Kinsey, written on February 20, 1950, shortly after their first meeting. Steward had immediately realized that in Kinsey he had found someone to whom he could safely reveal his sexual cravings, his masochistic strain, and his detailed sexual recordkeeping—someone whose genuine professional interest in his sexual practices would validate aspects of his life that he could reveal to no one else. Casting about for a way to cement a relationship with Kinsey, Steward decided to send him copies of all fifty-six of his *Illinois Dental Journal* essays. "I sat down the other day to pick out the ones I thought might be especially revelatory—but after some consideration, I decided to send you the whole lot," he wrote, explaining that taken together, the *Illinois Dental Journal* essays "contain an almost complete psychological revelation of my personality should anyone ever want to dig for it."[35] In short, it is not only the choice of subjects after 1944 that brings his essays to life but also the dimensions of his personality that he consciously projects through Philip Sparrow.

At the end of his life, Steward was known mainly for his earlier friendship with Gertrude Stein, for his career as a talented tattoo artist, and for the series of erotic novels that he wrote under the name Phil Andros in the 1960s and 1970s. The fifty-six essays he had published earlier as Philip Sparrow in an obscure journal for midwestern dentists were a part of his distant past in Chicago; few of his friends in California knew of them, and even fewer had read any of them. Yet the *Illinois Dental Journal* essays had occupied a pivotal position in Steward's life between his conventional careers as a novelist and college professor in the 1930s and 1940s and his emergence after 1950 as a tattoo artist, a contributor and consultant to Kinsey's research into American sexual behavior, and a gay essayist and novelist writing in publications explicitly intended for gay readers. These essays gave Steward the opportunity both to explore a new genre of writing and to experiment for the first time with creating a publicly gay alter ego in Philip Sparrow, the forebear of his later gay identities in print—Ward Stames, Donald Bishop, Thomas Cave, John McAndrews, and, of course, Phil Andros. The *Illinois Dental Journal* essays not only offer a kaleidoscopic perspective on Steward's life and personality in the 1940s; as an early example of the lifelong delight he found in constructing and performing new versions of himself in new circumstances, they also illustrate what was for him a defining feature of his life as a gay man.

1

THE VICTIM'S VIEWPOINT

On Sublimated Sadism; or, the Dentist as Iago

January 1944

Steward's debut as Philip Sparrow in the *Illinois Dental Journal* was prefaced by a note from the journal's editor, Dr. William P. Schoen, explaining that this essay was "the first in a series of articles executed by a nonprofessional writer" that would present readers of the journal with a "'worm's-eye view' of the dentist, the dental office, dental methods, etc."[1] The constraints of this rhetorical situation rigidly predetermined Sparrow's identity (dental patient), subject (dentistry), and audience (dentists), but in this first essay Steward partially escaped these limitations by ignoring the journal's actual readership and writing *about* dentists rather than *for* them, thereby casting his dentist readers in the role of eavesdroppers as he hyperbolically condemns the "diabolic gleam in their eyes," their "ghoulish glee" and "foul deliberation," and, perhaps most startling during World War II, their "Gestapo technic of delayed execution."

The constraint that Steward could not escape in the first of his *Illinois Dental Journal* essays was his defined role as a dental patient, which left little room for developing Philip Sparrow's persona as the writer. Here Steward attempts to compensate for this restriction with an outrageous premise, witty language, and clever allusions, but the effect is a somewhat contrived, bookish feel, and Sparrow remains a shadowy entity, referring to himself only abstractly—and rather awkwardly—in the plural ("We have opened our mouth widely. . . . We have worked ourself into a cold dribble."). Once Steward and Schoen had agreed to abandon the pretense of the dental patient, however, Steward would be free to create his distinctive version of the twentieth-century familiar essay by marrying his characteristic wit and allusiveness to a persona whose experiences and subjectivity become the focus of each piece.

Dentists are extraordinary, indeed.

There are some people of unjaundiced and unprejudiced eye who can admire in the digital dexterity of the dentist the same finger facility that marked a Rachmaninoff or a Paderewski; or who can perceive an aesthetic analogy between the delicate and torturing way a dentist plays on one's nerves and the smooth drawing of the bow across the strings that a Kreisler or a Heifetz is capable of; or profess to hear in the head-shuddering noise of a burr against an eyetooth the deep organ diapason of a Bach or a Pietro Yon. But we have never been able sufficiently to overcome our mundane emotions to appreciate such comparisons.

No, our associations are almost wholly literary and psychoanalytical, and after some thought on the matter we have come to a conclusion which we think is correct. And that is that every dentist has in him something of Iago.

All of us remember Shakespeare's archvillain, and the heinous way in which he tormented his master, Othello, and eventually brought destruction to all concerned. Why he did has long puzzled some of the best critical minds, who have described his conduct as being one

---

There are some people. Steward develops a series of witty comparisons between the dentist and his or her equipment and famous pianists, violinists, and organists known for the technical mastery of their instruments. With the obvious exception of Johann Sebastian Bach (1685–1750), all were in the news during the 1940s when Steward wrote: after leaving Russia in 1917, Sergei Rachmaninoff (1873–1943) lived for many years in the United States and became an American citizen just before his death in 1943 in California; a Polish statesman as well as a world-renowned pianist, Ignacy Jan Paderewski (1860–1941) died in New York in 1941 and was originally buried in Arlington National Cemetery; Austrian-born violinist Friedrich "Fritz" Kreisler (1875–1962) settled permanently in the United States at the outbreak of World War II and became an American citizen in 1943; Jascha Heifetz (1901–1987), a child prodigy whose family emigrated from Russia to the United States in 1917, made a number of famous recordings in the 1940s with RCA and Decca; Italian-born Pietro Yon (1886–1943) moved to New York in 1907, became an American citizen in 1921, and held the high-profile position of organist at St. Patrick's Cathedral until his death.

Iago. The villain of Shakespeare's tragedy *Othello*, who orchestrates a number of deceptions that result in other characters' deaths by murder or suicide.

of "motiveless malignity," and have said that he himself seemed not to know why he acted as he did. But lately a clever scholar discovered the reason, in Iago's soliloquy at the end of Act I. There, Iago says:

Let me see now:
To get his place and to plume up my will
In double knavery—How, how?—Let's see—

To plume up his will! Let us scan that for a moment. "To plume" in Elizabethan times meant to "heighten." And why should he have wanted to heighten his will? Because he was a man of superior intellect, and his position as mere ancient or servant-companion to Othello offended him; therefore, if he could do something devilish—involving a perilous intrigue—that would harm his master, his own sense of superiority would be heightened.

Why does a husband bully the wife and child he loves? Why are little short people so aggressive on street cars, squeezing between the standing rows of people with such belligerency as to knock one from one's feet? Why do policemen shout so loud and act such unreasonable stinkers when they give a ticket, or catch you on a sly U-turn? Why do nasty little boys pull wings off flies, or impale them on pins, or tie tin cans to dogs' tails? The answer to all these questions is very simple: such acts heighten their sense of superiority over their victims, and the sufferer's pain increases their own feeling of importance.

Freud and others say there is a bit of the sadist in each of us; and that such is all right provided it is sublimated. This seems in point, but the question is: do dentists sublimate their sadism?

"motiveless malignity." The often-quoted description of Iago's behavior in *Othello* as "the motive-hunting of a motiveless malignity" is found in the notebooks of Samuel Taylor Coleridge (1772–1834).

a clever scholar. Steward seems to refer to A. C. Bradley's analysis of Iago in *Shakespearean Tragedy: Lectures on Hamlet, Othello, King Lear, Macbeth,* 2nd ed. (London: Macmillan, 1905). Steward's next two paragraphs borrow loosely from page 229.

Freud. Sigmund Freud (1856–1939) discussed sadism and masochism in *Three Essays on the Theory of Sexuality* (1905). By the time he was writing, Steward was well aware of his own inclinations toward masochism in sexual encounters.

We have opened our mouth widely for many of these torturers, from Maine to Montana, and we are ready to swear that on more than one occasion—as we have been approached, lying there helpless and trembling—we have seen a diabolic gleam in their eyes as they reached for their tools. There is one certain prober, doubtless invented by Beelzebub, which they use when they begin their preliminary surveying. It is shaped vaguely like a sophisticated corkscrew, and is evidently intended to search out the secret places of one's heart; we personally have felt it go even lower, and are sure it once left a scar on our right kidney. With what ghoulish glee they brandish this! Of course, all such minor manipulations pale when they begin to adjust the burr and prepare really to get down to work. There is a certain foul deliberation in the way in which they insert the thing, and lock it with a click. Then they hang the whole apparatus up, so that you may be given an exquisitely painful, sweating moment to see if the burr is small and round, or terrifyingly long with spikes on it. They watch you with a cold eye and a false smile on their faces, noting your every reaction, while pretending to say something innocuous about the weather. But you know what is in their warped minds: they are employing the Gestapo technic of delayed execution, and you are well aware they are playing with you as a cat worries a mouse. Then they begin—but let us draw a curtain over this painful scene; even in thinking of it we have worked ourself into a cold dribble.

Freud adds that the most successful surgeons—nay, even the most skillful carvers of turkey at a table—owe their repute to the fact that they have turned their love of slicing into useful channels.

But as for dentists—*we* know better! We know that they've never heard of sublimation and that they like their torture straight, and our gums bloody and raw. We feel this way because our appointment is on the books for next Thursday.

Gestapo. The national secret police in the Nazi government of Germany, organized in 1933.

2

ON CRYPTOGRAPHY

When the United States entered World War II after the bombing of Pearl Harbor in December 1941, Steward was already thirty-two and too old to be among the first draftees, but he nonetheless began to consider how he could contribute to the war effort. Having had a long-standing interest in cryptography, he decided to enroll in a correspondence course in cryptanalysis through the Army Cryptographic Center at Fort Monmouth, New Jersey, imagining that such training could be the foundation of a wartime role in army intelligence. "During several months," he wrote later, "I faithfully did all the lessons they sent me, and enjoyed working with all the wonderful devices that arrived by registered mail—enciphering machines and such like."[1] In the spring semester of 1943, officials at Loyola University Chicago, where he had been teaching since 1936, agreed to let him offer a course in cryptanalysis, for which six students registered. One measure of Steward's classroom success may be the fact that all six enlisted in the military for cryptographic training when the course ended in June. "I was left—on the night of final exam—with a set of questions and an empty classroom."[2] It was time for Steward himself to take another step.

By this time, though, he had changed his mind about pursuing a career in the army, drawn instead to the navy by its long-standing homosocial mythology—as well as by the appealing dark blue of the sailor's uniform.[3] Steward enlisted on June 10, 1943, and was sent to the Great Lakes Naval Training Station north of Chicago, but his incapacitating food allergies—described in the *Illinois Dental Journal* essay "On Fifteen Years of Lent"—earned him a discharge within a week, and he returned to teaching at Loyola.

Like other early essays that Steward wrote for the *Illinois Dental Journal* as he began to develop his persona as Philip Sparrow, this one is witty but impersonal and draws on material that he had ready at hand. But with its roots in the cryptography course that he taught at Loyola, it also offers a window into his classroom manner. Steward's easy command of the subject, clarity of presentation, and playfully engaging tone all suggest the qualities that made him a popular teacher throughout his academic career.

When Lysander of Sparta, who lived in 405 BC, wanted to send to one of his generals a message not intended for prying eyes, he used one of two methods: if there were no great hurry, he shaved the head of a slave, wrote the communication on the fellow's pate, let the hair grow in, and started him on his way. Or if the message was urgent, he used a small round baton called a *scytale*, on which he wound in spiral fashion a soft leather belt, and then wrote his message along the length of the stick; when the belt was unwound it showed only a meaningless jumble of letters and fragments. But his generals had similar-sized batons, and it was simple for them by rewinding the belt to discover Lysander's orders. Suetonius, the Walter Winchell of ancient Rome, says that Julius Caesar used a secret cipher which consisted merely of shifting the alphabet by four spaces: thus, if Caesar wanted an *a*, he used an *e*, if a *b* an *f*, and so on. Francis Bacon,

Lysander of Sparta (468–395 BCE). Commander of the Spartan fleet that decisively defeated the Athenians in 405 BCE, leading to the end of the Peloponnesian War. Lysander's method of encoding messages by writing them on a strip of parchment wound around a baton is described in Plutarch's *Lysander* (19.6–7). The story of writing a message on the shaved head of a slave involves not Lysander but Histiaeus, who used the strategy to send a secret message to Aristagoras in the city of Miletus in 499 BCE (Herodotus, *Histories*, 5.35).

Suetonius. Gaius Suetonius Tranquillus (69–122 CE), Roman biographer and chronicler of everyday life who wrote anecdote-filled biographies of twelve Roman emperors and of well-known Roman citizens. The story of Julius Caesar's code is found in Suetonius's life of Caesar (ch. 56). The comparison with Walter Winchell is witty but not original: Steward lifts this line directly from Fletcher Pratt's *Secret and Urgent* (see below).

Walter Winchell (1897–1972). Radio and newspaper journalist/commentator known for his gossip, memorable phrasing, and rapid-fire style of delivery in broadcast and print. Winchell's widely read column appeared in the *New York Daily Mirror* until his retirement in 1963.

Julius Caesar (100–44 BCE). Roman general who assumed dictatorial powers in Rome after provoking a civil war in 49 BCE.

Francis Bacon (1521–1626). English parliamentarian, essayist, and philosopher.

Lord Verulam, is said to have written a running story of his life into several of Shakespeare's plays by means of a cipher; and the whole wild argument over the authorship of the plays began with that crackpot idea.

Ciphers and codes—which are classed under the general term of cryptography, or secret writing intended for the purpose of conveying information to but a few chosen people—seem to be the particular joy and necessity of kings, diplomats, tramps, lovers, thieves, generals, and schoolboys. Especially in wartime is it imperative that communications be secret, because it would play hob with one side's plans if the enemy immediately knew what movements were contemplated, and acted to stop them. Ciphers in the last war had a tremendous role, and actually accounted in large measure for the defeat of Germany; in the present struggle, only one small story has leaked out about them; but that story told us that it was through the efforts of the cryptanalytic department in Washington that Axis messages sent to Germany from Argentina were broken down, resulting in Secretary Hull's stern denunciation of Argentina. It will be many years before the story is completely revealed, and perhaps it will never be.

In wartime, then, it is only natural that there be a renewed interest in this fascinating and complicated science. This enthusiasm is rather curiously handled; by a tacit and coy agreement, libraries in the Chicagoland area have withdrawn all books on cryptography from their shelves for the duration; yet for one dollar one may buy, over the counter in any bookstore, a reprint of one of the best books on codes and ciphers—

play hob with. Make mischief with.

Ciphers in the last war. That is, in World War I.

Axis messages sent to Germany. In June 1943, the new government of Argentina banned all embassies—including the German, Italian, and Japanese embassies—from transmitting messages in code. To the exasperation of the United States, however, the Argentine government persisted in remaining neutral in the war.

Secretary Hull's stern denunciation. On August 5, 1943, the Argentine foreign minister Segundo Storni wrote to American secretary of state Cordell Hull (1871–1955), stating that the United States would need to end its arms embargo against Argentina before Argentina could side with the Allies and break diplomatic relations with Germany. Hull's blistering response was considered "the most devastating criticism in the annals of modern diplomacy made by one Government of the foreign policy of another Government with which it maintains diplomatic relations" (Arnaldo Cortesi, "Argentines View Italy with Calm," *New York Times*, September 9, 1943, 12).

Fletcher Pratt's *Secret and Urgent*. One sometimes wonders just how a librarian's mind functions.*

In the layman's opinion, there is no distinction between the terms *code* and *cipher*, yet for the cryptographer they are miles apart. A *code* entails the use of a codebook, of which there must be many carefully guarded copies, on the field of battle, at the headquarters in the rear, and at the office of the general staff. Should a copy be lost, stolen, or photographed by the enemy, a whole new book must be composed, printed, and distributed. The codebooks that the battleships of our navy carry are bound in lead, and are the first things to be thrown overboard in case of disaster. In a codebook, groups of five letters are arranged alphabetically, although the meanings of the groups are not close together. Thus, a message such as AWKLM AWKLN might when deciphered mean: "Am arriving at [AWKLM] five a.m." [AWKLN]. The advantages of a codebook are several: economy, because one five-letter group may stand for a whole phrase; security, unless the book is stolen; and exactness in transmission.

Ciphers, on the other hand, are quite different. Here, each letter of the message to be sent is represented by another letter or character—or sometimes two or more letters represent only one letter of the plain-text message. They are of three kinds, the first of which is known as *substitution*. In a substitution cipher, some letter or character other than the one to be sent *stands for* the intended letter. The Julius Caesar cipher is one of these. For example, using a basic equivalent of A plain = D cipher, the word "Caesar" would be enciphered FDHVDU. There are hundreds of elaborations and complications that have been developed from this idea, the number of them limited only by the imagination and ingenuity of the inventors—and yet they are all easily solved. In every modern language, certain letters appear more often than others; in English, the order of descending frequency is E T A O N I S H R D L U. The cryptanalyst takes a *frequency count*, juggles a bit, and if he finds that in the secret message which he has intercepted the letter *P* occurs more times than any other, the chances are that it is the equivalent of the letter *E*.

Fletcher Pratt (1897–1956). Author of biographies and military histories. In the prefatory note in his Secret and Urgent: The Story of Codes and Ciphers (1939; Garden City: Blue Ribbon Books, 1942), Pratt claimed that it was one of only two books on cryptography in print in English.

A second type is *transposition*. In this, no substitution of the original letters is made: they themselves are used, but are scrambled in accordance with a plan previously agreed upon. The simplest form is something like this:

ILNI DNA JUNL
LIOS ETL ORA

—which the sender would transmit by horizontal lines: ILNID NAJUN LLIOS ETLOR A; it is called a "rail-fence" cipher. The varieties possible here are perhaps more endless than those of the substitution method; squares, rhomboids, trapezoids, geometrical patterns may be used; differing routes may be taken through the patterns; preestablished keywords may change from day to day, and so on. It may be said here, in passing, that *there is no cipher which cannot be broken*, if the cryptanalyst is given sufficient time and enough intercepted material to work upon. The only purpose of ciphers in wartime is to delay the enemy in his translation of the cipher until the information it contains is no longer of any value to him.

A third method is *concealment*; the Baconian cipher already mentioned may be regarded as this, because with it one can send a simple communication, a seemingly innocent discussion about friends or the weather, and have it carry a hidden meaning. Here, too, we get into the dark and mysterious world of Mata Hari, the world of the seductive and slinking spy and the espionage novel—with secret inks and formulae to write invisible messages on cigarette paper, or between the lines of open letters, or hidden—as in Marlene Dietrich's movie *Dishonored*—in the notes of a piano concerto. Although this is an extremely exciting branch

---

Mata Hari. Margaretha Geertruida Zelle (1876–1917), Dutch citizen who was a celebrated exotic dancer in Paris and alleged spy for Germany during World War I. Executed by the French on October 15, 1917.

Marlene Dietrich (1901–92). German singer and film actor who left Germany in 1930 for the United States, later working in films with such directors as Josef von Sternberg, Billy Wilder, Alfred Hitchcock, and Orson Welles.

Dishonored. 1931 film directed by Josef von Sternberg in which Dietrich plays a Mata Hari–like Austrian prostitute turned secret agent during World War I.

of cryptography, it is never practiced on the battlefield, but only in back-of-the-line espionage; and the chemical division of G-2 is adequately equipped to handle such things.

There is an immense literature on cryptography, and no political crisis, war, or international relationship exists without secret writing. There are thousands of exciting stories—such as the almost unbelievable accomplishment of Maj. H. O. Yardley in breaking the Japanese diplomatic code used at the Washington Naval Conference in 1922, and the destruction of the German U-boat fleet in November 1917.

For those who might like to try their hand, here is a little message in a Caesar substitution, with an A plain = L cipher:

LWWAS LDPDZ QESPH LCHTW WMPZG
  PCTYX LJZYP YTYPQ ZFCPT RSELO

* No offense intended to the very capable Mrs. Josephine P. Hunt of the A.D.A.! [Steward's note]

G-2. Military division dedicated to intelligence.

Maj. H. O. Yardley. Herbert Osborne Yardley (1889–1958), American cryptologist appointed to head MI-8, the cipher bureau of military intelligence created during World War I. Prior to the Washington Naval Conference, an international disarmament conference convened in 1922, Yardley and his staff broke the diplomatic code used by Japan, thereby giving the Americans advance knowledge of Japan's negotiating strategy.

destruction of the German U-boat fleet in November 1917. Steward seems to have in mind Pratt's comment that November 1917 "was the black month of the [German] submarines, with six sent to the bottom and their own sinkings [of other ships] falling to a low from which they never recovered" (*Secret and Urgent,* 248).

LWWAS. The decoded message reads "All phases of the war will be over in May 1948 AD."

Josephine P. Hunt. Librarian and secretary of the American Dental Association in the 1940s.

3

ON ALCOHOLICS ANONYMOUS

NOVEMBER 1944

Steward started drinking in high school and continued, mainly with Prohibition-era bathtub gin, during college and graduate school in Columbus, Ohio. By the time Prohibition was repealed, he was twenty-four and already "fairly well on the way to being an alcoholic."[1] His struggle with alcohol intensified after he completed graduate school in 1934 and took a teaching position at Carroll College, a Catholic college with barely a hundred students in Helena, Montana, at a salary of $100 a month with room and board included. The isolation, the harsh weather, the drab institutional housing, and the task of "trying to teach cowboys and the sons of cowboys about semicolons" wore on him, he wrote later, and "almost every evening I would be tanked on sherry."[2] His drinking grew worse when he moved to Chicago in 1936 to teach English at Loyola University. "These were the vacant years, the empty years," he wrote, looking back, "when the blackouts steadily increased—until sometimes I had to take to marking the calendar with crosses, the way a convict might in prison, so that I could remember what day it was—and whether I had to teach at that time."[3] Once he fell asleep while teaching a class, "and though it was a nap of perhaps only three or four seconds, it was nonetheless enough to startle me into complete wakefulness for the rest of the period."[4] Gertrude Stein and Alice Toklas recognized his problem with alcohol even though he was on his best behavior when he visited them in 1937, and without raising the issue directly, Stein talked at dinner one night about the way that "liquor kills all passion" in a writer.[5]

When Steward wrote this essay in 1944—still three years from his lowest point and his own membership in Alcoholics Anonymous—he was drinking at least a quart of liquor a day. "It was a period filled with dreadful scenes, the gradual loss of friend after friend, the deterioration of my health and sleep patterns, the inexorable growing loss of memory, and the slow ruin of my potency and my body," he wrote later.[6] Here, though, as in his other early *Illinois Dental Journal* essays, Steward as Philip Sparrow is for the most part an impersonal presence in the essay, attaching the somber details about life as an alcoholic to a fictional friend—and thereby, not insignificantly, distancing himself from the realities of his own existence as he writes. Still, underneath the essay's half-mocking tone is the suggestion of his early respect for AA's success in "unravell[ing] the twisted knots of the alcoholic mind."

> Affliction's sons are brothers in distress;
> A brother to relieve—how exquisite the bliss!
> —ROBERT BURNS

Tradition hath it that there are six stages in getting drunk: jocose, amorous, bellicose, morose, lachrymose, and comatose. Almost anyone can endure the happy bibbler, to whom the world is bright and every man a friend; and the amorous one can usually be kept in control with a few simple holds of jiujitsu tactfully employed. The belligerents are somewhat worse to handle, the lachrymose and morose a trial more often than not, and the comatose—well, they're a vegetable grater on everyone's nerves and patience.

Your feathered friend has for some time known one of the greater and better drunks of this area, a fellow who wondrously combined the last four stages. Like Housman's Shropshire lad, many's the time that down in lovely muck he'd lain, happy till he rose again; and frequently you could find him in the gutter, casting a lacklustre eye up at the Big Dipper, and inquiring of the chance pigeons passing on the curb if there

---

"Affliction's sons." Lines from the poem "A Winter Night" (1786), by Scottish poet Robert Burns (1759–96).

Your feathered friend. Starting with the October 1944 issue, Steward's column in the journal featured a sketch of a newly hatched chick next to the title.

Housman's Shropshire lad. Steward paraphrases lines from "Terrence, This Is Stupid Stuff," one of the poems published in 1896 under the title *A Shropshire Lad*, by A. E. Housman (1859–1936): "Oh I have been to Ludlow fair / And left my necktie God knows where, / And carried half-way home, or near, / Pints and quarts of Ludlow beer: / Then the world seemed none so bad, / And I myself a sterling lad; / And down in lovely muck I've lain, / Happy till I woke again" (lines 29–36).

were any messages for him from home. Fifteen years is a long time, and at the rate of more than a quart a day, he must have consumed a helluva lot of booze. From simple and childlike beginnings—such as the rotgut and needled near-beer of prohibition days—he progressed rapidly, until some few years ago certain subtle changes began to appear. The appetite vanished, the nights were sleepless, the temper quickened and the mind slowed down, the will weakened and the fingers shook. The agreeable opalescent fogs through which he had viewed the world swirled and darkened into damp mists and swamp miasmas. From the status of a controlled drinker, who merely looked forward to the usual weekend punctuation of his daily routine with a mild orgy, he stepped across the line into the dim and shuddery region of alcoholism. The morning eye-opener became a dreadful necessity, even when he had to loop a towel around his neck and draw the glass up to drink; he measured the day by counting the time between snorts and the distance between taverns. In short, he experienced all of the symptoms so brilliantly described by Charles Jackson in his recent novel, *The Lost Weekend*.*

We ran into each other not long ago, our paths not having crossed for a coupla years; and as we strolled down the street, my steps quite naturally turned into the nearest bar—and he followed. "Double bourbon—neat," I said; "Ginger ale," said he. I goggled at hearing that; it was as if Superman had asked for a pair of knitting needles.

Finally the story came out. He had been through everything: Manteno, several outhouses of theosophy, two "cures," pledges, and psychiatrists—nothing worked. His life had got out of hand; he had been fired innumerable times in those months, and been involved in

---

Fifteen years is a long time. The details of the friend's life presented in this paragraph closely match Steward's later description of his own life as an alcoholic ("Autobiography," 81–88).

Charles Jackson (1903–68). Author whose celebrated 1944 novel about a writer's binge drinking was made into a movie in 1945 directed by Billy Wilder. The book was reissued in 2013.

Manteno. Manteno State Hospital, a psychiatric hospital opened in 1930 in Manteno, Illinois. In the days before Alcoholics Anonymous, psychiatric treatment was one of the few options available to alcoholics.

theosophy. Apprehension of the divine through intuition and mysticism.

incidents increasingly unsavory and scandalous. Wholly by chance he had heard of Alcoholics Anonymous, a rapidly expanding organization of ex–clove hunters; he had investigated, and joined. He had a new *via vitae*; he could be happy without being tight; and he had not slipped from his "program," as he called it, for ten months. He was full of excitement and zeal about AA.

Alcoholics Anonymous, it seems, is a layman's group, including every stratum of society, from the gas hounds of Skid Row to professional men: physicians, lawyers, engineers—and as you may have guessed—dentists! Founded ten years ago by two experienced elbow-benders on the tail end of a prolonged alcoholiday, its membership of reclaimed heisters now includes over ten thousand, and its chapters number over three hundred. Fifty per cent of those wanting to control themselves had done so; twenty-five per cent had a few relapses, but went on; and improvement—if not cure—was the reward for the rest.

AA has twelve steps in its program, he told me, the first of which is a frank admission that one is an alcoholic, and cannot govern his life any more than he can predict what will happen after he takes that first drink; and the last of which is a kind of fieldwork, in which the renovated and dry-cleaned blossom-nose sallies forth to bring sobriety to those who want and need it, strengthening himself—incidentally—in so doing. He is not a crepehanging reformer in any sense, nor a windy evangelist; perhaps he still wants a drink, but realizing that in the past he frightfully abused his privileges, he resigns himself to a dry existence—*only twenty-four hours long*. The twenty-fours add up eventually to weeks, months, and years.

Alcoholics Anonymous. Still a relatively new phenomenon when Steward wrote, the AA movement was founded in Akron, Ohio, in the mid-1930s by two alcoholics, Bill Wilson and Dr. Bob Smith. In 1939, Wilson published a discussion of their principles and methods for treating alcoholism in a book entitled *Alcoholics Anonymous*, which gave the organization its name.

clove. A clove-spiced alcoholic cordial (*OED*).

via vitae. Way of life (Latin).

crepehanging. From the nineteenth-century tradition of hanging black crepe over the windows of a home in which someone was dying or had died, the expression as Steward uses it means someone of a morbid or pessimistic outlook.

Between the first and last points lie three other main ones: (1) a belief in a power greater than himself—be it called intelligence, or beauty, or God or Zeus—and a willingness to leave to this power the ordering of the mess of garbage that his life has become; (2) the making of an extensive and minute investigation of his faults and weaknesses, and the confession of them to an AA member or other sympathetic person; and finally (3) the remedying of injustices to friends and relatives wherever possible and feasible.

Somehow, AA succeeded where all other means failed. Its plan unravelled the twisted knots of the alcoholic mind better than could drugs and psychiatrists. It was not for my friend to say, he admitted, but from his point of view the basic curative principle seemed to be largely one of group therapy. There were many among its membership who did not subscribe to all its steps, who even gagged at a belief in a guiding power—yet something happened to one's way of thinking, and it gradually righted itself, as the saturated blood lost its alcohol and the off-center existence stopped wobbling and settled into a steady turning.

He had tried, at first, to argue with himself and his newfound friends, to rationalize and be convinced that he could take it or leave it; but he found himself a cul-de-sac. Every one of them, he soon discovered, had gone through the same things he had; consequently, in them was none of the cold Olympian detachment of the doctors who had never known the hell of alcoholism. These men and women had suffered, had been ruined, and had recovered. He could not fool them, because they knew all the answers and tricks: hiding bottles in toilet water boxes, under mattresses, or out the window on a string. As he had, they had lied, cheated, stolen, and injured others. They had guzzled for every conceivable excuse: because they had lost money, or made it; their wives or husbands didn't understand them; they felt tired, exhilarated; they wanted to be sociable, or to drown their sorrows in solitude.

---

a belief in a power greater than himself. For Steward, the key AA principle of surrendering oneself to a higher power—by which most members meant God—would remain a stumbling block until he found an AA chapter in Chicago that instead defined this power as "the stuff in the bottle" ("Autobiography," 90).

To end his tale, he compared himself to the little runaway boy who told his woes to an attentive and respectfully listening circle of monkeys in the jungle; after the detailing of each petty complaint, the monkeys nodded and solemnly said, "Ah yes . . . and *then* what?"

"So," said my friend, "the little boy finally felt foolish, and went home to his parents."

* Read it; it's the most exciting *tour de force* of 1944 fiction! [Steward's note]

4

ON FIFTEEN YEARS OF LENT

JANUARY 1945

Steward was in graduate school at The Ohio State University when he began experiencing severe digestive problems. His family physician sent him to Dr. Jonathan Forman (1887–1974), the unnamed "specialist" in this essay, who had begun to make food allergy the focus of his practice and who would go on to publish widely in this still-nascent field.[1] It was Forman who ordered the tests that revealed the broad range of Steward's food allergies,[2] which provide the material for this witty essay, one of the first in which Philip Sparrow's experiences and personality assume center stage.

On Steward's first visit with Gertrude Stein and Alice Toklas in France in 1937, Toklas developed a host of rice dishes to accommodate his restricted diet: "Cuban rice and Spanish rice, saffron rice (in balls and croquets), rice à la Dreux (without the eggs), cream of rice, rice Greek style, rice Impératrice, India rice, Maltese rice, rice pilaf (both plain and Turkish), and rice pudding (sometimes plain, sometimes with lemon or other flavorings)." "You know," said Stein as he was departing, "since you've been here and we've all been eating this Chinese food I've lost seven pounds and I feel just fine, and maybe from now on, yes certainly from now on if Alice agrees we'll eat more rice and thank Sammy for making us make it so much, so thank you very much."[3]

Steward would have one significant allergic attack in the following years. Two days after he enlisted in the navy in June 1943, he suffered a violent reaction to the mess-hall food he had consumed. "My tongue was white," he wrote later, "my eyelids were swollen nearly shut, and giant hives marched in triple-row formation across my back. By midnight I could hardly breathe. I crawled out of my bunk and staggered toward the swabbie on duty just at the barracks door. He took one look at me. 'Jaysus!' he said, 'what's the matter with you?'"[4] Steward was hospitalized, tested, interviewed, and discharged from the navy within a week. He returned to teaching at Loyola University.[5]

By the time he turned forty in 1949, Steward had outgrown the food allergies that had crippled him for almost two decades. Alice Toklas concluded that his recovery was the result of his having stopped drinking. "I did not contradict her," he wrote later; "it might have been so."[6]

> Famine is in thy cheeks.
>
> —SHAKESPEARE

When grandpa sneezed, grandma said "God bless you!" and told him to move out of the draft; today, when grandson ka-choos, it's "Been eatin' bananas agin, boy?"

And ten to one he has. Allergy, which is a commonplace-enough malady today, was a strange and wonderful thing fifteen years ago, a new-fangled ailment that took the country by storm. This month, when the crystal anniversary of my sniffling at crabs, rumbling at yams, and puffing over pineapple takes place, I feel impelled to take stock of those years of continuous Lent. In that time I have only infrequently tasted milk or eaten its products, and can say the same about eggs, wheat, potatoes, and pork, as well as a host of little chaps like pepper, coffee, chocolate, and nasturtium stems—the latter insignificant, surely, when

---

"Famine is in thy cheeks." Shakespeare, *Romeo and Juliet*, V.i.69.

a strange and wonderful thing. The modern study of food's role in illness began in 1905 with the publication of *The Food Factor in Disease* (London: Longman's, 1905) by the Australian physician Francis Hare (1857–1928). In a landmark paper published the next year, Clemens von Pirquet (1874–1929), an Austrian physician and pioneer in the field of immunology, coined the word *allergy* to describe an organism's hypersensitivity to such stimuli as pollen, bee stings, and foods like strawberries and shellfish (Thomas M. Daniel, *Pioneers of Medicine and Their Impact on Tuberculosis* [Rochester: University of Rochester Press, 2000], 141–42).

crystal anniversary. Fifteenth anniversary.

Lent. In many Christian denominations, a forty-day period of fasting and penitence before Easter.

placed beside the Big Five. But despite my abstinences I'm still alive and healthy—and hungry.

The newspapers and Sunday supplements have taught us in the past two decades how fearfully and awkwardly some of us are made. Hay fever has always been with us, and so has "food fever" for that matter, but blessed are those who are poor in health only three months of the year, when the pollens are going to town. We have learned that more than flowers can make men and women uncomfortable; we have come to realize that a lamb chop or a yank at a cat's tail can make us have hives or a rash or watery swellings or convulsions, or any ill we can't explain, from astigmatism to bad dreams and pain in the joints. The medical profession has shown us that anything from a powder puff to a bunion plaster, a silk petticoat to a cough drop, a bar of tar soap to a goose can upset us. I used to think my not being able to wear silk socks or neckties or sleep on a feather pillow was funny enough, but the other day I heard of a woman who was allergic to her hubby's hair—to no other man's, mind you, but only her husband's! The implications of that sensitization are particularly fascinating, and lead one into all kinds of esoteric speculation.

People accepted the new malady varyingly: some pooh-poohed the idea that a teaspoonful of passionless custard or a dog's sniffing at one's heels could give anyone convulsions serious enough to demand an injection of adrenalin; others took it up to explain their inexplicable ills; some believed it an organic disease, like ulcers; and some were experimental. I belonged to the last class; once I drank a milkshake, not knowing that after two years' avoidance of the poison, it would smite with particular vigor; within fifteen minutes I began to shrink and sneeze, not polite little gusts but great soul-shaking paroxysms, which at the end of a half hour left me as weak as a draftee's smile. I spent the entire day in bed recovering, but I convinced myself and vindicated science. I never voluntarily experimented again, but a skeptical aunt of mine once

---

tar soap. Antiseptic soap containing coal tar, a liquid by-product of processing coal into coke or coal gas.

a woman who was allergic. Steward heard this story from his allergy specialist in Columbus, Dr. Jonathan Forman ("Autobiography," 124).

craftily introduced an infinitesimal amount of butter into my meals; within two days I was flat on my back, gasping asthmatically. My aunt, contrite and convinced, promised never to experiment again, and put me in her will.

Perhaps grandpa was happier, going through life in his peaceful ignorance, than grandson, who sees more in a shrimp than was dreamed of in gramps's philosophy. Today we find out what is wrong with us and devote the rest of our lives to suffering scientifically; and people who have not been the center of attention since life was slapped into them can now hold the spotlight, boring their audience with tales of their physiological inability to enjoy an unpremeditated roll in the hay.

Those many years ago, feeling something was wrong, I went to the family doctor, a good old man who thought the world revolved around typhoid fever and measles. He cocked an ear, thumped me desultorily, and gave me a diet of *milk and eggs!* For three weeks I lived on egg milkshakes, flabby custards, and tasteless gelatine desserts—and lost eleven pounds. The doctor was perplexed, so he sent me to a specialist, a fellow who was a bit of a sniffler himself. There were lots of questions about family history that seemed very silly, such as—was my great-aunt Susan that way about dahlias? When he heard my father had hay fever, his eyes narrowed; I knew he thought he had something there. "Once it was enough," he said, "if a person's parents led clean moral lives, but now we know that flitting through a garden may visit its sins unto the third and fourth generations." Then he put me on a medical conveyor belt and sent me through the assembly line—or perhaps it should be called a dissembly line, because I was certainly taken apart. Assistant explorers took gun and camera through my alimentary canal, making reconnaissance photographs of every little tributary, creek, and lagoon, and clucking disappointedly over the results. After checking oil and

more in a shrimp. Cf. Shakespeare, *Hamlet*, I.v.185–86: "There are more things in heaven and earth, Horatio, / Than are dreamt of in your philosophy."

visit its sins. Cf. Numbers 14:18: "Yahweh, slow to anger and rich in faithful love, forgiving faults and transgression, and yet letting nothing go unchecked, punishing the parents' guilt in the children to the third and fourth generation."

gas and finishing with a bumper-to-bumper service, they were baffled. "Sound as a bell" was the verdict—I knew they were right; I was ringing inside. So the siege was lifted, and another battle plan employed: skin tests.

That did it. The doctor discovered the substances to which I was sensitive, and gave me a barren diet. But it worked magically, like a rubbing of Aladdin's lamp: in three days I returned to him with all symptoms gone and every little hormone happy. And for fifteen years, Allergy, I have been faithful to thee in *thy* fashion. Long forgotten are the tastes of potatoes, coffee, and cake—and long before rationing, I had nothing left but a vague and elusive memory of butter. I have eaten approximately five thousand breakfasts consisting of stewed prunes, and cornflakes with water on them—prepared that way they are faintly suggestive of moistened plaster and shavings, but they are mine and I love them. I have morosely watched the abnormally healthy people devour the elemental potatoes and the universal bread, while I tried desperately to conceive a tenderness for the humble parsnip. But my peas are always unseasoned, and the carrots always taste like carrots. I am desolate and sick of an old passion for other things besides bourbon and sherry, but rye makes me writhe, and in gin there is a secret something that gives me hives.

In a way it has been fun. It is a game to travel. One becomes friendly—nay, even intimate!—with dining-car stewards and hotel chefs. I have seduced dozens of cooks in several lands and languages into fixing my food properly; I have cajoled hostesses in many states into serving me my broccoli butterless. New environments are challenges to be met; one sometimes has to work patiently with boxes of candy and honeyed words on hardhearted pot wallopers, but most resistances can be broken—and the allergic sufferer becomes in time a master diplomat; if the storming of the wall does not work, the ruse of the Trojan horse generally will.

Allergy, I have been faithful to thee. Paraphrase of a recurring line in "Non Sum Qualis Eram Bonae Sub Regno Cynarae" (1894), by the British poet Ernest Dowson (1867–1900): "I have been faithful to thee, Cynara! in my fashion."

long before rationing. Butter was one of the first foods to be rationed during World War II.

The scientists may think that the injection of the cortical hormone of the suprarenal gland will relieve allergy, but I know that it will take years for all the vegetables to find it out. Meanwhile I eat my mush, bolt my rice, and think what a swell poem could be written about me after I'm buried. It could be called "Allergy in a Country Churchyard."

"Allergy in a Country Churchyard." Steward puns on the title of the famous poem "Elegy Written in a Country Churchyard" (1751), by Thomas Gray (1716–71).

5

ON SOLDIERS AND CIVILIANS

FEBRUARY 1945

References to psychological distress resulting from soldiers' participation in war may be found in literary texts stretching back to antiquity. In modern times, the particular horrors of warfare during World War I and the massive numbers of soldiers affected gave battle-related disorders unprecedented prominence and compelled the attention of the medical community. The common label at the time for such illnesses was "shell shock," a phrase suggesting that what soldiers were suffering from was primarily a physiological reaction to the noise and concussive effect of modern battlefield artillery.[1] Not until 1980 would severe and persistent psychological stresses following battle—and similar reactions to traumatic events outside of warfare—be understood as a diagnosable anxiety disorder and described as "posttraumatic stress disorder" (PTSD) in the *Diagnostic and Statistical Manual of Mental Disorders* of the American Psychiatric Association.

Though Steward himself had not served in war, this essay demonstrates a keen sensitivity to the potentially lasting effects of battlefield trauma, and its depiction of the persistent dissociation and alienation that soldiers may experience anticipates an aspect of what we understand today as PTSD. Written as the war in Europe was evidently coming to an end, the essay is fundamentally about how people at home will deal with the thousands of men who will soon be returning from years of battle. For Steward, the disturbing incidents he cites at the outset—mostly collected from articles he read in *Time* magazine during the fall and early winter of 1944—suggested an ominous lack of comprehension and sensitivity among civilians and highlighted the need for society to begin preparing for the stresses ahead. To underscore the urgency of the situation, in this essay he defines an intensely personal relationship with his readers by dramatizing the rhetorical situation in which he sees himself writing: "You and I—yes, *you*, sitting comfortably in your armchair, and I, pecking away at my typewriter—are going to be faced intimately and harshly, in a thousand now-unsuspected situations, with this conflict between those who went and those who stayed." Just six months have passed since the last of Steward's whimsical essays on dentistry, but the dental chair, the anonymous squirming patient, and the comic stereotype of a sadistic technician have all now vanished, replaced by a new relationship and an implied new equality between Philip Sparrow and his readers.

In the gilt and plush lobby of the Statler Hotel in Washington, two naval officers brawl in a fistfight with two members of a labor union. Along the sunny boardwalk at Atlantic City, a group of hard, unhappy-looking Air Force veterans, home on furlough, are "damn glad to be going back overseas" because they were unprepared for the shock of coming home to see people jamming the bars and hot spots and movies, and hear them say such things as "If this war lasts two more years I'll be on easy street." In the glacial ice of Normandy an insulted soldier, retching at the we're-fighting-so's-we-can-watch-old-Bessie's-pups-grow-up-in-a-brave-new-world idea of advertising copywriters, writes a series of bitterly sarcastic form letters about how cute the piggy-wiggies and ducky-wuckies and lambie-wambies are as they waddle through the orchards of France. At the University of Wisconsin, a fraternity pledge is deliberately injured during hazing, because he had offended the upperclassmen by his attitude towards their childish and sophomoric folderol. At the University of Southern California, the wounded returned veterans form their own fraternity, the Trovets,

In the gilt and plush lobby. See "Battle of the Statler," *Time*, October 9, 1944, 20.

Along the sunny boardwalk. See "Army & Navy: When the Boys Come Home," *Time*, September 11, 1944, 67.

In the glacial ice of Normandy. See "Army & Navy: Dear Mom," *Time*, August 14, 1944, 62. Steward's addition of "glacial ice" made the story better suit the February issue of the *IDJ*.

brave-new-world idea. An allusion to the grim futuristic novel *Brave New World* (1932), by Aldous Huxley (1894–1963). Cf. Shakespeare, *The Tempest*, V.i.183.

At the University of Wisconsin. See "Education: Veteran Hazed," *Time*, November 6, 1944, 51.

Trovets. Short for "Trojan [the USC mascot] Veterans." The clash between veterans and members of other fraternities at USC is described by Bill Boyarski (*Big Daddy: Jesse Unruh and the Art of Power Politics* [Berkeley: University of California Press, 2008], 39–42).

and associate with no other students and civilians—proud, reserved, mature, cliquish, hard to know. At Kansas University, girls who had complained that the cigarette shortage had forced them to smoke pipes, received from five frontline soldiers two packages of pipe tobacco and a letter that said: "Oh, you poor distressed girls! Gee, just think. It seems a shame that you must smoke corncob pipes. If it will make you happy we will give up our smokes to keep you *and your 4-F's* from being dejected. Gee, we just can't sleep for worrying about you." And in Chicago, a Marine veteran of three hard battles said, "I have applied for more duty in the Pacific. I can't find anybody to talk to. The people back here have not yet got the word."

Straws in the wind? Isolated instances? Trivia that will be erased in the frantic joy of homecoming? Or unquenchable fires burning slowly and deeply beneath this smoke, flames fed by resentments against labor strikes, unrealistic home-front attitudes, complaints about shortages of this and that?

There has been a great deal of talk about the military-civilian friction of late, in the newspapers and magazines, on the streets and in the offices. Most of it is as unhealthily optimistic as an abscessed tooth is clean-looking on the outside, or a rotten egg hidden behind its fresh shell. People are inclined to let George think about the knotty problem; they shake their heads and rub their jowls, admit it is serious, but are more than ready to let the appropriate governmental agencies take care of it: the Veterans' Administration, Selective Service, the GI Bill, and the War Manpower Commission.

At Kansas University. This story appeared in *The Stars and Stripes*, December 14, 1944, 4, and was widely carried in the same week by American newspapers.

4-F's. Candidates disqualified for military service on physical or psychological grounds.

And in Chicago, a Marine veteran. See "Army & Navy: The Word," *Time*, November 20, 1944, 72.

GI Bill. 1944 law that provided educational and other financial benefits to honorably discharged military personnel. Frequently revised, it remains in effect.

War Manpower Commission. Commission formed in 1942 to establish policies that would balance the personnel needs of the military with those of domestic industry and agriculture during World War II.

The important thing, however, is this: You and I—yes, *you*, sitting comfortably in your armchair, and I, pecking away at my typewriter—are going to be faced intimately and harshly, in a thousand now-unsuspected situations, with this conflict between those who went and those who stayed. We can fool ourselves all we want with cheery thoughts and tut-tut expressions; we will continue to do so until the payoff actually comes, and the whooping and hollering begins. We can console ourselves with the half-apologetic, self-justifying statements that *somebody* had to stay home and keep supplying the goods. This is quite true, but—with all possible credit to the veteran—he is emotionally and mentally incapable of realizing it just as we are unable to know what he has been through. Only those who have been shot at can love and understand each other. We at home can never comprehend the powerful fraternalism that unites the men who belong, by reason of their experiences, to the ghostly brotherhood of war. When death is behind a bush that trembles, when it explodes in burning phosphorus to kill the friend who was joking a moment before, when it surrounds you in bodies black with flies and bloated by the sun until they at last explode, when your foot slides upon the stinking decayed intestines of a thing that was once a man—only then, after the bony fingers have inscribed the membership card with your name, and you have looked into the fearful emptiness of the sockets in the fleshless skull, are your dues paid and you yourself a member of the League of War. And you and I will never belong, can never enter the closed clubroom.

What are these returned men going to be like? It would be foolish to try to say in full, or predict in part. But you can be sure that they will be changed. They will be older emotionally and physically, older beyond their calendar years, because war is the speediest artificial ager known; they may be violent—for you cannot train a man to kill for a half-understood or vaguely expressed reason and expect him not to use action in place of words. They may have their own code of morals which we cannot possibly understand, and which will baffle and dismay us utterly. They will be startled and chagrined by what they will consider our indifference, but is really only our inexperience slowly woven around us in our geographically and emotionally isolated chrysalis. They will be the men without a country, for they will return to a land that has not changed; they will wander among us as strangers, seeking with hard evasive eyes the pledge pin that will show them a comrade, one to whom they can talk of hell—or even sit beside silently, aware of the bond between. One is almost tempted to feel as much pity for those who have been excluded from the war as for those who were included in it— although the expression of such a sentiment would outrage the veteran and annoy the civilian, and could be given voice by God alone.

Already we have seen enough to show us in part the extent of the dangerous cleavages that arise between the military and civilian populations. We have glimpsed the gulf between, the chasm over which no bridge can be thrown, unless the engineers undertaking it are highly skilled and have a long time in which to work. It will not be the labor of a night or a day, and many times there will be mistakes made before the meeting of the span from each side is accomplished. It will require the patience and perseverance of the spider that Robert the Bruce watched fail seven times, and succeed on the eighth. The achievement, the success are our responsibility. There must be no intolerance or impatience in us, no inclination to minimize what they have done; and on the other hand, there must be no fawning, cringing, apologetic, or "understanding" pose before them. A straightforward shoulder-to-shoulder man-to-man attitude in conversation and relationship will do more to oil the disturbed waters than anything else.

This expression of one man's viewpoint of the shape of things to come is entirely pessimistic, and if it seems to end on a flippant note the psychologists in the audience will easily diagnose the trouble and agree with a wise and knowing nod that the poor fellow has worked himself into such a state that he is bordering on hysteria. But a thought occurs, and is clutched with the eagerness of a drowning man: All this is mere pother, mere fuss and feathers, a teapot tempest. And why? Well, six

Robert the Bruce (1274–1329). King of Scotland, about whom the legend is told that observing the persistence of a spider making a web gave him the resolve to disregard his military losses at the hands of the English forces and renew the battle for Scottish independence in 1306–7.

the psychologists in the audience. A reference suggesting that Steward no longer imagines his audience as confined to subscribers to the *IDJ*.

months after the signing of a peace, most of the warriors will be mustered out and returned home. They will no longer be connected with the military; they will be civilians once again. And if everyone is a civilian, how in the world can there be any "anti-civilian" feeling among the ex-soldiers? It would be silly to be anti-yourself.

You see? It really is hysteria. But at least one person is terribly, terribly afraid of the darkness ahead.

6

ON HOW TO COOK A WOLF

MARCH 1945

For most readers in 1945, the title of this essay would have immediately recalled the popular 1942 book by M. F. K. [Mary Frances Kennedy] Fisher (1908–92), the prolific writer on food in midcentury America. Published as wartime rationing and food shortages began to affect the public, Fisher's *How to Cook a Wolf* presented simple recipes embedded in reassuring commentary intended to prove to her readers that "you can still live with grace and wisdom, thanks . . . to your own innate sense of what you must do with the resources you have, to keep the wolf from snuffing too hungrily through the keyhole."[1]

Steward's actual inspiration for his essay seems to have been Fisher's first book, *Serve It Forth* (1937), whose title comes from the final words in many medieval and early modern English recipes. In it, Fisher offers an anecdotal history of eating from the time of the ancient Greeks to the first decades of the twentieth century, along with a sampling of amusing recipes through the ages—including several taken from the *Harleian MS. 279*, which Steward also used as one of his sources.

For modern readers, the homoerotic (not to mention sadomasochistic) element in Steward's final paragraphs may seem unmistakable, but in a decade in which virtually no one spoke or wrote openly about homosexuality, the passage probably struck most of his readership of Illinois dentists merely as a whimsical, if perplexing, joke. Of course, one can also readily imagine a small group of readers who followed Philip Sparrow's meaning clearly and looked forward to his future columns.

I like good bread, I like good meat,
Or anything that's fit to eat.
—FROM "DRIED APPLE PIES"

In the darkest and most profound book of the twentieth century, *The Decline of the West*, Oswald Spengler gloomily surveys the future, and what he sees is not a picture to make Poppa or Momma dream too happily of a brave new world. Viewing the uneasy pattern of the years ahead, he sees nothing but twenty-year intervals of peace sandwiched between increasingly bloody wars, the domination of the power of money growing until it is overthrown by blood, the formation of what he was pleased to call Caesarism and what we call dictatorships, the developing simplification of political forms [my cane and diaper, Charles—this is where I came in!] and suchlike direful and boding things. In the midst of his extended analysis of the old theme that history repeats itself is one fascinating statement: "Primitive human conditions slowly thrusting themselves up into the highly civilized modes of living."

Intriguing, what? In this day of substitutes and shortages, what he predicted in 1917 has been happening under our eyes. The horse-drawn vehicle appears on the city streets, the rubber we use has reverted in quality to that of the early experimental stages, the broom replaces the vacuum cleaner, the sugar is coarse and dark and the meat was killed yesterday, utensils of aluminum and metal are vanishing, and radios and pianos and batteries are definitely out. It will be only a little while until the scarcity of sheets and bed linens will drive

---

"*Dried Apple Pies.*" Nineteenth-century American poem (unknown author).

Oswald Spengler (1880–1936). German author whose two-volume *The Decline of the West* (1918–1922), begun during the cataclysmic final years of World War I, proposed that civilizations, like organisms, experience cycles of growth, maturity, and death.

brave new world. An allusion to the grim futuristic novel *Brave New World* (1932), by Aldous Huxley (1894–1963). Cf. Shakespeare, *The Tempest*, V.i.183.

direful and boding. Steward plays on the cliché "dire and foreboding."

substitutes and shortages. The nationwide rationing of food and of products needed for the war effort, such as gasoline and rubber, began in 1942.

us back to rolling ourselves in skins for the night. And in the grocery stores, the shelves have empty gaps like missing teeth; your own good huswife will tell you how her ingenuity has been stretched to fill your hungry maw.

Realizing that this trend will become more marked until its temporary relief by peace in 1948, we set about to be prepared for Spengler's worst, and decided to beat the draw on cooking and eating. Why not, we asked ourself, go clear back to the medieval days, the twelfth or thirteenth centuries, and see how the inner man was satisfied then? With the discoverer's gleam in the eye, we dug through some dusty tomes and wormy manuscripts, and came up with some ideas that are honeys. Having gone back so far, we certainly feel that we shall be prepared for come what may.

American cooking, though filling and full of calories, has never been a great shakes. The tradition has always been good plain food, and lots of it: steak, mashed potatoes, corn on the cob, apple pie, and coffee. Until very recently, when pressed by the lack of red points into making the cheaper meats more flavorsome, the American cuisine queen had rarely used herbs, or known of their existence beyond the pickling spices. She did not know the subterranean glow of thyme or oregano on lamb and chicken, the muted laurel leaf in gingerbread, the misty fennel, the vehement marjoram and mace, the saucy pert rosemary, the subtle saffron and the gentle peony, nor the made-in-heaven marriage of basil and tomato, nor the startling sailor's whistle of cumin seeds with cheese.

The people of the Middle Ages used spices and herbs for two good reasons: to preserve food without refrigeration, and to mask the taste of food that had begun to spoil. Taste was perhaps, though not always, incidental—but not even the coldest nose could remain unthawed at

red points. Small wooden tokens used to make change for the ration coupons used to purchase meat, cooking oil, and butter during World War II.

The people of the Middle Ages. This paragraph is closely paraphrased from a passage in the 1928 English translation by Keene Wallace of the novel *Là-Bas* (*Down There*), by Joris-Karl Huysmans (1848–1907), which Steward read as an undergraduate at Ohio State (*Chapters*, 27).

the savory fumes of the herb-laden roasts of heron, swan, stork, crane, peacock, and bustard that were set before it, the venison in verjuice, the perfumed and thirst-provoking tarts of elderflower and rape, the rice with milk of hazelnuts sprinkled with cinnamon and coriander, to be washed down with heady hypocras charged with anise, almonds, and musk, with raging liquors cloudy with flecks of gold.

The trouble with medieval recipes is that so many of the ingredients are unavailable today that only rarely can one follow them without a substitution here and there. There are no directions, neither about tea-spoonfuls or techniques, nor even pinches or smidgins; you take the recipe, look at it, and begin, feeling like some watcher of the skies when a new planet swims into his ken. But the adventurer can easily surmount such things, and he is rewarded by the language in which the meagre hints are written. Who could resist such a one as this, for medieval gin-gerbread? "Seethe a quart of heather honey and skim it and put in saffron and ginger and red pepper and fill it with grated bread till it be solid and then shape it and cast box-leaves on it and cloves and if thou wouldst have it red or gilt color it now." Small matter to us, with such a delightful recipe before us, that we were sticky from top to toe the first time, had every utensil in the kitchen dirty, were gasping from the grated ginger root and pepper, and stained with red and speckled with gilt—we had our gingerbread, and the memory of its taste is one of the things that help keep us alive.

We can recommend some others, too; one favorite is brown pears with thick cream. You take hard pears and pare them, and cut them

---

verjuice. Condiment or cooking liquor derived from sour fruit such as crab-apples (*OED*).

rape. "A spiced sauce made of dried fruit boiled in wine" (*OED*).

hypocras. "A cordial drink made of wine flavored with spices" (also *hippocras*) (*OED*).

feeling like some watcher of the skies. Cf. lines 9–10 of the sonnet "On First Looking into Chapman's Homer" (1816), by John Keats (1795–1821).

medieval gingerbread. This recipe and the one below for mutton sauce are found in *Two Fifteenth-Century Cookery-Books*, ed. Thomas Austin, Early English Text Society Original Series 91 (London: Oxford University Press, 1888), 35, 110. The first comes from the *Harleian MS. 279* (1430–40), the second from the *Harleian MS. 4016* (1450), both now in the British Library.

round ways thick, removing the cores; then put them in a pot with a measure of honey and sharp crab-apple juice and a little ginger and cloves, and seethe [boil] them. "And when they be soft let them cool and serve forth with sweet clotted cream."

Or perhaps you might want to try a very medieval bird pie, the directions for which read thus: "Make coffins of fine floure and put them in the oven till they be baked hard and fill them full of mutton knobs or pieces of bird, and cast thereon a lytil ginger and salt and y-bake, and when cold fill up the coffin with spiced crab-apple jelly, and if bird be used, stick the birds' feet uppermost in't to show it, and it is a royall Pye."

Or you may be satisfied to begin with a simple sauce for mutton: "Parsley and onion and mince them fine into vinegar and pepper and salt and eat him so." Anyone who does not feel the charm of that last "and eat him so" is in a stony March 15th mood indeed.

For all the bountiful table set in medieval days, there were evidently lean times, because tucked away almost apologetically in microscopic writing we found a recipe for cooking a wolf, the one animal most feared and hated in the Middle Ages; and to have it on the table must have been as much a comedown for the medieval hostess as for Eleanor to serve forth a family dog. But here it is:

"Take a wolfe and draw him and smite off his head and cut him in four quarters and cleave him through his joints and put him upon a bed of worts, leeks, and herbs and much spice and vinegar and leave him three days until he grow restive and is soft. Take him up and put him in a pot and seethe him uncovered in his own juices and cast thereinto wine and salt and pepper. Take a handful of sage—wash it—grind it up—and pound it with hard yolks of eggs and draw it out with vinegar and pepper and ginger and salt. And couch the beast in dishes and cast the sirop on him and few will know what meat has come therein."

coffins of fine floure. Pastry shells.

a stony March 15th mood. March 15th—the Ides (i.e., middle) of March—was the date of Julius Caesar's assassination in 44 BCE—hence an ominous or portentous date.

for Eleanor to serve forth. Presumably a reference to First Lady Eleanor Roosevelt (1884–1962) and the Roosevelts' famous dog, Fala (1940–52).

For my part, I cannot rest until I find a wolf to try it. Unfortunately, there is in these parts a scarcity of the four-legged kind, so I have a notion to call up "Esquire Escorts" [Bonded Male and Female Escorts for All Occasions] and ask them to send me out an unbonded one, a tall, husky, grey-eyed blond of the two-legged variety. Then, clutching my trusty cudgel, I'll lay him flat as he enters the door, and set to work.

After all, to what better use could you put such animals, now that the midnight curfew is on?

a wolf to try it. In the urban parlance of the early twentieth century, George Chauncey notes, men known as "wolves" were not necessarily considered queer but "combined homosexual interest with a marked masculinity" (*Gay New York: Gender, Urban Culture, and the Making of the Gay World, 1890–1940* [New York: Basic Books, 1994], 89)—that is, with the physical dominance that Steward preferred in a sex partner.

the midnight curfew. On February 26, 1945, a midnight curfew on nightclubs went into effect nationwide (Patrick Burke, *Come In and Hear the Truth: Jazz and Race on 52nd Street* [Chicago: University of Chicago Press, 2008], 168).

7

ON HOW TO BE A SPY

April 1945

Espionage on the home front was a constant concern during World War II, and to illustrate the danger of idle talk about military armaments and installations, Steward may well have conducted the experiments in extracting sensitive information from enlisted men that he describes in this essay. But it was first of all the sailors themselves who drew him to Chicago's bars during World War II. The city was just a short train ride south from the Great Lakes Naval Training Station, which processed a million recruits during the war, and was awash every weekend with thousands of sailors on leave.[1] Steward's own hopes of joining the navy had been dashed by his discharge for health reasons just a week after he had enlisted in June 1943, but he was still drawn to the navy uniform and the men who wore it. A trim man in his early thirties who was adept at engaging anyone in conversation, Steward discovered in the bars of wartime Chicago endless opportunities to mingle with "bell-bottomed boys in their cups."

A surprisingly large number of them followed him home to his apartment on the north side of Chicago. Steward later estimated that over the years in Chicago he had had sex with "a coupla hundred" sailors.[2] The encounters were documented not only in the Stud File, his card-file index of all the sexual partners of his life, but also in the many photographs of sailors in his apartment that Steward took with the new Polaroid Land Camera that he bought in February 1951.[3]

> She leaned her ear
> In many a secret place . . .
> —WORDSWORTH

"She leaned her ear." Paraphrased from the poem "Three Years She Grew in Sun and Shower" (1799), by William Wordsworth (1770–1850): "and she shall lean her ear / In many a secret place" (lines 26–27).

Three years ago America was much more spy conscious than it is today. Dramatic posters were everywhere: a hand just sinking beneath the water, a spaniel looking mournfully from a chair whereon rested a sailor's blouse, a waiter resembling Hitler cocking a large and tremulous ear at the conversation between a soldier and his girl. And to accompany the object lessons there were admonitions and warnings: *A slip of the lip may sink a ship. Little pitchers have big ears. Somebody blabbed. Don't talk.* Daily the radio during its station breaks croaked shuddery examples to remind the listener that spies were at work piecing together vital information, and that one should not breathe a word about defense work or transportation or anything else unless one had heard it on the radio or read it in the newspaper.

I must confess that such drivel left me cold. By nature being somewhat a skeptic and a bit overmuch a cynic, I permitted what I thought was my good hard American common sense to come forward, and let my innate babbittry convince me that such things didn't happen here. This was America, by gum; we had no slinky furriners like Mata Hari around, sneaking information to the enemy. Even such things as the landing of the saboteurs on the eastern coast did not change my viewpoint: the Fibbies had made short work of them, hadn't they? Caught 'em right off. No-siree, they couldn't get away with that sorta stuff in America.

Having reached this brilliant intellectual conclusion, I decided that I would test it before I took a definite stand against the Office of War Information directives, or began a subversive whispering campaign against

---

babbittry. Smug conformism to middle-class values, from the central character in the 1922 novel *Babbitt*, by Sinclair Lewis (1885–1951).

Mata Hari. Margaretha Geertruida Zelle (1876–1917), Dutch citizen who was a celebrated exotic dancer in Paris and alleged spy for Germany during World War I. Executed by the French on October 15, 1917.

landing of the saboteurs. On June 13, 1942, four German agents left a German U-boat off the east coast of the United States and landed on Long Island; on June 17, four more were put ashore from another U-boat off the Florida coast. Their apparent mission was sabotage, but several turned themselves in to the FBI shortly after landing, and the rest were quickly tracked down and arrested. Six were subsequently executed; two were imprisoned and deported to the American zone in Germany after the war.

Fibbies. Agents of the Federal Bureau of Investigation (FBI).

the necessity of having such an organization as the FBI. I, too, would be a spy, and my failure to secure any valuable information would give me a strong talking point when I wrote to my congressman to recommend the dissolution of such nosy groups as the Fibbies and the O'WIseys. I cast about, then, two years ago, to find the subject that was considered the most secret—"top drawer," I think, is the picturesque phrase the War Department uses to designate its most private information; and naturally radar presented itself, for at that time "radar" was scarcely a word to be spoken aloud. Luckily I already had one hint about it: an uncle who had made a career of the army had told me, eight years before, how work was progressing on a new method of locating enemy planes; they were endeavoring, said he, to use rebounding radio waves instead of sound waves, thus reducing the margin of error and the extended mathematical calculations necessary to compute distance away from time lag.

The next thing to be decided upon was a plan of action. Considered but quickly discarded was the idea of disguise: I would go out simply as a young man-about-town, turning on Personality No. C-34, the hail-fellow-well-met one, and meet and mingle with servicemen in the bars in Chicago's Loop and around the railway stations. There were some preliminary steps to be taken; I brushed up on all the insignia which indicated the branches of service in which I was interested: four horizontal forks of lightning for a Navy radioman, three forks crossed by an upward pointing arrow for radarman, and two crossed flags for the Army signal corps. With me I took (a) my discharge papers from the Navy—always a good introduction to a sailor, (b) my Selective Service card, and (c) the lapel button, at that time different from the gold eagle now adopted. Thus armed, and with my stomach fortified against alcoholic

---

O'WIseys. Steward means agents of the Office of War Information, created during World War II to promote patriotism and warn the public against espionage. Among other responsibilities, the OWI produced the kind of posters that Steward mentions in the first paragraph of this essay.

Personality No. C-34. Behind Steward's joke is the psychological reality that throughout his life, he enjoyed creating and performing different versions of himself.

my discharge papers. Steward enlisted in the navy on June 10, 1943, but immediately suffered a serious allergic attack after eating the food served to recruits. He was honorably discharged a week later ("Autobiography," 132–36).

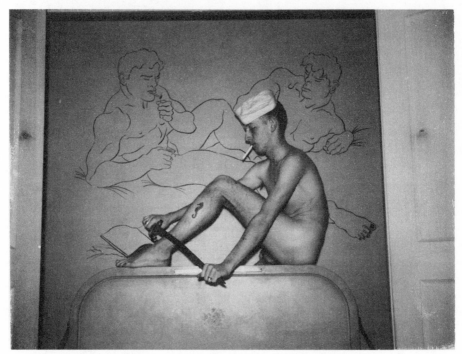

Polaroid of a sailor in Steward's apartment on North Kenmore Avenue, Chicago, in front of a mural by Steward, early 1950s. (Courtesy of the Estate of Samuel M. Steward)

bombardment by a heavy jolt of mineral oil, I sallied forth in search of bell-bottomed boys in their cups.

It is much harder to become a self-made spy than it is to become a self-made man. There are no books of instructions in the art of espionage available to the layman, no simple little manuals intriguingly entitled *The Care and Feeding of Spies* or *The Science of Eavesdripping*. One has to learn by the primitive method of trial and error if one enters the field

bell-bottomed boys in their cups. A Steward pun: "in their cups" can mean "drunk" or "wearing dixie cups," the slang term for a sailor's round white cap.

The Science of Eavesdripping. Steward seems to engage in characteristically erudite word play based on the fact that the word *eavesdrop* in the sense "to listen secretly" is likely a back-formation from the older word *eavesdrip*, denoting the area next to a house defined by rainwater dripping from the eaves—hence, to stand near a house in order to listen to conversations within (*OED*).

Sailor with a photo album of Polaroids in Steward's apartment, early 1950s.
(Courtesy of the Estate of Samuel M. Steward)

cold. The training schools at Berlin and Washington [1435–7 K Street, N.W.] are not open to the public, of course. But if one has patience and knows a little psychology—enough to realize that any expert will

1435–7 K Street. In 1945, the building at this address was the Washington headquarters of the Federal Bureau of Investigation. Espionage training during World War II was actually under the purview of the Office of Strategic Services, whose complex of buildings was located at 2430 E Street NW.

instinctively correct a misstatement relating to his particular field—the task is not too difficult. And each tiny bit of information gained is a talking point to be used on the next victim, who when he hears it is the more easily convinced that you have had some experience with the matter, and is inclined to open up, especially if you buy him a coupla drinks. *In vino veritas* was an old and true proverb even in the days of Pliny the Elder. Thus slowly, carefully, never posing as something I was not, in the space of two experimental months I built up a flabbergasting amount of information about things which at that time had not been discussed in print.

In that time I had learned the general working principle of radar. I knew of the existence and function of the master signal board placed ten or more miles from the actual combat, whereon was indicated by blue and orange lights the actual air position of our own and enemy planes; I had become familiar with the system of warning signals, and the workings of the small companion plate indicator in each cockpit. Naturally, I could not have constructed one, but an expert might perhaps have received valuable aid from the information accumulated.

And there were other things, too, picked up along the way. From a succession of young Canadian and American pilots I got the story of the "Franks Flying Suit" long before it was announced in the journals, the skintight green nylon underwear with inflatable rubber pouches over the groin and elsewhere, which by counterpressure kept the pilot from "blacking out" during the long power dives. From the Army I wormed the secret of the Type M-209 Converter, a small ingenious cipher device, precision manufactured by a large watch company, its two keywords

---

In vino veritas. "In wine there is truth"—a saying with origins in ancient Greek and Roman cultures.

Pliny the Elder. Gaius Plinius Secundus (23–79 CE), Roman naturalist, author and—more important in the context of Steward's essay—naval commander.

"Franks Flying Suit." Suit designed to counteract G forces on pilots, invented by the Canadian scientist Wilbur R. Franks (1901–86) in 1940.

Type M-209 Converter. A compact mechanical encryption device that printed the coded or decoded message on a strip of paper. Designed by Swedish inventor Boris Hagelin (1892–1983) and adopted by the US military in 1940, it was mass-produced by the Hagelin Cryptograph Company and by Smith & Corona Typewriters, Inc.

and interlocking wheels on the Wheatstone principle furnishing some ninety thousand [or was it 900,000?] variables for each letter of clear-text message—printing out on paper tape in five-letter groups the message that was put into it in regular-length words, and reversing the procedure for the decipherment. I heard that a Navy text on Japanese gun emplacements had just come off the press, and that in a certain Arkansas garret there was a complete duplicate set of the plumbing and communications systems of the Great Lakes Naval Training Station, just waiting for a saboteur . . . but why go on?

Admittedly there is a moral to this story, one that should be written in letters of fire, shouted in every street. My experiment left me disheartened, unhappy, and worried, for I realized what easy prey these innocents might be for an accomplished agent. They had doubtless been warned, these gallant trusting young fighting men of ours, but had forgotten and grown careless, thinking it not important, or believing the war to be nearly won. It is such unguarded relaxed moments the enemy awaits.

If you remember your son's or brother's quick smile, his voice, the crinkle of his eyes, and if you want to enjoy them again—then remember this little story.

If on the other hand it makes no difference to you, if you will be satisfied to have left of him only a three-starred telegram from the War Department, a returned box of neatly folded clothes and worn shoes, and a white wood cross growing grey and weatherbeaten under the lashing storms of France or in the loneliness of an island in the Pacific, then by all means talk all you please.

---

the Wheatstone principle. An encryption scheme developed in 1854 by the British inventor Charles Wheatstone (1802–75) that prevents multiple appearances of the same letter from being encoded in the same way, thereby thwarting attempts at code breaking through letter-frequency tables.

8

ON PSYCHIATRY

MAY 1945

Although the word *psychiatry* was first coined in the nineteenth century, the true beginnings of psychiatry as a professional field in the United States are often traced to a twentieth-century event that Steward alludes to in this essay: a series of five lectures on psychoanalysis that Sigmund Freud delivered in September 1909 at Clark University in Worcester, Massachusetts, as part of a symposium celebrating the twentieth anniversary of the university's founding. Today such a destination for Freud's only visit to the United States might seem a curious one, but in 1909, Clark's renown as a distinguished graduate-level institution provided Freud with a highly visible venue for advancing his theories of psychoanalysis at a time when, as Philip Manning notes, he was "still struggling to establish psycho-analysis as a legitimate field with an institutional home."[1] In his autobiography, indeed, Freud later commented on the personal significance of the invitation to speak at Clark: "As I stepped on to the platform at Worcester to deliver my *Five Lectures upon Psycho-Analysis* it seemed like the realization of some incredible day-dream: psycho-analysis was no longer a product of delusion, it had become a valuable part of reality."[2]

The translation into English and publication of the lectures in 1910 quickly made Freud's work a reality among American mental-health professionals as well; in Richard Skues's words, "This was the point at which psychoanalysis began to become not merely a method, but also a body of thought."[3] A decade later, the American Medico-Psychological Association formally acknowledged the status of the new field by changing its name to the American Psychiatric Association. In the humorous way in which Steward describes this evolution, medicine married psychology "and shocked the world with the mating and the Thing produced."

Psychiatry in the 1940s, therefore, was the kind of subject that Steward especially liked to exploit for humor—a relatively new arrival on the cultural scene that was widely known but not yet widely understood. Here Steward adopts the role of the skeptical outsider with a wry perspective on his subject, a stance he will also assume in later essays on such topics as pet cemeteries, bodybuilding, and the Women's Christian Temperance Union.

> Faith, thou hast some crotchets in thy head.
>
> —*THE MERRY WIVES OF WINDSOR*

Through the unhurrying years of history, the sciences of the modern world have grown from small and sometimes strange beginnings. Medicine began with invocations and spells, and herbs brewed into poultices in the dark of the moon. Physics is associated with Galileo leaning over the rim of a windy tower in Pisa to drop his bundles of lead and wood, with apples falling on Sir Isaac's head, with Archimedes dashing naked through the city streets, and with the alchemist's long-discarded crucible—in which he sought the secret of making gold from lead— reappearing in the atom-smashing cyclotron.

The progress in a science is inevitably from quackery to legitimacy, and it is a thorny road. None better illustrates the difficulty than the new one called psychiatry. In its highly suspicious family tree are faith healing, mesmerism, phrenology, astrology, Couéism, and many more

"Faith, thou hast some crotchets." Shakespeare, *The Merry Wives of Windsor*, II.i.144.

a windy tower in Pisa. Galileo Galilei (1564–1642) was said to have dropped items of different weights from the Tower of Pisa, observing that they hit the ground at the same time and thereby disproving Aristotle's assertion that the rate of acceleration toward the earth varies according to the mass of the falling object.

apples falling on Sir Isaac's head. A reference to the surely apocryphal story that Sir Isaac Newton (1642–1727) developed his theory of universal gravitation while sitting under a fruit tree.

Archimedes dashing naked. Archimedes of Syracuse (287–212 BCE) is said to have come upon his famous principle of bouyancy—that a body will float if the amount of liquid it displaces weighs at least as much as the body itself—while he was in his bath, and in his excitement he ran naked through the streets shouting "Eureka!" (Greek for "I have found it!").

Couéism. From Émile Coué (1857–1926), a French psychologist who taught a method of positively affecting the subconscious through autosuggestion by repeating optimistic phrases.

lunatic dishonesties. Its illegitimate mother, psychology, was herself a mongrel of many alley adventures before she made her weird wedding with reputable medicine, and shocked the world with the mating and the Thing produced.

Certainly old Doc Freud never realized what he was doing when he let loose his new vocabulary upon mankind around 1909. Up to that time people had lived comparatively happy lives, shooting their mothers-in-law when they deserved it, playing at two-backed beast with a certain devil-may-care attitude, and drinking because it made them feel good. But as Freud's shadow lengthened across the land, first falling upon the psychologists and then filtering down by a kind of osmotic process to the common man, people stirred uneasily and began to look at their neighbors with misgiving. Nonetheless they followed Freud with all the enthusiasm that the children of Hamelin felt when they trooped after the Pied Piper; if he were leading them to a river, that river was not very deep or dark. Here was explanation, here was the reasonable answer to the *why* of human action! So many unclear events were now perfectly comprehensible. It was easy now to understand why that Hardin feller calmly poisoned his old man, and then carved him up with the butcher knife into neat pieces and put him in with the salt pork; it was all because of a compulsion neurosis, brought on by an Œdipus complex dating from his fourth birthday when his father would not let him play post office at a party. Simple as all that. Served the old man right, too.

People fell upon the new method with howls of delight. The novelists and dramatists found an inexhaustible treasure house in the new explanations of conduct; what they had been doing by intuition for centuries, they could now accomplish by the simple application of a system and a formula. The confused layman was forced into familiarity with the new words, and was soon reeling under the baggage of his inhibitions, inferiority complexes, psychoses, defense mechanisms, and sublimations. If Johnny broke the hall mirror with a hammer and then undressed and sat upon the broken glass, Mother simply shrugged it off as a mild case of masochism induced by his erotomanic loathing for the umbrella stand,

---

two-backed beast. Cf. Shakespeare, *Othello*, I.i.126–27.

instead of walloping the daylights out of the little brat as she should have. Has little Helen developed an appetite for crickets and white garden slugs? Poor child, give her a little bicarbonate; she has a morbid fixation on Orson Welles and seed catalogues. Does the dentist hurt you with a mad and gleeful gleam in his eye? Be tolerant; he is merely sublimating his sadism.

It was the inferiority complex, however, that really nailed America to the floor. That could be blamed for everything, or used as a convenient excuse for any action from belching at the opera to collecting stamps. Most easily understood because most prevalent in humankind, it became the property of everyone from farmhand to senator, and even extended itself to the nation's conduct in world affairs. Do we beat the drum for isolationism? We are afraid of the rest of the world. Do we yell that America is the best country of all? Sheer defense mechanism, to hide the inferiority that our youth and inexperience induces—or so the psychoanalyst with a worldview would say.

Many years ago Oscar Wilde wrote that Dorian Gray wanted "to cure the soul by means of the senses and the senses by means of the soul." In a much more literal sense than Wilde meant it, the psychiatrist attempts that very thing. By law, the psychoanalyst found the hypodermic put into his hand, and the prescription pad opened before him. He was legally entitled to practice medicine upon the mind. He has—to be fair—had a measure of success with his benzedrine sulfate in narcolepsy, alcoholism, and manic-depressive states of schizophrenia; his barbiturates and morphia have aided him in treating neurasthenia and the shattered nerve; his testosterones and androgens have guided fragile

---

a morbid fixation on Orson Welles. Orson Welles Theater, a radio program hosted by actor and director Orson Welles (1915–85) in 1941–42, featured occasional appearances by the actor Cliff Edwards (1895–1971), who reprised his popular role as Jiminy Cricket from Walt Disney's 1940 film *Pinocchio* (John Dunning, *On the Air: The Encyclopedia of Old-Time Radio* [New York: Oxford University Press, 1998], 525).

sublimating his sadism. Phrase borrowed from Steward's own humorous discussion of dentists' sadism in his first *IDJ* essay.

Dorian Gray. The line is found in chapter 16 of Wilde's *Picture of Dorian Gray* (1891).

benzedrine sulfate. Amphetamine first developed in the 1930s.

and perplexed beings across the whirlpools of the climacteric; and his metrazol and insulin shocks have convulsed divided personalities into a healthy whole again. Being a stubborn creature, however, I refuse to let the psychiatrists additionally complicate the process of living by pouring their buckets of loose jargon over me; and I have been considering hanging out my own shingle inviting the limp victims of their treatments to hobble over to my better door. My advice would be patterned after that of Nat Gubbins: To the spinster who does not like eggs: "I sometimes wonder how *anyone* can eat them. Think where they come from!" To the young lady afraid of snakes: "Who isn't? They're loathsome." To the young bachelor frightened of women: "That's perfectly all right. Go on being frightened and leave them alone." To the wife who dreams recurrently of Robert Taylor: "Why not? No one knows, and it's fun." To the sailor who hates water: "You'll get over it." In this way, one might do more to untangle the knots of life than by fumbling around in the dark pit of childhood and memory and coming up with a slimy mess of neuroses that dirties both patient and physician before it can be thrown away.

Perhaps Medicine, in marrying Psychoanalysis, thought to give the ungovernable trollop the decent home she had been denied, and hoped that she would mend her ways and bring forth fine children. So far as we can see, the only product is this misshapen monster. It may seem a little old-fashioned and stodgy to say it, but we believe there is a certain realm in every man that ought to be safe from the attacks of science.

metrazol and insulin shocks. In the 1930s and 1940s, treatments for the mentally ill included the drug metrazol, used to induce convulsions, and high doses of insulin, used to place patients into therapeutic comas.

Nat Gubbins. Nathaniel Gubbins (1893–1976), popular British humorist whose newspaper column, "Sitting on the Fence," began in 1930 and featured characters with the perspectives and expressions of the British person on the street ("The Press: Nat Gubbins," *Time*, March 8, 1943, 66–67).

the young bachelor. The gay implications of the term *bachelor*—well established since the nineteenth century—are reinforced by Steward's following comment that it is "fun" to dream about Robert Taylor (whose heterosexuality was widely doubted during his acting career).

Robert Taylor. Handsome American actor (1911–69) cast in leading-man roles in the 1930s and early 1940s.

You may try to analyze the soul in the laboratory, but it is very hard to get a slice of its tissue under the microscope, and even if you should be able, the clinical report will reveal no actual findings and few suspected presences.

So I have sealed off my little room, and I will never open it to any psychiatric explorer who comes knocking inquisitively on a night of storm and tempest. It may have been a Herculean labor to wash the Augean filth away, but it is accomplished, and things are clean and straight as a pin. Not even my feathered namesake could find so much as a grain there to keep him alive. The only trouble is that I have to share the room with a guy who thinks he's Philip of Sparta. He's crazy, of course, because that's *my* name.

Herculean labor. In Greek mythology, Hercules was assigned twelve tasks of atonement, the fifth of which was cleaning an impossibly large amount of manure from the stables of King Augeas.

my feathered namesake. Steward again plays with his pen name, Sparrow.

Philip of Sparta. An imagined character.

9

ON BALLETOMANIA

June 1945

Steward saw his first ballet performance, by the Ballet Russe de Monte Carlo, while he was in Washington, DC, in the early 1930s doing research at the Library of Congress for his doctoral dissertation at Ohio State. He seems to have been genuinely overcome by the beauty of the art form (not to mention of the male dancers) and plunged into reading about the Ballet Russe. In the early years of the Depression—and in the remote places where he found himself living after completing his PhD—an opportunity to see the company again did not materialize until the winter of 1934–35, when, amazingly, they performed in Billings, Montana, just three hundred miles from where he was teaching, at Carroll College in Helena. But seeing that performance only left him longing for something more: "Still I yearned," as he writes below, "sick with an old passion, to be closer to the Ballet Russe."

That opportunity came after he moved to Chicago in 1936 and a friend—an "'impresario' for extras," as he called him[1]—offered Steward the chance to be an extra in a Ballet Russe performance of *Scheherazade*. In this essay about the experience, the humor rests in the deflation that comes from discovering that what one thought was perfect turns out to be not just imperfect, but shabby. The essay ends with Sparrow virtually cured of his "balletomania," but in reality, Steward continued supering for years more whenever a ballet company performed in Chicago, and his faithful participation won him several regular roles, including a eunuch in *Scheherazade*, a violinist in *Gaîté Parisienne*, and the gondolier in *The Nutcracker*, the sleeveless costume for which he enhanced by getting his first tattoo—an anchor on his shoulder, visible to the audience as he rowed across the stage.[2] Over the years, he collected many signed photographs of famous dancers—and more than a few dancers themselves: "With how many," he recollected later, "were there small romantic encounters high in the wings among the flats and catwalks, with flies whispering ghostily in the hot rising air from the stage below. Or in the bedrooms of the Loop? Or even in my own apartment?"[3]

> dance mehitabel dance
> caper and shake a leg . . .
> —DON MARQUIS

As we grow older and our tubing begins to crack, when our breath gets shorter and our hearts flutter not at the view of well-turned limbs but only after climbing stairs, and when we realize in a bleak moment of desolation that we must reach for our glasses before looking up a number in the telephone directory, we sadly discover that those golden dreams that we wove in the rose-white days of our youth slip away from us one by one, and no new ones arrive to take their place. The loom is broken, the thread is brittle, the pattern lost.

When a man, however, unwittingly but nonetheless completely destroys one of those old bits of magic through his own doings, he deserves the severest censure it is possible to give; and so it is with a full consciousness of my guilt, and a penitent acceptance of the world's scorn and loathing, that I pull from the vasty deeps of my past this unhappy tale to unfold before what I hope are sympathetic eyes. Do not judge me too harshly; I was very young . . .

For exactly three years of my life I was afflicted with balletomania, a peculiar kind of sensory disease involving certain parts of the nervous system. The onset of the ailment was abrupt and painful, and I remember it quite distinctly. It was a wet wintry afternoon in Washington, DC, many years ago, when through a shimmering champagne fog I first watched the cavortings of the Ballet Russe. Perhaps the old fortress had

"dance mehitabel dance." Lines by Donald Robert Perry Marquis (1878–1937), author and humorist whose fictional characters included Archy, a cockroach who typed poems on his typewriter (always in lower case) by leaping from key to key, and his friend Mehitabel, an alley cat.

pull from the vasty deeps. Cf. Shakespeare, *1 Henry IV*: "I can call spirits from the vasty deep" (III.i.52).

Ballet Russe. The Ballet Russe de Monte Carlo, a ballet company founded in 1932 as the successor to the Ballets Russes, the great Russian ballet company that traveled the world from 1909 to 1929.

been weakened by repeated submergings in the grape, but I do know that I was a crumbled ruin at the end of the performance, when the orchestra crescendoed to the stormy conclusion of Strauss's *Blue Danube* and all of the *artistes* whirled giddily about in what the program notes described as the "gaiety of the hour." This, I said to myself as I stumbled into the bar to recoup, is Art; it is the only romance left on earth; I am going to follow the ballet around the world.

Of course, the next morning I had to be at work, and the business of being a camp follower had to be called off. But the malady was firmly implanted. I began to read books on the ballet—histories of its past, intimate memoirs of its internal life, snooty discussions of its aims, naughty anecdotes about its personnel. I learned all of the technical terms from *entrechat* to *glissade*, I worshipped Nijinski and flung the names of Diaghilev and Fokine into all my talk, and panted to be among the members of its glamorous world; I would have gladly given a gland to have been present at that fantastic banquet when my brother balletomanes in Europe supped a consommé made from the boiled slipper of the *première danseuse*.

This went on and on, as the bugs multiplied within me. I thought, I dreamed the Ballet Russe. I wanted to write a story for it, or help with the choreography, or paint a backdrop, or compose some music—but I was gangling and clumsy, had no musical or artistic talent, and could

---

Strauss's Blue Danube. Famous waltz written in 1866 by the Austrian composer Johann Strauss, Jr. (1825–99).

entrechat. A ballet movement in which the dancer begins with one foot in front of the other and jumps with a scissorlike movement of the legs that alternates the positions of the legs in the air.

glissade. A sideways ballet movement in which the dancer leaps with the leading leg and slides the following foot along the floor to create the impression of gliding.

Nijinski. Vaslav Nijinsky (1890–1950), Russian-born star of the Ballets Russes from its founding in 1909 and one of the most celebrated dancers of the twentieth century, whose career was cut short by mental illness.

Diaghilev. Sergai Diaghilev (1872–1929), founder of the Ballets Russes and lover of Vaslav Nijinsky, whom he fired from the company when Nijinsky married in 1913.

Fokine. Michel Fokine (1880–1942), choreographer with the Ballets Russes from 1909 to 1912.

première danseuse. Prima ballerina.

not think of a tale decent enough to get by with Minsky. Thus thwarted, all I could do was missionary work in an attempt to spread the disease, a thing I did accomplish by skillfully dropping spicy suggestions at the right moment, by eye-rollings and lewd grunts and hand-claspings. The most spectacular conversion was that of twenty-five Montanans in thirty-below weather, when we rode six hundred miles to see the troupe shiver upon a creaking stage. But still I yearned, sick with an old passion, to be closer to the Ballet Russe.

And then after three years of frustration it happened! In Chicago a friend called me up one evening and asked me if I wanted to be a "super" in *Scheherazade*. Momentarily befuddled by purple visions of proximity to the white-tulled nymphs floating by me through the blue light, I got everything wrong, but a second call set things straight, and on the wonderful night I stood nervously at the stage door a full thirty minutes before it opened. I was among a coupla dozen other lads and lassies all there for the same purpose; they were heavy laden with pictures to be autographed, and while we waited they gurgled over the photographs, telling stories about the ballerinas and discussing Massine's sartorius and gluteus muscles. It all seemed too sacrilegious for words.

The supers' dressing room was on the fifth level above the stage, and I was hot and breathless when I got there. It was tiny, full of costumes hanging on the walls, and had a long rough wooden table down the middle of it. Into the little space crowded twenty-four of us, undressing like sailors on shore leave in Panama, and fighting over clothes hooks instead of bags. The smell made that of a locker room seem dainty and fresh as

---

Minsky. Burlesque theater operated by Minsky brothers in New York until it was closed down in 1937 for indecency—in short, the cultural antithesis of the Ballet Russe.

The most spectacular conversion. Steward was teaching at Carroll College in Helena, Montana, in 1934–35, when he led this trip to see the Ballet Russe de Monte Carlo perform in Billings ("Autobiography," 11).

"super." A supernumerary—that is, an extra on stage.

Scheherazade. Ballet by Michel Fokine set to the 1888 symphonic suite by Nikolai Rimsky-Korsakov (1844–1908); it premiered with the Ballets Russes in 1910.

Massine. Léonide Massine (1896–1979), dancer and choreographer with the Ballets Russes and later with the Ballet Russe de Monte Carlo.

Photograph inscribed to Steward: "Pour Sam—who even makes Chicago even more exciting than it is—Fernand Nault Ballet Theatre." (Courtesy of the Estate of Samuel M. Steward)

a new-mown field by comparison. The weird and tacky costumes were evidently never laundered, but simply worn until they dropped off and embarrassed someone, after which they were replaced.

A few quick strokes by the make-up man transformed us into bearded Arabs, and then we stumbled downstairs, holding our skirts high. My

Nault, Fernand   345
               13-VI-50. New York

L Tk

                                                    px³¹ 9

6-19; 6-20 [2x]; 3-2-51; 3-4; 12-29[Chgo];

Intro: Baron
Amer. Ballet Theater. Canadian. Lovely hard granite body.
    Jeans. Cruel. Wonderful! Used sailor's belt.
    Chancres, Feb, 1953

Steward's Stud File card documenting his sexual encounters with Nault. (Courtesy of the Estate of Samuel M. Steward)

costume looked like a cross between a peppermint stick and a mint frappé, and I was achingly self-conscious. But no one noticed us except a stagehand, who bawled to get the hell outa the way. I slipped towards a wing, and hidden there, saw Danilova rehearsing with Lichine. I blinked—was this my goddess, my incomparable wing-footed dove? Her practice tights looked like a trackman's winter sweatpants, her face without make-up was colorless and vapid. And Lichine! The handsome faun, the Prince Charming of ballet, was an undersized barrel-chested young Russian, thin-lipped, lank-haired, and hirsute-jowled; he wore a vomit-colored wool jersey fastened at the back with two large diaper pins. For very shame I unconsciously rubbed my moustache down into my goatee.

I saw and heard too much—the cracked and scaling backdrops for *Swan Lake* rustled ghostily in the dank foul backstage air, the dust arose

Danilova rehearsing with Lichine. Alexandra Danilova (1903–97), prima ballerina with the Ballets Russes and subsequently with the Ballet Russe de Monte Carlo, and David Lichine (1910–72), principal dancer with the Ballet Russe de Monte Carlo from its founding in 1932. Both had long careers as performers and teachers.

Swan Lake. Ballet composed in 1875–76 by Pyotr Ilyich Tchaikovsky (1840–93).

from the dirty floor when Danilova thumped noisily back to it from an upward leap, the smell of greasepaint and canvas and ancient perspiration and kerosene was heavy over all. Was this the magic world of moonlight and music that one saw from the other side of the footlights? Sickened and unhappy, I was relieved when the distrustful property man snatched our silver-painted wooden swords from us after our brief prance across the stage, and we could grope our way back upstairs. There I tried to dress as best I could without chair or shoehorn, and to find some cold cream to take the mess off my face. I backed into the wooden table and picked up a splinter, very lovingly centered. There was no cream left—someone tossed me a towel, already a dark chocolate shade; I took it with a little prayer to Dr. Parran and rubbed like hell. There wasn't enough light to see if I had it all off; I just had to pull down my hat and beat it for home through all the alleys I could find.

Once there, I dug into my trunk and found all my carefully treasured souvenir programs. With one last "where-are-the-snows-of-yesteryear" look, I stuffed them down the incinerator. The next day I took my remaining ballet tickets and turned them in, deciding to get as drunk as possible on the proceeds. It was all over. The last bubble was busted, the last dream shattered. No more the tingling ecstasy, no more. O lost and by the wind blown——.

Excuse me, while I answer the phone. . . .

*   *   *

Well, it was a friend who called to tell me that he had an extra ticket for the ballet tonight. So, if you don't mind, I'll finish this some other time. I'm sure you'll understand. You know how it is, when a man's gotta go.

Dr. Parran. Thomas Parran, Jr. (1892–1968), surgeon general of the United States from 1936 to 1948.

"where-are-the-snows-of-yesteryear." English translation by Dante Gabriel Rossetti (1828–82) of a line from the poem "Ballade des dames du temps jadis," by François Villon (1431–63?).

O lost and by the wind blown——. Paraphrase of a line from *Look Homeward, Angel* (1929), by Thomas Wolfe (1900–1938): "O lost, and by the wind grieved, ghost, come back again."

10

ON BOOKS FROM PRISON

Σεπτεμβερ 1945

When Steward wrote this essay, nine years had passed since the publication of his novel *Angels on the Bough*, but since that early success, he had not published anything other than the first eighteen of his *Illinois Dental Journal* essays. In 1934, he had drafted a novel about his religious development in the 1920s and 1930s that his publisher asked him to recast as a sequel to *Angels*, but with his interest in religion waning, he never pursued the needed revisions. A second project—a Southern gothic novel drawing on his experiences while teaching for a summer at Davis and Elkins College in West Virginia immediately after graduate school—never developed beyond a longhand draft. After arriving in Chicago in 1936, he wrote a novel about homosexuals in the city—"a fearsome thing ending with a murder . . . and the subsequent actual emasculation of the protagonist."[1] Gertrude Stein hadn't liked it—"the ending was horrible, everything cut off that poor fellow"—and summarized the manuscript's problem by telling him, "You tried to do Henry Miller but without the gusto."[2]

The financially independent Stein advised Steward that he could not successfully pursue a career as a writer while teaching because "teaching wore out the word-finding part of your brain and left it exhausted when you came to write."[3] In fact, Steward's teaching schedule at Loyola University starting in 1936 involved a staggering number and variety of courses that left little time for writing, whether or not his brain could find the words needed. In his first two years, he prepared and taught more than two dozen different courses—first- and second-year courses in writing and literature and upper-level courses in almost every imaginable specialization, from Anglo-Saxon and medieval grammar and literature to the modern novel, from sixteenth- and seventeenth-century drama to eighteenth-century poetry and romantic poetry and prose, from literary criticism to linguistics, semantics, and bibliography. "The wonder of it," he wrote in retrospect, "is that I managed to accomplish these, what with my drinking and my new sexual liberty."[4] He was still teaching a heavy load of courses, still drinking, and still seeking out sexual encounters when he wrote this whimsical essay on the benefit of free time that comes with being locked in jail.

> Stone walls do not a prison make,
> Nor iron bars a cage.
> —RICHARD LOVELACE

Sometimes one wonders how in the world people find time to write books. The mere routine of living clutters up one's life too much. Such ghastly necessities as showering, shaving, and shampooing leave one with barely any time at all for the important things, like eating and swilling and reading the evening paper. It is easy to understand the frame of mind that the man was in when he committed suicide. He left a simple note saying "Too many buttons to button."

But there seems to be an answer to the problem. All one has to do is get thrown in the jug, and then there is all the time in the world to write books. It is rather astonishing to consider just how many people have written books in prison, thus gaining a kind of freedom from the bars which their bodies are denied. They must have felt very much like the convict who gave so many pints of blood that the Red Cross congratulated him. The con winked at the field director, and said: "Dat's one way I puts it over on de warden. Part of me gits out."

There was first of all that handsome young villain of a Villon, back in the fifteenth century. François was in more brawls over skirts and in

---

"Stone walls do not a prison make." Oft-quoted lines from the poem "To Althea, from Prison," by Richard Lovelace (1618–57), presumably written when the House of Commons imprisoned him for seven weeks in 1642 because of his outspoken royalist sympathies.

Too many buttons. From a passage in the novel *Le Grand Écart* (1923), by Jean Cocteau (1889–1963): "He was still thinking of the Englishman who committed suicide having written: *too many buttons* to do up and undo, I'm killing myself."

There was first of all. As Steward doubtless knew, the history of famous books written in prison actually goes back at least to the Roman scholar Boethius (480?–524?), whose *Consolation of Philosophy*, composed while he was awaiting execution, powerfully influenced philosophy and literature for more than a millennium. Steward starts at a more recent point to present a tighter chronology of writers from the fifteenth century to the present.

Villon. François Villon (1431–63?), French poet known for his criminal activities.

tangles with the pinch-and-padlock boys than a butcher had friends in 1944. He was in and out of the klink for almost every crime on the book, from mayhem to church robbing. And while he languished scratching his neck among the vermin of the prisons of Paris, Meung, and Angers, he found time to write some of the most touching of his ballades: the poignant "Where are the snows of yesteryear?," the grim "Ballade of the Hanged Ones," and the sincere and humble "Song for My Mother," full of piety and devotion.

And there was that genial rakeheller, Raleigh. Sir Walter had his brushes not only with Queen Elizabeth but with her successor, James I. He offended the queen by seducing one of her maids of honor instead of herself. He was clapped into the Tower of London, where he frittered away his time by feeding the ravens and writing verse until he was released. Under James, he was again confined because he was thought to be involved in a conspiracy. This time he made chemical experiments, and if report be true, he discovered a quack stimulant that would make even testosterone propionate seem like soothing syrup. But he also composed many treatises, and wrote one volume of a vast *History of the World*. Unfortunately, the quality of the *History* was not good enough to save Sir Walter's head; and there are those cynics who say that it was so bad it actually hastened the swinging of the axe.

John Bunyan must have got a little tired of hearing the prison gates clang behind him, and then open again. They were certainly real swinging doors for him. Poor John was just a little batty, and he always managed to be in hot water with the Royalists. He spent about a third of his

---

than a butcher had friends. A reference to the wartime rationing of meat.

Meung. The twelfth-century Château de Meung-sur-Loire, a bishop's residence that included a dungeon in which, Villon claimed, he was imprisoned in 1461.

Angers. Ancient city in the Loire Valley that in Villon's time was dominated by a thirteenth-century castle, the Château d'Angers.

Raleigh. Sir Walter Raleigh (1554–1618), writer and explorer, imprisoned by Elizabeth I for marrying one of her maids without permission and by James I for treason.

testosterone propionate. Anabolic steroid developed in the 1930s to treat male hormone deficiencies; Steward mentions it again in his *IDJ* essay "On Getting to Be Forty" (May 1949).

John Bunyan (1628–88). Nonconformist Christian writer and preacher who was repeatedly imprisoned for preaching without having been ordained.

life in prison, one session lasting twelve years. Naturally, then, almost everything he wrote was produced behind bars. *Pilgrim's Progress*, the one book about which the educated few had to come over to the opinion of the common people, was written during a short session in the old gaol on London Bridge in 1675.

Daniel Defoe fell afoul the church on both sides by writing *The Shortest Way with Dissenters*. He was put in the public stocks three times. One cannot of course write while one's hands dangle helplessly beside one's ears, and the jeering people throw ripe eggs and old cabbages into one's face. Defoe must have been glad when he was at last taken to prison. He was there for two years, and should have been given the literary "E" for mass production. In that time he wrote forty long treatises, innumerable short pamphlets, and even began a kind of newspaper called *The Review*, which appeared three times a week and ran to a bulk of over eight volumes!

Leigh Hunt got his when he libelled the Prince Regent, George IV, in the newspaper which he edited. In the columns of *The Examiner*, Hunt called George a liar, a libertine, a gambler, and a corpulent fool of fifty. George happened to be all those things, it is true, but no government except the United States could allow such statements to be published about its rulers. During the two years Hunt was in the cooler, he must have had a very, very good time. He decorated his room with wallpaper *aux trellises de roses*, colored the ceiling with clouds and sky, and brought in his books and piano. Charles Lamb said that nothing like it had ever

---

Daniel Defoe (1660–1731). English journalist and early novelist whose political tracts resulted in repeated pillorying and imprisonment for libel.

Leigh Hunt (1784–1859). English journalist and friend of many of the leading literary celebrities of his day. Jailed in 1812 for libeling the Prince Regent, Hunt was lodged in an unused prison infirmary consisting of a suite of rooms that he famously decorated with extravagance: "I papered the walls with a trellis of roses; I had the ceiling coloured with clouds and sky; the barred windows I screened with Venetian blinds; and when my bookcases were set up with their busts, and flowers and a pianoforte made their appearance, perhaps there was not a handsomer room on that side the water. I took a pleasure, when a stranger knocked at the door, to see him come in and stare about him" (*The Autobiography of Leigh Hunt*, new ed. [London: Smith, Elder, 1870], 217).

Charles Lamb (1775–1834). English essayist and friend of Leigh Hunt. Steward paraphrases Hunt's *Autobiography*: "Charles Lamb declared there was no other such room, except in a fairy tale" (217).

been known outside a fairy tale. Hunt continued to write and to edit *The Examiner* and to work on a long poem called *The Story of Rimini* while he was jugged.

Oscar Wilde, poor dear orchidaceous Oscar, was on ice for two years. A libel action which he had brought against the Marquis of Queensbury unluckily backfired. The Marquis forgot all about his famous rules, and hit Oscar below the belt by proving in no uncertain way that Oscar's tastes ran to fauns and satyrs instead of nymphs and dryads. It was a great scandal in England, and one of Wilde's biographers says that when the trial started there was an exodus across the Channel of practically everyone who was worth knowing. But while in prison Wilde wrote two of his best things: the superb and haunting "Ballad of Reading Gaol," and the moving cry from the depths of his oblique and tortured heart, *De Profundis.*

William Sydney Porter comes next in this little catalogue of crime and literature. He is better known under his pen name of O. Henry, of course. Porter was a southern gentleman of small means and education, who was always running short of shekels to buy his juleps. His checkered career finally landed him in the state coop at Columbus, Ohio, for embezzlement. While he was there he began to dicker with the short story, and evolved a style and technique which made him immensely popular on both sides of the big drink.

Oscar Wilde (1854–1900). Celebrity London playwright known for his wit and, ultimately, for his homosexuality, Wilde was convicted of gross indecency in 1895 and sentenced to two years of hard labor. His health and spirit broken by the experience, he died three years after his release.

orchidaceous. "Exotic, extravagant, or florid" (*OED*); also appropriate because Wilde was well known for wearing an orchid in his lapel.

William Sydney Porter (1862–1910). Convicted of embezzling money from the First National Bank of Austin, where he worked as a teller from 1891 to 1894, Porter wrote and published his first stories under the pen name O. Henry while in an Ohio prison, where, he once commented, he had "enough spare time to take up fiction seriously" (Richard O'Connor, *O. Henry: The Legendary Life of William S. Porter* [Garden City: Doubleday, 1970], 139).

shekels. A term derived from Hebrew but also denoting coins from many ancient Middle Eastern cultures. Steward apparently chooses the word from its humorous clash with *juleps.*

juleps. Cocktails of bourbon and mint associated with the American South.

Of course, one cannot neglect a mention of Hitler. Nursing his paranoia, and impotently chewing at the frayed edges of his ego, he scribbled away at *Mein Kampf*. How the old Landsberg fortress must have quivered from the throbbing hate that he spat upon those sheets of paper back in 1923! What twisted joy must crack his thin lips as he looks upon the world from whatever hole he is hiding in! It really does not matter whether he is alive or dead; the shimmering gates of Valhallah have long since swung shut upon the little Austrian mouse. He sits at the right hand of his father Wotan, and is sealed among the Teutonic legends. He has left his mark upon the world with *Mein Kampf*. Who killed ten million men? I did—I did it with my little pen-and-ink. Although his book was merely an evil offshoot of Spengler's *Decline of the West*, it was a translation of it into blood and fury and violence, a dogma of battle and murder and sudden death. Its poison will be felt in the world for many years, and like malaria it will return at intervals to plague the globe and make it sweat and shake.

At any rate, these examples are certainly the answer to my problem. If I can only think of a crime heinous enough to get me hoosegowed

---

Landsberg fortress. For his part in an attempted coup in 1923, Adolph Hitler (1889–1945) was sentenced to five years of imprisonment in the Bavarian town of Landsberg am Lech. In "conditions more akin to those of a hotel than a penitentiary," he served less than a year, during which he composed his autobiographical-ideological tract *Mein Kampf* (Ian Kershaw, *Hitler: A Biography*, one-volume ed. [New York: Norton, 2008], 136).

whatever hole he is hiding in! Although the Soviets had used dental records as early as May 11, 1945, to identify the charred remains they found near Hitler's Berlin bunker as his (Kershaw, 958), Joseph Stalin continued to suggest publicly that Hitler might have escaped from Berlin. Thus the question of his whereabouts was still an open one when Steward wrote in late summer 1945.

Valhallah. The home of the gods in the four-opera cycle *Der Ring des Nibelungen* (1876), by Richard Wagner (1813–83), whose work was a particular favorite of Hitler.

Wotan. Leader of the gods in Wagner's *Der Ring des Nibelungen*.

ten million men. Steward wrote with limited information; modern estimates put the death toll in World War II well above fifty million.

Spengler's Decline of the West. Oswald Spengler (1880–1936), German author whose two-volume *The Decline of the West* (1918–1922), begun during the cataclysmic final years of World War I, proposed that civilizations, like organisms, experience cycles of growth, maturity, and death.

for a long time, there may be time to write a novel. Or maybe I can be another Villon or Wilde. The difficulty is that I can't think of anything serious enough to get me in for the time it would take to write a sonnet. I have considered such things as a brick through a department store's window [30 days], speeding [10 to 30], and bigamy [difficult if one is single]. Murder is out, because the hotsquat would cut everything short.

But I shall go on thinking, and perhaps the next communiqué will be issued from the local Bridewell. If out of your vast experience you have any suggestions as to how to get in, I'll be glad for your help.

---

hotsquat. The electric chair.

Bridewell. Famous London prison opened in a converted royal palace in 1553; also the name of the central prison in Chicago from the city's founding until 1871 (Perry Duis, *Challenging Chicago: Coping with Everyday Life, 1837-1920* [Urbana: University of Illinois Press, 1998], 337–38).

11

ON CEMETERIES

October–November 1945

The occasional burial of domestic animals in prehistoric and ancient cultures has been well documented, but the establishment of entire cemeteries expressly for pets is a much more recent phenomenon. The first such cemetery in the United States was the Hartsdale Pet Cemetery in New York, which opened in 1896 and has since interred more than eighty thousand pets.[1] The Hinsdale Animal Cemetery, which Steward writes about in this essay, was laid out in the farmlands west of Chicago in 1926 and is the oldest pet cemetery in the Chicago area. Since Steward visited it in the 1940s, the "wheat fields beyond" have been replaced by the housing and traffic of an upscale suburb that surrounds the cemetery's twelve acres, but gravestones from its early decades—like that of Admiral Togo, whom Steward mentions in this essay—are still to be found in the oldest parts of the cemetery.

As in his essays on Alcoholics Anonymous, psychiatry, and bodybuilding, Steward casts himself here in the role of a droll commentator on what was in the 1940s a relatively new cultural phenomenon. What he could not have known is that thirty years after writing this essay, when age and illness had closed the door on the sexual encounters that had occupied so much of his younger years, he too would come under the spell of canine companionship. After the death of his Berkeley neighbor in the early 1970s, Steward tried unsuccessfully to find a new home for her longhaired dachshund, Fritz, before gradually making a discovery: "I fell in love with Fritz—and began to adore every hair on his bullnecked, broad-chested, bandy-legged black and tan body." The emotional attachment he felt for the dog astounded and even unsettled him: "It was as if all my life I had been waiting for an object on which to pour out all the accumulated love that I had been storing up for so many years," he wrote tellingly.[2] A succession of dachshunds—Blackie,

Cranford, Harper, Charlie—would be Steward's companions for the rest of his life, and their deaths would be wrenching emotional experiences. Perhaps the most revealing lines about the place of dogs in his life are found in the obituary he composed for Cranford in September 1988: "For nine years, nearly ten, he has been the repository of nearly all my love, the keeper of all my secrets, a small beast who gave me love and affection in his reserved way, and asked for nothing except an occasional treat. . . . He understood and loved me, with all my faults, as no one else in the human world ever could."[3]

> O bury me, friends, with my face to the ground,
> For all the world soon will be turned upside down.
>
> —DIOGENES LAERTIUS

This has been a month of ghouls and open graves for me.

It all began on a peaceful Sunday morning some days ago. I was lying in bed minding my own business when the phone rang. One of those impossibly bright and cheery voices inquired if it were really Sparrow on the wire, to which I sleepily answered yeah. Then, said she, she was speaking for the Palisade Park Memorial Association, and would I be interested in buying a cemetery lot.

Well, there is nothing quite like being sold a cemetery lot at an early hour of a Sunday morning to make a person perk up a little, and to shake the old sandman out of one's eyes, so it was almost at once that I was wide awake. N-no, I stuttered, I didn't think I would be interested in buying a lot in Palisade Park Cemetery.

"Oh," she said, and you could feel the hurt in her tone. I had begun to sweat a little by then, when all of a sudden she said very brightly, as if the idea had just hit her: "Well, perhaps you are more interested in cremation?"

I allowed that I hadn't given much thought to the matter one way or another. She then got to work in earnest.

"O bury me." Quotation by the cynic philosopher Diogenes of Sinope (412–323 BCE) as recorded in the anecdotal biographical work *Lives of Eminent Philosophers* (VI.ii.31–32) by the fourth-century CE writer Diogenes Laertius.

Sparrow on the wire. A play on Steward's ornithological pseudonym.

"We have the loveliest columbarium in all Chicagoland," she said effusively. Just what, I responded, is a columbarium? Why, she said, it is a place where you store the cinerary urns, you put them in niches sunk in the walls.

That gave me a talking point. I was decidedly against, I said firmly, any such practice of public exhibition, and I wanted my ashes divided into three parts and hauled gaily away by my best friends. That rather wounded her, and she sounded as if I weren't being exactly decent. Whereupon I told her of an old French countess I knew, who had her husband's ashes made into an egg timer, saying "Time he should be of *some* use!"

She gargled throatily on that one, and I said why not send me your brochure on measurements and rates of admission, and she mumbled something about me that contained a small insult to my grandmother, and we both hung up. The more I lay thinking of her, the clearer grew the picture in my mind of her speaking over the telephone. She probably held the instrument with a half-decayed hand that had shreds of flesh clinging around the exposed bones. A king-sized rubber band supported her lower jaw. She was dressed in a rotting shroud with a withered corsage on it, and thin and wintry vines were trailing from her. There were lumps of earth in her hair, and sere brown leaves falling from her dress now and then. What a lovely way to spend one's life—pimping for an open grave!

By all counts, that should have ended my contact with death. But it seemed to be my cemetery day. In the afternoon we went riding out towards Hinsdale, and we stopped at a cemetery. It was a very unusual cemetery. It was for pets.

I have nothing against pets. Along with W. C. Fields, I will say that the man who hates children and dogs cannot be entirely *bad*, but that is neither here nor there. I once knew a dear old lady who had her pet parrot stuffed and put in an inlaid box, specially made at a cost of a hun-

an old French countess. Variations on this story have long been enshrined in folklore.

W. C. Fields. William Claude Dukenfield (1880–1946), American film and radio actor who cultivated the comic persona of a man who hated children and dogs.

Gravestone (foreground) of the horse Admiral Togo (1902–1937) in the Hinsdale Animal Cemetery, Willowbrook, Illinois. (Author's photograph)

dred and fifty smackers. That was all right—she could afford it, she had piles. And I'd heard of the old maid who had her monkeys stuffed and holding hands. But never have I seen such monuments erected, such money spent, as in that holy burying ground.

I must confess I was shocked. The inscriptions on the tombstones ranged all the way from a dignified "Bill" on a boulder inset with a photograph of a Boston bull to a sonnet of Shakespeare's on a huge memorial over someone's horse. It seemed to be the custom to append the

Steward late in life with one of his dachshunds. (Courtesy of the Estate of Samuel M. Steward)

family name to the animal's monument, which might lead one to say
something about the Mothers of Dogs if this were not a family magazine. And here were such things as "Our beloved baby, 1925–1937," and
on a Christian cross above Sancha, our beloved fox terrier, were the
words: "As a mark of gratitude and fidelity this sacred spot has been
reserved." For a beast named Kahn of Kabul, who dwelled in this vale

of sorrow from 1941 to 1944, John Keats tore out his soul a century ago to furnish the information that "A thing of beauty is a joy forever." Our Chiqui Girl reposed beneath a simple little *décor* of Holland wooden figures, painted white and looking very rustic and tranquil. The horse named Admiral Togo [1902–1937] had a tree growing from his grave, abundantly in leaf and fertilized by his superior manure. Here was a fine granite in loving memory to Prince, Nora's baby puppy boy, Jerry's little pride and joy. And there was Tuffy, a perfect little lady, never to be forgotten. Trudy our Lover, Sugar our Pal.

We wandered about looking at the graves. It was a pleasant and delightful spot, with late summer flowers in bloom, and the cool wind rippling the wheat fields beyond. Willows bent and swayed, as proper and decent willows should bend and sway in cemeteries. We saw some cement caskets four feet long, and learned that a hearse could be rented, and that something could be said over the grave—a few dignified words—for a mere twenty-five bucks more. Perpetual care? Oh, yes indeed! Flowers for the summer season, evergreen covering for the winter season. There was a sign that said "Dogs not permitted except on leash" but it was worn and illegible, so the dogs couldn't read it, of course. And there were several lively ones scampering around, blissfully lifting a leg against the laurels over the graves of their dear departed comrades. But in one far corner, almost obscured beneath a clump of shrubbery, we found our greatest triumph of the day. It sat upon a little flat tombstone inscribed with a family name. It was a quart Mason jar full of religious cards, all properly made out to the dog beneath.

Need these distressing remarks be continued? It was with emotions jiggling between tears and laughter that we left, laden with leaflets about rates and the number of tenants [fourteen hundred, with room for two thousand more]. Can any sane person with the slightest vestigial remain of a sense of social justice look upon this macabre farce and think of

---

this vale of sorrow. Cf. lines from the eleventh-century hymn *Salve Regina*: "Ad te suspiramus, gementes et flentes / in hac lacrimarum valle" ("To you do we sigh, mourning and weeping / in this vale of tears").

"A thing of beauty." Oft-quoted first line of the poem *Endymion* (1818), by John Keats (1795–1821).

human beings starving and not do something about it? Have we worked hard at civilization for ten thousand years to see this end product?

As we were leaving, we passed two hatchet-faced women who had evidently just arrived by broom. One of them suddenly burst into tears. "Oh, I'm so unhappy," she blubbered. "I just lost my pussy last week."

"You poor dear," rasped the other. "How old was it when it died?"

The French have a word for it. They call it *le mot de Cambronne*.

---

pussy. A term with many sexually related slang uses, including (as early as 1904) "a male homosexual" (*OED*).

le mot de Cambronne. A French euphemism ("Cambronne's word") for the alleged one-syllable reply of General Pierre Cambronne (1770–1842), a commander of the French forces at the Battle of Waterloo in 1815, to British demands for his surrender: "Merde!"

12

ON A CALL TO PARIS

MARCH 1946

Steward first became familiar with the early works of Gertrude Stein through Clarence E. Andrews, a charismatic professor at Ohio State who lived part of each year in Paris, had been invited to Stein's salon, and taught her poetry at a time when she was not widely known. When Andrews died in 1932, Steward, then in graduate school, decided to write to Stein with the news of his death. A regular correspondence between the two followed, and in 1936 Steward sent Stein a copy of his just-published novel, *Angels on the Bough*. Stein liked it—she wrote back to Steward that he had "really created a piece of something"[1]—and started addressing her letters more informally to "Sam."

Traveling to Europe for the first time in August 1937, Steward arranged a stay with Stein and Toklas at their summer home in Bilignin, and the three hit it off, Steward slightly awed to be in the presence of Stein, whose reputation was now well established,[2] and the older women taking a somewhat maternal interest in their bright young friend, whom they now called "Sammy." Steward visited a second time in the summer of 1939, leaving hurriedly as war was breaking out. On both occasions, he spent each night making extensive notes on the day's events and conversations. Steward's 1977 edition of Stein's and Toklas's letters to him begins with a 115-page memoir in which he drew on this material to create a vivid account of their conversations and mannerisms and of daily life in Bilignin.[3]

As the ebullient tone of this essay suggests, Steward's friendship with Stein and her confidence in him as a writer marked a high point in his early life. But only four months after this piece was published, he would be devastated to read in the newspapers of her unexpected death in Paris following surgery for stomach cancer—a turn of events that makes this essay's final paragraph especially poignant.

In the years after Stein's death, Steward's friendship with Alice Toklas deepened; he sent her frequent gifts and visited her regularly in Paris until her death in 1967. "Nothing in my life has ever had any more real meaning for me than my knowing these two," he wrote in 1977, "and to the end their presence will still be tenderly and happily alive for me."[4]

It is with great pleasure that we announce the restoration of civilian telephone service to France.

—THE ILLINOIS BELL TELEPHONE COMPANY,
IN SEPTEMBER, 1945

All the world knows of Gertrude Stein, that famous American expatriate writer who because of her obscurity and her haircut has a wider and more varied audience than almost anyone since Saint Paul. Her name is news for all the journals in America. Limericks are composed about her, and rugs for nurseries are woven on her themes in children's stories. She is called, among other things, the "Grandmother of Modern Literature"; and it is certainly true that every writer deserving of a hoot in the last forty years has at one time or another come under her influence. She has had countless imitators but no rivals. Secure in her position, lonely and immortal, she has for the past half century kept hammering away at words—and frequently knocking the daylight out of them, it may be said in passing.

All the world knows. Steward's opening sentence is deliberately and humorously hyperbolic. *The Autobiography of Alice B. Toklas* (1933) had finally gained Stein a wide readership, but her other works remained inaccessible to most readers in 1946 and were not likely to be known by many in Steward's putative audience of Illinois dentists.

rugs for nurseries. Six of Clement Hurd's illustrations for Stein's children's book *The World Is Round* (1939) were used as designs for hand-hooked wool rugs sold in 1939 for $14.50 by the famed W. & J. Sloane furniture and design store in New York. The patterns included "Rose Is a Rose," "Eyes a Surprise," "Willie and His Lion," "Is a Lion Not a Lion," "There," and "The World Is Round" ("Nursery Steins" [advertisement], *New Yorker,* October 31, 1939, 36).

Time has put a circle of legend around her, like the magic fire around Brunnhilde. Sitting in her rocking chair in Paris or down in the south of France at Bilignin, she is like a grey squat Buddha as she makes her *ex cathedra* pronunciamentos about modern literature. And she has gradually come to acquire that dusky mage-like character that Coleridge had at Highgate . . . prophet and seeress, her oracles are sibylline and profound, and invariably correct. Few there are who can match her in conversation, and none at all who can outshout her.

The war did not change Gertrude much. I was with her in France in 1939 when it began to pop. She was flustered, but she got a check cashed and laid in two hundred litres of petrol—"because money and gas stop when a war comes and then how do you get anywhere and what do you use to get there with now tell me." When I finally escaped from France,

Brunnhilde. The name of a figure in Norse mythology who appears in Richard Wagner's four-opera cycle *Der Ring des Nibelungen* (1876) as a valkyrie, a type of powerful female spirit who decides human destinies—especially who shall triumph in battle and who shall be defeated. In Wagner's telling, Brunnhilde disobeys her father, the god Wotan, and is put to sleep surrounded by a ring of fire that can only be vanquished by a fearless hero. In operatic tradition, the role is performed by a soprano of formidable physical size and vocal power.

Bilignin. The French village not far from Geneva where Stein and Toklas rented a summer home. When the Germans occupied and divided France in World War II, Stein and Toklas closed up their Paris home and moved permanently to Bilignin in order to be in the unoccupied zone. They spent the last part of the war in nearby Culoz before returning to Paris.

ex cathedra. A Latin phrase ("from the chair") referring to a doctrine defined by the Roman Catholic Church in 1870, according to which the pope's pronouncements when he invokes the authority of his office are infallible. In secular contexts, the phrase is often used sarcastically to suggest unwarranted authority; here Steward pokes gentle fun at Stein's "pronunciamentos."

mage. "A person of exceptional wisdom and learning" (*OED*).

Coleridge had at Highgate. In 1816, the English poet and literary theorist Samuel Taylor Coleridge (1772–1834) moved to the house of his physician in Highgate, in the north of London, where he lived until his death. Among the pilgrims who came there to hear his pronouncements on literature and philosophy was Thomas Carlyle, who offers a vivid portrait of the elderly Coleridge in his *Life of John Sterling* (1851).

When I finally escaped. At Stein's urging, Steward left Bilignin for LeHavre on August 29, 1939, with plans to board the *Normandie*, scheduled to depart for New York on September 6. Once in LeHavre, Steward discovered to his shock that the *Normandie* was still in New York, but he managed to book passage on the crowded S. S. *President Harding* (Steward to Stein, ALS, September 15, 1939, Steward Letters).

sweating and scared, I sent her a Mixmaster from Chicago. It arrived, and was a minor sensation in the province of Ain.

Time went on, and the postal service failed. There was a trickle of letters during the war, but not many. But last October there came an epistle from her. She would not mind, I am sure, if one were to quote a few lines from it:

> My dearest Philly: It's a long time between drinks but there is so much to do these days and then there is still more, there always is still more, what can we tell you, first is the Mixmaster still re-created, that is to say can one get spare parts, we could do with the two twirlers our two got busted in the country and the bowl in which the twirlers twirl, would it be too much bother, these days one asks for what one wants, since you cannot buy you have to ask and asking mostly works such is the way of life . . .

I immediately called the company, and asked. "You will have to find out," someone said, "if it has an automatic whipper and ejector." Then

---

Mixmaster. The Sunbeam Mixmaster electric mixer, first manufactured in 1930, was available in fall 1939 as the Model 5, which came with either milk-white or jadeite-green glass bowls (Taylor Evan, "Sunbeam Mixmaster," http://taylorevan.com/sunbeam-mixmaster/). Steward chose the latter, had the wiring and plug adapted for use in Europe, and in late November 1939 shipped it to Stein and Toklas in a wooden crate (Steward to Stein, TLS, January 26, 1940, Steward Letters). It arrived on Easter Sunday, March 24, and sparked a series of effusive letters of thanks from Stein: "oh so beautiful is the Mix Master, so beautiful and the literature [directions for use] so beautiful, and the shoe button potatoes that same day so beautiful and everything so beautiful" (Stein to Steward, ALS, March 25, 1940, Stein Letters). In July, Toklas accidentally dropped the jadeite mixing bowl, which "fell into little pieces on the kitchen floor, such lovely green little pieces," and Stein wrote to ask if Steward could send a replacement (Stein to Steward, ALS, July 8, 1940, Stein Letters), repeating the request in subsequent letters: "you see you can use other bowls but they do not twirl around in that lovely green mix master way and when they do not twirl then they instead of staying down rise up and spill and therefor [sic] the mix master will have to be a mix master still" (Stein to Steward, ALS, November 18, 1940, Stein Letters).

Ain. District in France where Bilignin is located.

My dearest Philly. Stein's actual salutation is "My dearest Sammy"; the letter is dated October 27, 1945 (Stein to Steward, ALS, October 27, 1945, Stein Letters).

the two twirlers. The Mixmaster 5 used two twin beaters. Steward eventually sent a new bowl and beaters (*Dear Sammy*, 155).

it was that I saw the wonderful, wonderful advertisement from the Bell Telephone Company. Rates were down, the war was over, the world was bright! I would call Gertrude Stein in Paris!

Sunday was the only day to call—if you wanted the rates, and I did. And between eight in the morning and noon were the only hours, for after all, the time lag and Gertrude's advancing years made it rather imperative that the dear girl be not disturbed after early evening on any day.

Full of high hope, I called on the morning of October 28, last year. Some adenoidal bobby-soxer took the call. "Where?" she said, and when she finally realized, she gasped "Oh my goodness!" and her voice vanished into the switchboard maze. In a few moments, a dour and elder lady from the chorus line in *Macbeth* questioned me, told me to wait, connected me with the overseas operator in New York—and then broke the connection.

Well, I tried it again. Not for nothing is my name what it is; I have learned to keep pecking away. This time I was gravely informed that the lines were open only for government business. I stuttered and talked loosely about the ad I'd seen in the papers, but to no avail. Sunday morning wore on, noon came, and I sank back exhausted from my labors.

The next Sunday I tried it again. Nothing doing. The ad was "a mistake." The fourth supervisor I talked to threatened to charge me double, and finally said that the circuits were in order for only five minutes a day, and that they were out now, and would I kindly hang up and free the line.

The third Sunday they came out with a brand new one. You had to place a call, it seemed, and then you had to wait in line. They had had calls placed for almost six months. That, said I, was rather strange, since the announcement of the resumption of service was only three weeks

---

Bell Telephone Company. Popular name for American Telephone and Telegraph, the company that owned and operated telephone service in most of the United States in the 1940s.

on the morning of October 28. Since Stein's letter was written on October 27 and posted from France on October 29, Steward's first attempt at calling in response to it had to be later than October 28.

the chorus line in Macbeth. Steward refers humorously to the three witches in Shakespeare's play.

old. Grudgingly, the gal finally took my call; she would place it, and I would be able to get through on December 2.

Since I am a gentleman, that stopped me for two weeks. But what do you think happened on December 2? Of course, the same thing that happened on the earlier trials. No wires. No connections. Then the next Sunday [or was it earlier? The chronology gets a little confused] there was a telephone strike in New York. No operators. No answers. No hands.

If there ever were a fit candidate for the degree of Doctor of Frustration in the Boswell Club, it was myself by then. To be so handled by a public utility is almost too much. After you express yourself in no uncertain terms, the *click!* and the dead wire are almost enough to make one look for a homing pigeon. But I met the frustration magnificently with a coupla fifths of whisky each Sunday, and time went by.

On January 13, 1946, there seemed to be signs of life in the telephone company. Bright and early at seven a.m. an operator called. "Did youse have a call placed to Danton 65-06 in Paris, France?" she whinnied. I allowed as how I did.

"Well," she announced, "it may go through next Sunday." And hung up.

The shock was pretty great, but it took only a pint to get over it. I began to get ready for the Great Day, January 20. At eight that morning I was up and dressed in my best suit, freshly shaved, and with a new necktie on. The hours slipped slowly by. Ten, eleven o'clock came and went, noon passed, the symphony came on—and I couldn't even get an operator. My line was sealed against all incoming and outgoing calls.

At four the phone rang. It was the overseas operator. "We have your party," she said. Then—after all the months—I'd forgotten what I had been told to ask her about the Mixmaster! Frantically I pawed through the scraps of paper on the desk—no information! I tried to think whether it was an automatic injector or a twirling whipper or a skipping turtle that she wanted.

Doctor of Frustration. Humorous degree awarded by the Boswell Club, a literary club founded in Chicago in 1942 to study the works of Samuel Johnson, James Boswell, and other eighteenth-century authors.

Then I heard her wonderful voice, straight from Olympus, neo-Valkyrean, thrilling and delightful. Space and time were no more. But something was dreadfully wrong. I could hear her voice, and get the inflection—but I could not understand a single word. For three full minutes we shouted at each other, neither of us knowing what the other said. But it was joyous, after all. I know damned well I was sweating when we hung up, and I'll bet she was, too. Telephone conversations are lovely things, but it is very hard to carry them on without words.

Well, I'm twelve dollars lighter and not very much wiser, but I do know that I won't try it again. It will really be cheaper for me, considering the wear and tear on the nervous system over a period of three months, to wait until 1947 and then go over to Paris and talk to her face to face. And meanwhile, I think I'll go to my favorite medium to see if she can't get in touch with the shade of Alexander Graham Bell. I would like her to convey to him a few rather pointed words.

Olympus. In Greek mythology, the mountain home of the twelve major gods.

neo-Valkyrean. Steward continues the comparison between Stein and Brunnhilde.

twelve dollars lighter. The equivalent of about $150 in 2015.

the shade of Alexander Graham Bell. That is, the spirit of the inventor of the telephone, in 1876.

13

ON THE IMPORTANCE OF DYING YOUNG

APRIL 1946

When Alfred Edward Housman died in 1936, he was widely recognized as one of the leading classical scholars of his age. "He had a vast knowledge of classical literature," wrote C. M. Bowra in a contemporary appreciation, "and he knew Latin as few can ever have known it."[1] Through his lifelong study of the Latin poets Manilius, Juvenal, and Lucan, Housman had single-handedly raised to a new level the field of textual criticism—the branch of literary study devoted to determining the text of a work that is closest to the text originally written by the author. The Kennedy Professor of Latin at Cambridge when he died, he was an exacting scholar who had developed a reputation for acute intelligence and undisputed integrity—and for little patience with sloppy thinking, the purveyors of which he didn't hesitate to ridicule. As he put it in his famous lecture "The Application of Thought to Textual Criticism" (1921), "Knowledge is good, method is good, but one thing beyond all others is necessary; and that is to have a head, not a pumpkin, on your shoulders, and brains, not pudding, in your head."[2]

Housman's esoteric scholarly career was balanced by his work as an accessible and popular poet, and in this essay, it is primarily that Housman whom Steward writes about. Housman wrote his first book of poetry, *A Shropshire Lad*, in 1895, at the very time that Oscar Wilde's trial for indecency in April and May of that year was demonstrating the danger that faced anyone whose homosexuality came to public notice. The book's preoccupation with male comradeship but also with transience, loss, death, and the grave no doubt derives from Housman's lifelong but unrequited love for his heterosexual undergraduate roommate, Moses Jackson, but may also more broadly reflect the sensibility of a gay man alone in a hostile world.[3] The world was anything but hostile to his poetry, however. Housman himself paid to have the first edition of five hundred copies printed in 1895, but by the 1940s, when Steward wrote, the book had sold more than 130,000 copies.[4]

Steward no doubt exaggerates when he states that the entire world mourned Housman's death, but presumably the gay world did, for his poetry had clearly suggested his homosexuality to the knowing reader at a time when gay men like Steward eagerly sought signs of kindred souls in the world around them. As a young man, indeed, Steward had written to Housman and had received a reply, and while teaching in Washington state, he had consciously imitated Housman's poetic style in "scores of melancholy poems about handsome young men I couldn't have."[5] During Steward's first trip to Europe in 1937, the year after Housman's death, he traveled to Cambridge "to visit Whewell's Court and Great Court B2 where A. E. Housman had lived for twenty-five years (to stand silently weeping, with chills along my spine)."[6]

The idea and epigraph of Steward's essay come from one of Housman's most famous poems, "To an Athlete Dying Young," a work to which Steward frequently refers in other writings. While the poem does not exactly celebrate early death, it does, as Steward writes, offer the consolation that dying at the height of one's accomplishments is preferable to living on into mediocrity. With that as his starting point, Steward interweaves lines from Housman's poem with reflections on people whose fame endures despite—or, he suggests, perhaps because of—their premature deaths.

> Eyes the shady night has shut
> Cannot see the record cut . . .
> —A. E. HOUSMAN

On a gray day, when the sky is glooming outside and the dark is gathering, there is no one better to read than Alfred Edward Housman. Turn low the lamp, set the slow hourglass on end, and stare into the empty sockets of a skull, remembering the saddest of all mottoes: *Remember, man, that thou art dust, and to dust thou shalt return.* For Housman is the poet of the shortness of youth and the nearness of death, the mourner for the golden friends, the rose-lipped maidens and the lightfoot lads. To

---

Remember, man. From Genesis 3:19, words traditionally said by a priest in the Catholic ritual of marking the foreheads of the faithful with ashes on Ash Wednesday.

the rose-lipped maidens. Cf. Housman's poem 54, lines 1–4: "With rue my heart is laden / For golden friends I had, / For many a rose-lipt maiden / And many a lightfoot lad."

read him is to feel the clutch at the heart, the unendurable sadness when youth is struck down, the anguish because the frosty scythe carelessly cuts off the unripe heads of wheat along with the others.

A strange man, Housman. His themes are youth and love and death. On his death in 1936 the world felt as Tennyson must have, when as a boy he climbed far out on a rock jutting into the angry sea, and carved the words, "Byron is dead." An incomparable sense of loss fell upon those of us who loved him. Housman was a Latin scholar, and taught at Cambridge in England. Before the scarlet lightning of his criticism, the world of classical scholarship quaked. He could forever demolish the pretensions of any scholarly fake with one lone paragraph. Yet there was another side to him, mellow, suffering, romantic, that made him write three thin volumes of verse: *A Shropshire Lad, Last Poems,* and a posthumous volume—*More Poems.* Within this slight compass, there is contained more genuine poetry than in a half hundred volumes of his contemporaries. The presence of Housman in a library is more surely a sign of good taste today than was a copy of the *Rubaiyat of Omar Khayyam* on the table in 1900.

Among the sixty-three poems of *A Shropshire Lad,* there are many that make one pause to consider the great questions of life. There are some that in simple words tell of love ended by death, and there are brave and bitter ones that tell us to train for ill and not for good. There are universal truths, and subtle analyses of the way-things-are-but-should-not-be. One hesitates to say which is a favorite, when all are of such excellence. But there is one which always starts me pondering, and it is "To an Ath-

---

felt as Tennyson must have. The story's source is Frederick Locker-Lampson, whose daughter married Tennyson's son Lionel; it is repeated, among other places, in Hallam Tennyson's biography of his father (*Alfred Lord Tennyson: A Memoir by His Son* [1897; Cambridge: Cambridge University Press, 2012], 2:69).

Last Poems ... More Poems. Housman published *Last Poems* in 1922, just before the death of Moses Jackson, to whom he sent a copy. In 1936, Laurence Housman edited and published his brother's remaining unpublished poetry as *More Poems.*

a copy of the Rubaiyat of Omar Khayyam. The number of new editions of Edward Fitz-Gerald's nineteenth-century translation rose dramatically between 1899 and 1909 (William H. Martin and Sandra Mason, *The Art of Omar Khayyam: Illustrating FitzGerald's Rubaiyat* [London: Tauris, 2007], 8).

lete Dying Young." The lines at the top of this page are from it, and state the theme. The athlete, cheered by the people and brought home on their shoulders, is today set down at the threshold of a stiller town. But his glory and record and reputation can never be lost, because he died at the right moment, in the full robe of life.

The poem always sets me thinking of the many in the past who died young, at the moment they should. There was Keats, for instance. What promise he showed! What things he accomplished in his twenty-six years! Sonnets cut in crystal, odes carved from chalcedony and onyx, lines as divine as anything in the English language—all came from his magic quill in a few brief years. And then he died, alone in the ancient city of Rome, just as the world awakened to his greatness. What would have happened had he lived to be as old as Wordsworth, scribbling verse that became flatter and more prosaic, turning out lines from which the hard clear flame had vanished?

> Smart lad, to slip betimes away,
> From fields where glory does not stay . . .

And there is Isadora Duncan, she of the lithesome body and the graceful arms, who brought to the world of dancing more bright loveliness and charm than the ballet has seen since. She was the goddess of two continents—kings wept at her thistledown grace, and all men adored her. She was driving recklessly with the wind down a dusty road in France one day—her long dramatic scarf whipping out behind her,

---

Keats. John Keats (1795–1821), English romantic poet and today a major figure in English literature, who died of tuberculosis in Rome at the age of twenty-five with only a handful of publications to his name.

chalcedony. A type of quartz found in many colors and varieties, of which onyx is one.

Wordsworth. William Wordsworth (1770–1850), major romantic poet and theorist of poetry whose early work had a profound impact on the nineteenth century but whose conventional poetry later in his long life is rarely read today.

Isadora Duncan (1877–1927). Dancer whose freely interpretive style and break from the positions of traditional ballet are often considered the beginnings of modern dance; on September 14, 1927, while she was riding in an open automobile, her long scarf became entangled in the spokes of a wheel, and she was pulled out of the car to her death.

her eyes shining under the great blue sky and the white pilings of clouds low on the horizon behind the poplars, her ears filled with the melody of unheard song. Who can say if it were not lucky for her scarf to touch the wheel of the car, to hesitate a moment, then wrap itself firmly around the axle, and snap her swan-like neck?

And silence sounds no worse than cheers
After earth has stopped the ears . . .

And lucky Chopin, to die when you did! The melodies that burned your brain might have faded, for no man can go on being good forever. As music comes forth, it leaves behind a grey and brittle ash. Your valses, your "Polonaise," your sparkling lovely etudes—would you have made them still? Might not those harmonies have grown dull and common-place? Might not the brilliance have turned to singsong monotony? You, too, have Death to thank, for now the year 'round—winter and summer—your grave in the cemetery Père Lachaise in Paris is banked with flowers and wreaths from those over all the world who love your music.

Now you will not swell the rout,
Of lads that wore their honours out . . .

Light tall white candles around the bier of the loved dead Valentino, set sweet incense to burning in the braziers, and have for the mourner a dove in a cage of sandalwood! Dream of a fair place graced by his slim

---

Chopin. Frédéric Chopin (1810–49), Polish pianist and composer whose funeral in Paris drew thousands of mourners.

Père Lachaise. Large Parisian cemetery laid out in 1804.

Valentino. Rudolph Valentino (1895–1926), handsome Italian-born silent film star and sex symbol whose funeral in New York following his death from peritonitis was attended by tens of thousands of women. As a teenager in Columbus, Ohio, Steward learned that Valentino was staying at a hotel in the city, went to his room to get an autograph, and left with a swatch of Valentino's pubic hair that he kept in a monstrance for the rest of his life. He described the encounter in a 1989 interview (Carl Maves, "Valentino's Pubic Hair and Me," *The Advocate*, June 6, 1989, 72–74).

brown hands . . . or so might say a woman now near forty, as she remembered the tempestuous passion of *Blood and Sand*, *The Son of the Sheik*, and *The Cobra*, in which the muscular and classic-profiled young Italian wrought his way with women. He did not grow old like John Barrymore; the muscles did not sag in his belly, nor the jowls droop into a satyr's mask. Swift as an arrow, he was struck to the heart, and died.

> And round that early-laurelled head
> Will flock to gaze the strengthless dead . . .

When Ernie Pyle raised his head just a little too far above his foxhole on the tiny isle of Io, was it lucky that the bullet came along? Could Ernie have found again, after the war was over, people to write about as movingly as he did about Captain Waskow? Could his audience be held by stories of tramps and hoboes, mill workers, and gas-station attendants in Arizona? On the wave of terror and love and agony of the war just past, Ernie rode high. Perhaps he would have continued.

> But set, before its echoes fade,
> The fleet foot on the sill of shade . . .

The list could go on and on, naming the names of those who died when they should, and it would include the range from Joan of Arc through

---

Blood and Sand . . . The Cobra. Three of Valentino's films, released between 1922 and 1926 (*The Son of the Sheik* posthumously).

John Barrymore (1882–1942). Dashing American stage and screen star whose good looks and acting acumen were eventually lost to alcohol.

Ernie Pyle (1900–1945). American journalist and Pulitzer Prize winner whose informal writing style and interest in the lives of individual soldiers made him a popular correspondent in World War II.

Captain Waskow. Henry T. Waskow (1918–43), subject of Pyle's most famous column, "The Death of Captain Waskow" (January 10, 1944), about the affecting tributes paid to Waskow's body by soldiers in his company after his death in combat.

Joan of Arc (1412–31). Military supporter of French king Charles VII in the Hundred Years' War with England who was captured by pro-English forces, tried for heresy in a pro-English religious court, and burned at the stake on May 30, 1431, in Rouen.

Knute Rockne and Will Rogers to Franklin Roosevelt. They were all fortunate in a way. They can never be those "runners whom renown outran,
and the name died before the man." Their glory is secure, their place in
history established, they can never fade into nothingness. And the world
will go on, speaking their names with reverence and regret. . . .

Oh, *hell*, James! Bring me the cyanide—*QUICK!*

Knute Rockne (1888–1931). Legendary Notre Dame University football coach whose death
in a plane crash in Kansas on March 31, 1931, sparked a national interest in airline safety.

Will Rogers (1879–1935). Cowboy, vaudeville performer, film actor, journalist, and
national celebrity who died in a plane crash in Alaska on August 15, 1935.

Franklin Roosevelt. Physically ill but still mentally acute, Roosevelt had died a year before
this essay appeared, on April 12, 1945.

14

ON CHICAGO

August 1946

Steward moved to Chicago from Washington state in 1936 to teach at Loyola University. His first novel, *Angels on the Bough*, had been published that spring and favorably reviewed in the *New York Times*, but on the day after commencement at the State College of Washington in Pullman (now Washington State University), he had been abruptly fired from his teaching position there by the college's president, who had been told that Steward's book was a "racy novel with a streetwalker in it." Shocked and outraged but in need of a job, Steward responded to an announcement of a position in English at Loyola University in Chicago by sending the dean an explanation of his situation and a copy of the novel. "He found it innocuous, and I was hired."[1]

Until this time, the largest city Steward had lived in was Columbus, Ohio, and he was initially repelled by the grittiness and dirt of Chicago in the 1930s and the extremes of wealth and poverty he found there. The more he wandered through the city, though, the more he fell under the spell of its skyscrapers and the allure of Lake Michigan. "The lake at midnight was sometimes wild and blowing, with the air full of King Lear," he wrote later. "I would stand on an embankment overlooking darkness and see no line between sky and water, only a sullen noisy void with whiteness fretting and circling at my feet and a coiling black film of water sweeping over a sanded beach, ending finally in a thin and crisping edge of foam."[2] Chicago also offered far more opportunities for sexual encounters than any place where Steward had lived previously, as suggested by his mention in this essay of "walk[ing] along the Oak Street beach at night" and "prowl[ing] the dark alleys of the Loop." And his closing description of the city as a naked, hairy giant lying "relaxed and smoldering along the lakefront" adds a decidedly homoerotic dimension to Sandburg's earlier celebration of Chicago as "City of the Big Shoulders."

Steward lived in Chicago for nearly thirty years, teaching first at Loyola and then at DePaul University, and subsequently pursuing his career as a tattoo artist on the city's Skid Row, until he moved to Berkeley, California, in 1964.

> Stormy, husky, brawling,
> City of the Big Shoulders.
> —CARL SANDBURG

There is a quality to the City of the Big Shoulders that grows on a person, like the taste of a martini, like learning to like pineapple and cottage cheese. There are so many things against it that have to be forgotten. When we first arrived we hated it—the dirty papers flying loosely on the streets, the sprawling quality it had, the "maryann" backs of the apartment houses that you see from the elevated tracks as the train groans and screeches on its way to the Loop. We loathed the dirty clothes hanging on the little wooden back porches, we suffered over the unbelievable squalor and filth of the south-side tenements, the naked babies playing in the mud of the backyards—and the incredible hypocrisy of the bright shops on Michigan Boulevard, and the white lights on the whiter Wrigley Tower.

The paradox of State Street, beginning in nothingness at the river, and running down through the proud stores . . . into what? Once you

"*Stormy, husky, brawling.*" Lines 4–5 of "Chicago" in *Chicago Poems* (1916), by Carl Sandburg (1878–1967), Pulitzer Prize–winning journalist, biographer, and poet whose poems about Chicago made a lasting contribution to the city's mythology.

Loop. The central business district of Chicago acquired this name after 1897, once the city's new elevated train tracks encircled the downtown area.

Michigan Boulevard. North Michigan Avenue, between the Chicago River and Oak Street, which became an elegant retail street after the opening of the Michigan Avenue Bridge across the Chicago River in 1920.

Wrigley Tower. The Wrigley Building (1921–25), an iconic Chicago landmark clad in white terra cotta and always illuminated by floodlights at night.

State Street. The "proud stores" of Chicago's main shopping district in the 1940s included Marshall Field's (in a building designed by Daniel Burnham) and Carson Pirie Scott (in one designed by Louis Sullivan).

the river. The Chicago River.

cross Van Buren, going south, what happens? Tattoo joints, burlesque houses, prostitutes, pimps, and ten-cents-a-shot saloons. Westward, the stumble bums of Madison Street, the dives on Clark Street—only a mile or two from the stately tower of the Tribune, and less from the elegant hotels of the Gold Coast. And for sharpest contrast, walk a short distance from the Gold Coast. You find yourself in one of the most unsavory sections of the city, if indeed you get there without being knocked cold.

Yet after a few years you come to love the city. You love its filth, and at the same time its strange holiness. It is the only human city in America. It has everything one could ask. Carl Sandburg called it the City of the Big Shoulders, Freight Handler to the Nation, Hog Butcher for the World, Tool Maker, Stacker of Wheat, and Player with Railroads. It is all that, and more.

It is only slowly that the quality of the city grows on you. You find that it breaks up into little neighborhoods, each with a distinct personality of its own. It falls apart into a hundred or a thousand or ten thousand small communities. It divides itself into north, south, and west sides—and the Poles and Italians live on the west, and the Negroes and the Germans elsewhere, and the Jews and the Catholics on the north side, and yet the whole city fits together, differently colored pieces in a jigsaw puzzle that is two hundred and fifteen miles square.

Gradually you learn about the city. It takes you six months to discover how to ride the elevated and find your way around. Policemen growl at you when you ask directions, and mumble something that only a native could understand. You walk along the river and watch the lights

Once you cross Van Buren. State Street south of Van Buren Avenue was Chicago's Skid Row in the 1940s, a seedy, crime-ridden stretch of the street that just a few blocks north featured the city's most fashionable department stores. Within ten years of writing this essay, Steward himself would open his own tattoo business here.

stately tower of the Tribune. The Tribune Tower (1925), a neo-Gothic skyscraper whose design won an international competition.

Gold Coast. The northside neighborhood along Lake Michigan that attracted many of Chicago's wealthiest residents in the first half of the twentieth century.

ride the elevated. The first stretch of the Chicago El, from downtown south to Jackson Park, was completed by 1893. By the 1940s, the system encircled the downtown area and reached far to the north, south, and west.

of the tall buildings around Wacker Drive break and glitter in the dirty water. You walk along the Oak Street beach at night, with the thunderous rush of the water washing against your eardrums, when the lake is white with a nor'wester blowing. And in winter the ropes stretched along the windy corners help you to stand on your feet. In spring you prowl the dark alleys of the Loop, see a street fight, look for a babe on a street corner, and get drunker than hell at a half buck a shot. In summer you tangle with the miscellaneous arms and legs on Foster Beach, get your nose burned, and pick up a case of skin rash from somewhere. But still you hear, obscurely in the back of your mind, a quotation from some second-rate poet that seems quite appropriate: "I cannot live away from water." And much as you swear at Lake Michigan, its tantrums, its unpredictability, its hot and cold—you know very well that it's yours, and you're its, and that its green and grey and blue and brown are there when you want to see them. You're discovering Chicago, you're learning that something other than a human being can have life in it. A city can, and Chicago is that city.

One night on the elevated platform you meet a mousey little man with a small suitcase. He is busily engaged at work on the billboards of

---

Oak Street beach. A mile-long sand beach along Lake Michigan at the north end of North Michigan Avenue. In the 1930s and 1940s, it was a popular gathering place for gay men (Chad Heap, "Gays and Lesbians," in *The Encyclopedia of Chicago*, ed. James R. Grossman, et al. [Chicago: University of Chicago Press, 2004], 331).

you prowl the dark alleys. Steward's search for sexual partners frequently led him into the alleys of the city and more than once resulted in his being robbed or beaten up (Spring, 58–60).

Foster Beach. In 1946, Steward lived only a few blocks from Foster Beach on Lake Michigan, in an apartment at 5441 North Kenmore Avenue.

"I cannot live away from water." Title of a 1929 poem by Benjamin Musser (1889–1951). In 1928, while an undergraduate, Steward met Musser at a poetry reading in Columbus, and the encounter developed into a sexual relationship that lasted for two years. Twenty years older than Steward and then poet laureate of New Jersey, Musser arranged for the publication of Steward's first book, *Pan and the Firebird*, in 1930 ("Autobiography," 97–101). Steward also quotes this line in his erotic novel *The Boys in Blue*, where the narrator calls it "the only good line of poetry that old Ben Messer [sic], one of my earliest scores, had ever written" (Phil Andros [Samuel Steward], *The Boys in Blue* [San Francisco: Perineum Press, 1984], 139).

the platform. He is using the implements in his case. You watch him idly, and hear him swear. What is he doing? Well, he's erasing moustaches from the billboards. He has all sorts of substances—wallpaper cleaner, art gum, typewriter erasers, ink eradicator, ether, and Energine. You are so fascinated that you follow him around for ten stations. "The lipstick is hardest to git off," he complains. "What about all the telephone numbers and messages?" you ask. "Oh, I hates to rub 'em off. Might be spoilin' some romance." He sighs wistfully. "But orders is orders," he says.

You go with a physician friend of yours to Harrison Street, to a little Italian bakery. You watch the hot bread being pulled out of the great stone-floored oven, just as they do it in Italy and Greece. You drink homemade wine, eat pizza and lamb baked in grape leaves. You go to the south side with a Negro friend, and drink in the black-and-tan joints. And then in the early dawn you ride home on the Outer Drive, with the lovely grey light on the skyline's buildings, and the steady *swush!* of the early traffic around you. And if you don't love Chicago at such a magic moment, you never will.

We came from a fairly small town in Ohio, and knowing Chicago was our first experience with a Big City. We were frightened and terrified at first. Ben Hecht's stories in his *1001 Afternoons in Chicago* had been our

---

Energine. A naphtha-based spot remover.

You go with a physician friend. Steward refers to his friendship with Dr. Stephen Anthony, the subject of the *IDJ* essay "On Ulysses, Grown Old" (May 1948).

black-and-tan joints. In largely segregated Chicago during the 1940s, music clubs open to both black and white patrons.

Outer Drive. Lake Shore Drive. When Steward wrote, the Lake Shore Drive expressway was complete between Belmont Avenue on the north and 47th Street on the south.

a fairly small town in Ohio. Steward grew up in Woodsfield, Ohio, which he elsewhere described as "a sleepy little town . . . arrested in time" (*Chapters*, 1).

Ben Hecht's stories. A leading writer of the so-called Chicago Literary Renaissance, Ben Hecht (1894–1964) was a journalist, novelist, and (later) celebrated Hollywood screenwriter whose column of Chicago sketches, "Around the Town: One Thousand and One Afternoons in Chicago," appeared in the *Chicago Daily News* between June 1921 and October 1922. Steward refers to the book of the collected sketches that was first published in 1922.

reading since we were old enough to know what Ellis and Freud were saying. They were fascinating stories. But of course such things could never really happen to people. They were the mad dreams of the man who wrote *Fantazius Mallare*. And the City was frightening. It was more lonely than the city of a quarter million from which we had come. And it is a commonplace that one can be more lonesome in a city of four million than in a city of one million. But if you find no single person to love, you begin to love them all. Then slowly but surely, they begin to love you.

There is, however, always your first holdup, and you are not a native Chicagoan until that happens. Mine occurred one evening long ago, when the old Stratosphere Club atop the Pure Oil building was still in existence. In those days the building wore a little blue neon Juliet cap, and beneath it was the fantastic, expensive club. From its windows you looked down on the misty abyss that was the cavern of the City. The

Ellis. Havelock Ellis (1859–1939), British physician whose *Studies in the Psychology of Sex* (7 volumes, 1897–1928) was the first comprehensive study of human sexual behavior. Steward writes that while in high school, he found a library copy of volume II, *Sexual Inversion*, left under a bed in the Woodsfield, Ohio, rooming house operated by his aunts: "The book opened the wide tall doors of the world for me. . . . Not only did I discover that I was not insane or alone in a world of heteros—but I learned many new things to do" (*Chapters*, 12).

Freud. Sigmund Freud (1856–1939), physician who lived and worked for most of his life in Vienna, where he founded the field of psychoanalysis; his works stressed the centrality of the erotic in human development. In the 1920s, Steward wrote later, he and his fellow college students "looked to our midsections as the glow from Freud filtered down to illuminate our crotches" (*Chapters*, 21).

Fantazius Mallare. Ben Hecht's novel *Fantazius Mallare: A Mysterious Oath* was published in 1922. The story of a mad artist unaffected by "the excitement of his neighborhood, his city, his country and his world" and consumed instead by "an intolerable loathing for life, an illuminated contempt for men and women" (22, 29–30), it was seized by government officials for obscenity on the basis both of the text and of the book's nude illustrations by Wallace Smith (1888–1937).

Stratosphere Club. Popular nightclub located at the top of the Pure Oil Building's forty-one-story central tower in the 1930s. The club's blue-and-silver matchbooks were inscribed with the slogan "There is atmosphere in the Stratosphere."

Pure Oil building. Office building (1926) at 35 East Wacker, commonly called the Jewelers Building.

little men, who always follow me when I'm in my cups, and whom I thought had long since gone home, began to appear. Gramps perched on my shoulder, and little Isaac crept from my pocket. "It's time now to go home," Gramps growled, so I went. I walked westward, and from an alley across LaSalle street, a guy came out with a gun. He took my watch and wallet and told me not to move for five minutes. La! I sat on the curb until the cops came (thirty-five minutes) and my knees couldn't have supported me even if I'd had crutches. So after that I was a native, and without batting an eyelash I now say that I was born in the city.

Well, Chicago, you can see now that we love you. Oh, yes, you're cultural enough, but it isn't for that we like you. We know you have the World's Largest Aquarium (with eleven cute seahorses and an octopus) and a museum of natural history (with some wonderful sculptures by Malvina Hoffman), and an orchestra and a band shell and an art institute and many other things (please see the front section of the classified Red Book directory)—but that doesn't count. You have a soul. Paris has one too, and London has none. New York has a metronome for a heart, and Los Angeles a woman's wristwatch ticking.

World's Largest Aquarium. The John G. Shedd Aquarium (1926; addition 1991).

a museum of natural history. Established in Chicago in 1891, the Field Museum of Natural History moved into its present building, designed by Daniel Burnham, in 1921.

Malvina Hoffman (1887–1966). New York–born sculptor commissioned by the Field Museum of Natural History in 1930 to create more than a hundred bronze, marble, and stone sculptures of people from a wide range of ethnicities and cultures, based on models from her own extensive travels around the world. At the time that Steward wrote, the complete set of works—life-size sculptures, busts, and heads—was displayed in the museum's Hall of Man.

an orchestra. Founded in 1891 under the direction of Theodore Thomas, the Chicago Symphony Orchestra occupied Orchestra Hall, designed by Daniel Burnham, in 1905. The building is now known as Symphony Center.

a band shell. The Grant Park Band Shell that Steward refers to was erected in 1935 to offer free summer concerts. It was renamed the Petrillo Bandshell in 1975.

an art institute. Founded in 1879, the Art Institute of Chicago first occupied its current main building, designed by Shepley, Rutan, and Coolidge, in 1893.

Red Book. Telephone directory.

I think of Chicago as a man-city, healthy, sweaty, and sensual. It is Gargantua with his head in Evanston, his feet in Gary, and he lies relaxed and smoldering along the lakefront. The trees of Lincoln Park are the curling man-hair of his chest, the trees of Jackson Park the foliage upon his legs, the tall buildings of the Loop his sturdy muscles, and the whole anatomy of the city his outstretched body.

This is my song of love to Chicago. I could not live anywhere else save in this city. I could not live away from the sound of the water of Lake Michigan. I love Chicago.

Gargantua. Giant who figures in five novels by François Rabelais (1494–1553) published between 1532 and 1564.

his sturdy muscles. In the same description of Chicago in his 1981 memoir, Steward recasts this phrase more explicitly (and logically) as "his sturdy upstanding phallus" (*Chapters*, 40). His alternative wording here suggests something about the boundaries of sexual explicitness that he imposed on himself when writing for publication in the *IDJ*.

15

ON OPERAS AND OPERATING

DECEMBER 1946

When Steward moved to Chicago in 1936, the city boasted a world-class opera theater that had opened only seven years earlier. The Civic Opera House, designed by
the Chicago architectural firm of Graham, Anderson, Probst, and White, was a spectacular art-deco space that included a gilded two-story atrium, a grand staircase in
the European style, and a stunning theater with 3,500 seats, excellent sight lines,
a gigantic stage, and state-of-the-art mechanicals. Unfortunately, the venerable
Chicago Civic Opera, which moved into the building when it opened in 1929, collapsed in bankruptcy only three years later in the depths of the Great Depression.

The experiences as an opera "super" that Steward describes in this essay occurred
later, between 1940 and 1946, when grand opera was remounted in Chicago by
the new Chicago Opera Company, which also performed in the Civic Opera House.
After the war, this company too went bankrupt, and until the founding of the Lyric
Opera of Chicago in 1954, opera in Chicago consisted mainly of traveling productions from the Metropolitan Opera and the New York City Opera.[1] The most
famous Chicago-based production of this period—for which Steward was again a
super—was an extravagant benefit performance of Wagner's *Tristan and Isolde*
on November 16, 1947, with Artur Rodzinski conducting the Chicago Symphony
Orchestra and two international stars of Wagnerian opera in the lead roles—the
Norwegian soprano Kirsten Flagstad and the Swedish tenor Set Svanholm. "As a
newly dead soldier on the field," Steward recalled later, "I lay on the stage floor
with armor faintly clanking as I heard, trembling, the magic love duet between
the two, singing fifteen feet away, the 'Liebestod.'"[2] The *Milwaukee Journal* called
the production "the greatest musical occasion of Chicago's recent history, with
undoubtedly the greatest singer [Flagstad] in the world today,"[3] and the apprecia-
tive audience demanded twenty-two curtain calls.[4]

When the Lyric Opera of Chicago was born in 1954, Steward got the job of "curtain boy," one of two invisible stagehands who pulled the closed curtains apart after each act to permit the principal singers to step out and recognize the audience's applause. For its fall 1954 premier, a grandly staged production of Bellini's *Norma*, the new company had scored an opera-world coup by booking the celebrated Greek-American soprano Maria Callas, now at the peak of her fame, in her American debut. Yet Steward, seated on stage just out of the audience's view behind folds of the open curtain, had a curiously ambivalent reaction to Callas's incomparable voice, and his recollection of the event decades later suggests that the first paragraph of this essay accurately describes his mixed feelings about opera as an art form: "[She] sang for seven weeks, three or four nights a week, seemingly directed at me, a few feet away," he wrote. "Her voice was lovely, the trills and fluting falls most effective—but it was like eating too many sweets at once. I foundered on it. And ever since, I have not been able to endure the sound of the human voice singing. I have not heard an opera for twenty-five years, and will never hear one again."[5]

> O toreadoro, don't spit on the floor-a,
> Use the cuspidor-a; that's what it's for-a.
> —ARIA FROM AN OLD OPERA

I always hated opera. First of all, it offended my aesthetic taste. Then it hurt my dramatic. And last, it pricked my realistic. A bastard art form that requires so much of what Coleridge called the "willing suspension of disbelief" should not be allowed to exist. It is hard enough to believe the ordinary play or movie, but to accept the fact that people acted out their lives and destinies in song is very, very thick for me. But that's opera for you—the last, the greatest, and the weakest of all illusions.

But I am a sucker for novelty. At the awful hour of six on a Sunday morning, my favorite uninhibited Brunnhildish friend of the Chicago

---

"*O toreadoro.*" Parody of lines from the bullfighter's aria in act 2 of the opera *Carmen* (1875), by Georges Bizet (1838–75).

"*willing suspension of disbelief.*" Famous phrase coined by Samuel Taylor Coleridge (1772–1834) in his *Biographia Literaria* (1817) to describe the necessity that the reader of a literary text accept its conventions, however unrealistic they may be.

Brunnhildish. From Brunnhilde, the name of a figure in Norse mythology who appears in Richard Wagner's four-opera cycle *Der Ring des Nibelungen* (1876). In operatic tradition, the role is performed by a soprano of formidable physical size and vocal power.

Opera called me to come down for a dress rehearsal. And I went, arriving there at eight on the dot.

The opera house at that hour is a magic and mysterious place. There were about ten persons there—sitting mummified in the first few rows, in the dark red-cushioned silence of the great auditorium. Then down the aisle came a man in a sweatshirt. He hopped over the retaining wall of the orchestra pit, and landed directly and business-likely on the podium. It was the "general artistic director," who was to direct the orchestra for the day.

The few operas I have seen were not "dress" rehearsals, and as we have said, it was hard enough to believe the illusion even when the actors were in costume. But nothing can compare to an opera done with as little scenery as possible, and the singers in street clothes! The harsh white lights, the frequent interruptions by the conductor as he swore in Italian at someone who hit a wrong note—these were shattering. The chorus went about its own business when not singing: I saw one girl open a paper bag and eat lunch while the aria "Celeste Aida" was being sung. Another was placidly crocheting a doily of some kind. And one of the stars calmly sat on the king's throne and applied a fresh coat of lipstick. When the great portable throne bearing the king was brought in, we could hear him loudly whispering: "Mygawd, you'll drop me, I know you will!"

When I left that early Sunday afternoon, I was quite sure I had attended my last opera. Yet curiously enough, a coupla weeks later—when another "dress" rehearsal was announced—I was right there, sitting absorbedly in one of the front rows. This time it was *Lohengrin*, a long and stuffy thing at best, full of idle song and little action. There was a new conductor who was very precise. He kept continually rapping to interrupt the music, and then he would throw his hands in the air and say, "Can dis be possible? How can dis ting be?" To confuse us more, he started out with the overture to the third act, then called for a singing of the second act, followed that with the first act, and finally went into

"*Celeste Aida.*" "Heavenly Aida," aria sung by Ramades in act 1 of the opera *Aida* (1871), by Giuseppe Verdi (1813–1901).

Lohengrin. Opera (1850) by Richard Wagner (1813–83).

the third. I was completely confused and exhausted, for the thing had kept us there for five full hours. And I was sure this time I was finished with opera.

Yet the human spirit is a curious thing, always questioning and alive to new experiences. So when my darling Brunnhilde spoke to me about "supering," about standing mutely around in costumes to lend "atmosphere," I once more tumbled. It was *Carmen*, and she got me on the list of supers.

I showed up at seven, trembling a little. I heard my name called, and within moments was being whisked up the elevator to the fifth floor above the stage, where the men supers dressed. Here all was tumult and shouting, and people climbing in and out of tights and knee-length Spanish breeches with white stockings and black pumps. The costumes looked rather frightful at close range. Gold braid was tarnished, velvet was patched, buttons were off, and safety pins were everywhere.

The costume master handed me a mustard-colored costume: a pair of breeches, a short bolero jacket, a string of red cheesecloth for a necktie, and a salmon-colored cummerbund to wrap around my manly form. And a round Spanish hat.

Within a short while I discovered that the breeches were size 46, which is a little large for my svelte thirty-inch waist. I was soon madly fumbling at my rear, trying to pull in the straps and pin myself together. To add to the complications, the buttons were all off on one side of the front. At last a kind old gentleman saw my troubles. "Come here," he said. He applied two safety pins, took an extra long cummerbund, and twirled me into it. Then he took two three-inch folds in my rear, and warned me not to turn my backside to the audience. And we went down to the stage, where a little man rubbed our cheeks briefly with bright rouge, and with a black eyebrow pencil gave us romantic sideburns, and let us go.

It was a wonderful night, especially that second act. My Brunnhilde, strangely metamorphosed now into a black-haired gypsy, squired me to the front of the stage, to the table where Carmen would later come, and Don José. There we sat during the exciting music, while a lusty and wonderful Carmen flirted with me, snatched my wine cup, and then turned her attention to Don José, of course. At the end of the scene, there was almost a tragedy. I did not know she was going to spring on the table to do a brief fandango, and I damned near got a heel in my eye.

Then we were smugglers in the third act, and picadors in the last, carrying banderillas and going to the fights. How many costume changes did it all involve? I dunno, but by the time it was over, I had the feeling that I had handled more safety pins, strange garments, and funny hats than anyone else on the stage. My white cotton stockings were always coming down, and I was always having to pull them up and give 'em an old-fashioned 1920 twist.

I fell again for *Samson and Delilah*. This time I was a high priest, with a smelly wig and goatee, and lots of black lines on my face. The big moment in that came when Samson, blinded in Gaza, pushed aside the pillars of the temple of the god Dagon. Lightning flashed on the stage, thunder roared, and down came the whole shebang. We all ducked, because when *Samson* was first put on, two stagehands got hit by a column section when a cable broke.

This was on a Friday night. Sucker that I am, I went back for *La Traviata* on Saturday afternoon. Here I was a romantic young dandy, encased in tight brown trousers, a green jacket with a frilly white jabot in front, and a beautifully embroidered vest. This time I made no mistake: I had borrowed a garter belt from a friend, and my stockings stayed up beautifully. But I had forgotten I had it on in the dressing room, and it was not until much later that I knew why all the boys were tittering behind my back as I undressed.

Oh, we were such a gallant and polite crew with our white gloves and sideburns, bowing and scraping to all the lovely ladies, while the fragile consumptive Violetta coughed out her life in delicate song.

---

banderillas. Decorated barbs that the bullfighter thrusts into the neck of the bull.

1920 twist. A reference to a women's hair style of the 1920s that involved pulling long hair straight back and twisting the ends together at the back of the head to keep them in place.

Samson and Delilah. Opera (1877) by Camille Saint-Saëns (1835–1921).

La Traviata. Opera (1853) by Giuseppe Verdi (1813–1901).

jabot. In eighteenth-century men's fashion, a decorative piece of lace attached to the neckband and falling on the chest like a modern necktie.

Poor Violetta! Weak as she was, it took her forty minutes of singing in the last act before that brave spirit finally expired.

There you have it, and I hope you'll all be warned by my experience. Long ago, an evening of supering in the ballet *Scheherazade* cured me permanently of my balletomania. I suppose the case is altered, however, with opera. For I had loved the ballet to begin with, and had hated opera. I seem to have begun at the rear end in this instance. And now I think I will put on my red tights, don my black cap with horns, and go out with my staff to scare the living bejeepers out of little kids. For, look you, do you not recognize Mephistopheles from *Faust*?

Poor Violetta! Steward gently mocks the operatic convention that requires the consumptive female character to keep singing until the opera ends.

an evening of supering. See Steward's *IDJ* essay "On Balletomania" (June 1945).

Faust. Steward refers to the opera (1859) by Charles Gounod (1818–93).

16

ON MEN AND THEIR FEATHERS

JANUARY 1947

Ostensibly about the way in which contemporary men's clothing runs counter to nature by drably attiring the male of the species, this gender-bending essay can also be read as a coded celebration of drag. In the context of references to feathers, straight seams, "the genus *homo*," and radio personality Tom Breneman trying on women's hats, even the "little white aprons and white gloves" worn by Masons assume a possible gendered meaning. From sailors' earrings to the rising popularity of fragrances for men, there are signs, Steward suggests, that "the shell is cracking" and men have not completely lost "the subterranean memory of their former fine feathers." On New Year's Eve they delight in being "strung with festoons and ribbons," and on Hallowe'en they prefer those costumes that allow them to wear tights rather than pants. In that connection, the Victorian poet Alice Meynell appears as an unlikely witness in support of the assertion that "the more [men] can show of their legs, the happier they are."

In short, "Man still likes to dress up"—a statement that certainly applied to Steward himself, for whom clothing and role playing were interconnected, lifelong interests. In graduate school, he became interested in Catholicism partly through reading Joris-Karl Huysmans's novel *Against the Grain* but more intensely through the "panoply" of the liturgy: "How richly colorful the vestments of the Church seemed when I first attended a mass!"[1] Though his military career lasted only a week, he had joined the navy rather than the army in 1943 in part because of the appeal of the uniform: "I loathed the color of khaki! Blue was better for me."[2] At the time that he wrote this essay, he had been supering in Chicago ballet and opera productions for almost a decade and had so often performed several parts on stage—the gondolier in the *Nutcracker*, a eunuch in *Scheherazade*, a smuggler in *Carmen*—that he had a standing claim on the costumes and the roles.[3] But perhaps the link between clothing and fantasy in Steward's life is clearest in the studio portraits of himself that he had made in Paris during visits to Alice Toklas in the 1950s, in which, abandoning the dapper attire of an English professor and imagining himself as a sailor or a street tough, he could fulfill the "driving hidden urge" to reclaim "his birthright of color and costume."

> The redder the wattles, the prouder the cock.
>
> —OLD ARABIAN PROVERB

Somewhere along the way, the male of the species has lost his birthright of color and costume. Whether he willingly cast it aside or whether he was robbed of it is hard to say. But even the briefest glimpse into the animal world should call up in the modern man feelings of shame, loss, and desolation.

Consider the world of creeping and crawling and flying things. Has not the peacock a wider fan, glistening and glittering with purple and green and gold, than the mousey little peahen? Does not the scarlet-crested male pheasant with his graceful tail outshine his nondescript wife? Has not the proud strutting cock of the barnyard a finer comb, longer wattles, and a more piercing black eye than the little red domestic who lays his eggs for him? The nightingale's song is sweeter than that of his spouse, and the whale's breath lovelier than the she-whale's. The damask moth is brilliant beside his mith, and the color of the cardinal outdazzles that of his mistress.

But what of the genus *homo*, the *sap* of today? Encased in dull drab woolens, bevested, noosed around the neck with a stiffened collar, creased in his long hot pants, he goes sombrely and soberly about the business of try-

---

Consider the world. In this paragraph, the series of similar rhetorical questions ("Has not . . . Does not . . ."), the parallel and balanced sentence elements, the emphasis on contrasting examples, and the frequent alliteration ("creeping and crawling . . . glistening and glittering . . . moth . . . mith . . . color . . . cardinal") evoke the style popularized by the English dramatist and prose writer John Lyly (d. 1606) in his narrative *Euphues: The Anatomy of Wit* (1578).

genus homo, the sap of today. On one level, Steward seems to refer humorously to the only surviving species of the genus *homo*: *homo sapiens.* Read differently, the phrase could refer to homosexuals who have to wear confining, drab clothing when they would actually be more comfortable in a "furtively" purchased "pair of mauve pajamas edged with yellow."

ing to attract a wife with his sad colors. And the curious reversal remains unexplained—for the female has borrowed the male's plumage, and now with earrings and bracelets, scents and pomades, feathers and "hairdos," she has made of herself the quarry that the male used to be.

Today we often forget that it was not always so. Man lost his decorative coloration less than a hundred years ago. The ancient Greeks wore silken chitons and chlamys, embroidered with bands of purple and gold, with silver fillets around their hair. When Leonardo lived, men were exquisite in their puffs of lawn and gold, green jackets sewn with silver herons, collared with jewels of rose and violet and seed pearls. They carried pierced perfume balls, and rosaries of black amber and gold. In Shakespeare's day, there were two-foot starched ruffs around the neck, lockets, rings, slashed bodices through which scarlet and green silks showed, and perfumes from the Orient. In the eighteenth century, at the courts of France and England, the male outdid himself. Jeweled snuffboxes, elaborately curled wigs of shoulder length, walking sticks encrusted with precious stones, rings on all fingers, velvet and silken knee breeches, scents and oils, powders and paints—all these were his heritage, and his person paled the woman's.

It is a sunken state in which man finds himself today. His normal love of color is suppressed, his desire thwarted. Only adolescents can get away with bright sweaters, trousers, and shirts—unless, of course, the male lives in Hollywood, which is really not a part of our time or civilization at all. Frustrated, inhibited, suppressed in his desires, man tries to find some outlet. But what can he do? He rather furtively buys some red-striped shorts or a pair of mauve pajamas edged with yellow, wears a little tufted feather in his hat, and lets his neckties do the rest. For, after all, the shorts and pajamas are scarcely to be worn outside his

---

chitons. Loosely draped, belted garments worn by men and women in ancient Greece.

chlamys. Normally an outer garment pinned at one shoulder and worn only by men in ancient Greece (plural: chlamyses—Steward seems to mistake the singular form for plural).

a little tufted feather. The gay associations of a feather in a hat go back to the eighteenth century: in the familiar (and originally satirical) song, when Yankee Doodle stuck a feather in his cap, he became a "macaroni"—contemporary slang for a fop or dandy, and by implication a homosexual.

suits—and the whole burden of his repression falls upon the five inches of colored cloth that is tied around his neck.

But we submit that there is still another angle to the problem, one which accounts for many phenomena of modern life. Man still likes to dress up. The subconscious hangover of what he used to be, the subterranean memory of his former fine feathers, is still with him.

To fulfill this driving hidden urge, he makes many efforts. He joins things like lodges, where he can wear little white aprons and white gloves, fezzes with quarter moons and tassels on them, gold-shaking epaulets, and silver braid and buttons. He becomes an Oddfellow, a Mason, an Elk, or a Knight of Pythias. He parades in mystic formations and at funerals. He may even—heaven help him!—join the Ku Klux Klan, and in sheet and pillow case, emblazoned with a fiery cross, combine his innate sadism with the fecal symbolism of his dress.

Tom Breneman in his Hollywood restaurant has built a fantastic reputation for himself by trying on women's hats. He says he does it because they're so silly, and because it makes people laugh. But I often wonder. Is it not done simply because Tom cannot any more escape the urge to dress up than any other man can? Men welcome New Year's Eve because they can wear silly hats, be strung with festoons and ribbons, and in so doing can feebly clutch at the peacocks they used to be. And think of men at masquerade balls on Hallowe'en! If they are not too much the babbitt, what happens? They go as sinister pirates with cloak and dagger,

---

little white aprons and white gloves. Elements in the traditional attire of Freemasons.

join the Ku Klux Klan. At the age of nine, Steward saw hooded Ku Klux Klan members abduct the African American chiropractor from his hometown of Woodsfield, Ohio; the event left him "paralyzed with shock." Later in his boyhood he frequently witnessed cross burnings by the Klan (*Chapters*, 5). As an adult, he had no tolerance for racism, the theme of his last *IDJ* essay, "A Modest Proposal" (July 1949).

Tom Breneman (1901–48). Host of a popular morning radio program in the 1940s, *Breakfast in Hollywood*, and proprietor of Tom Breneman's Restaurant in Hollywood, from which the program was broadcast after 1945. It consisted largely of unrehearsed banter between Breneman and his live audience of women (John Dunning, *On the Air: The Encyclopedia of Old-Time Radio* [New York: Oxford University Press, 1998], 112–14).

not too much the babbitt. Not too much preoccupied with conforming to conventional middle-class behavior, from the central character in the 1922 novel *Babbitt*, by Sinclair Lewis (1885–1951).

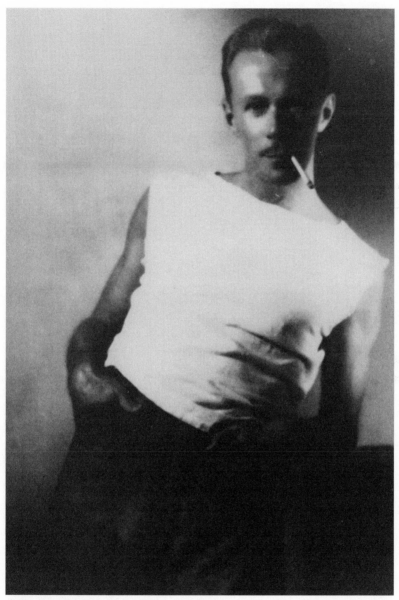

Studio photograph of Steward posing as a street tough, Paris, 1952. (Courtesy of the Estate of Samuel M. Steward)

Polaroid self-portrait of Steward dressed as a sailor, early 1950s. (Courtesy of the Estate of Samuel M. Steward)

or as romantic toreadors in velvet breeches, or as Colonial gentlemen, Robin Hoods, monks, sailors, huntsmen, or devils. And invariably, another vestigial remain of their former glory is shown in this fact: the more they can show of their legs, the happier they are. Dear old pious and proper Alice Meynell once wrote in an essay: "It is principally for the sake of the leg that a change in the dress of man is so much to be desired. . . . The leg is the best part of the figure . . . and the best leg is the man's. Men should no longer disguise the long lines, the strong forms, in those lengths of piping or tubing that are of all garments the most stupid"—which is quite a statement for Victorian Alice. For my part I am not so sure. An afternoon on the beach amid the knobby knees and the bowed and hairy underpinnings of the American male leaves one not quite so convinced as she seemed to be.

One final point remains, and that is the problem of the uniform in wartime. City fathers, social workers, ministers, and moralists in general always loudly deplore the increase of juvenile female delinquency when young girls (and some not so young) run after the jaunty sailor in his tight bell-bottomed trousers, and the solid marine in his red and blue and gold. It is probably as Proust said: that the uniform represents a special way of life that the gals can never know, and that the uniform makes them less particular about the man's face. They believe that beneath the gallant cloth there beats a heart different from the rest—more gallant, more adventurous, and more tender. It is perhaps not too much to say that the first donning of a uniform gives the wearer a thrill, a feeling of romance, and a satisfaction of his love for "dressing up." But when he comes home from the wars, the glamor gone—ah! then it's another story.

The modern male does not dare wear a scarlet hibiscus behind his ear, as the Bali native does. But there are little signs that the shell is cracking, and that he is making a feeble struggle to regain a part of his former self.

Alice Meynell (1847–1922). English journalist and poet whose verse was much influenced by her Catholic faith. The lines quoted are from her essay "Unstable Equilibrium" in The Rhythm of Life and Other Essays (1893).

as Proust said. Steward paraphrases a passage that appears near the end of "Part I: Combray" in Swann's Way, volume 1 of the novel À la recherche du temps perdu (1913–27, most recently translated as In Search of Lost Time), by Marcel Proust (1871–1922).

Take a look around the perfume counter in any store for men. There are ruggedly attractive colognes, soaps, and powders for the Man. The last war did a lot to make them popular, and GIs from Tokyo to Berlin soused themselves in Tumbleweed, Old Spice, Russian Leather, and Boots and Saddle. Sailors in the South Pacific sometimes wore one earring, as they did long ago. And the identification bracelets grew larger, heavier, more ornate as time went by—and the lads still wear them, secretly liking them, and at last having a legitimate reason to bedeck themselves.

All, well—maybe the pendulum is swinging. I do not know. I'd just like to ask a question. Should I wear Aphrodisia or Le Dandy when I go skating tonight? And tell me, dear, are my seams straight?

Aphrodisia or Le Dandy. These fragrances create some presumably deliberate gender confusion in the essay's concluding paragraph. Aphrodisia was a women's cologne introduced in 1938 by Fabergé, which subsequently also developed a men's version with the same name. Le Dandy, despite its name (and its distinctly gay associations since Oscar Wilde) was a women's fragrance introduced in 1925 by D'Orsay (James Eli Adams, "The Dandy," in *International Encyclopedia of Men and Masculinities*, ed. Michael Flood, et al. [New York: Routledge, 2007], 129–30; Barbara Herman, *Scent and Subversion: Decoding a Century of Provocative Perfume* [Guilford: Lyons Press, 2013], 41, 69–70).

are my seams straight? While this question could possibly refer to the seams in an article of men's clothing, in the 1940s it was more typically asked by women about their seamed nylon hosiery.

17

ON GERTRUDE STEIN

February 1947

Steward owed his early familiarity with Gertrude Stein's work to Clarence E. ("Claire") Andrews, the "favorite professor" alluded to in this essay. Urbane and witty, a brilliant lecturer and a discreet homosexual, Andrews spent half of each year in Paris, where he had met Stein, and the other half winning his Ohio State students over to her notoriously difficult early poetry. "One day in class he read [Stein's] As a Wife Has a Cow A Love Story," Steward recalled, "and he read it so well we were all thenceforth readers of Gertrude Stein."[1] Andrews's death while Steward was in graduate school was a severe blow: "When he died of pneumonia on December 12, 1932 . . ." he wrote years later, "my world was darkened—even shattered."[2]

But sharing the news of Andrews's passing provided Steward with a plausible reason to write to Stein. Steward had been sending letters to literary and other celebrities since high school to augment his sizeable collection of famous autographs,[3] but from the first, his correspondence with Stein—undertaken as it was in Andrews's memory—was something different. In this essay, he accurately describes his early letters as "rather timid and hesitant" (a typical excerpt: "I am happier than I can tell to think you answered me and I only hope I won't ruin things by being too impulsive and frequent."[4]), but they also included sympathetic and intelligent comments on Stein's work. And as Steward advanced from graduate student to professor to published novelist between 1933 and 1936, his correspondence with Stein became less fawning and increasingly personal and informal.

Steward's first visit with Stein and Toklas at their summer home in Bilignin in 1937 cemented his relationship with the two women, which was reflected in the new familiar tone of his subsequent letters and the often whimsical ways in which he began them—"Dearest Twain," "Dearest Duad," "Dearest Geralicetrude and

Algertrudice." The letters themselves give ample evidence of his respect for Stein and of the intensity of his love for her and Toklas.

Written six months after Stein's death, as Steward sank into deep depression, this eloquent essay is based on daily notes that Steward took during his visits with the two women in 1937 and 1939. Both a tribute to Stein and a description of everyday life in her presence, it demonstrates Steward's skill at weaving evocative images and anecdotes into a rich and vivid portrait.

> Alas, poor world, what treasure thou hast lost!
>
> — SHAKESPEARE

On July 27, 1946, the newspapers carried the word to the world that Gertrude Stein was dead. There was the expected flurry in the expected circles: reviewers who had known her, and reviewers who had not, all said the same things over and over of herself and her writings—how she had influenced Hemingway and Anderson, how few people really understood her, and how she had become the grandmother of modern literature. They spoke of her sitting in her rocking chair in Paris or in Bilignin, surrounded by those who had come far to see her, to listen to her words on life and writing. They wrote of how she came gradually to acquire some of the dusky mage-like character that Coleridge had at Highgate, uttering oracles that were sibylline and profound, and usually correct. To teenagers reading of her death, she was vaguely associated with some mysterious lines of writing, like "Pigeons on the grass, alas!" and "Rose is a rose is a rose is a rose."

"*Alas, poor world.*" Shakespeare, *Venus and Adonis*, line 1075.

Anderson. Sherwood Anderson (1876–1941), American novelist who, like Ernest Hemingway, Thornton Wilder, and other writers, was among Stein's friends.

the dusky mage-like character that Coleridge had. Steward used the same comparison in his earlier *IDJ* essay "On a Call to Paris" (March 1946).

"*Rose is a rose.*" On his first visit to Bilignin, Steward asked Stein directly about what she meant by this famous—and famously baffling—line, and she explained that the word *rose*, which once "called up a beautiful picture to the reader," had gradually lost its meaning and impact. "Now," she continued, "when I wrote 'Rose is a rose is a rose' . . . I slowly brought the meaning back to the word by repetition, I put the picture back in the word and I am the first person in two hundred years to do that thing" (*Dear Sammy*, 24).

On that July evening there were many empty hearts in the world, and many lonely people remembered her. I walked along the lakefront in Chicago, almost as sadly lost as the young Tennyson who—hearing of the death of Byron—crawled out upon a finger of land jutting into the sea, and carved upon a rock the words "Byron is dead." With him an age came to an end, and so, too, was a door closed softly with the death of Gertrude Stein.

That was in July, six months ago. Now it is February, the month in which she was born, and it is still hard for me to write of her without those thoughts which are too deep for tears. For I was of the happy ones whose fortune it was to know her well, to have talked with her, eaten her food, and slept under her hospitable roof in the old chateau at Bilignin in the south of France.

It began fifteen years ago, when my favorite professor at the university died. He had known her, had lectured on her work in class, and started us to thinking about her writing. Knowing that Gertrude Stein might never hear of his death, I wrote to her, and she answered. So began a rather timid and hesitant correspondence that ended with a visit to her in 1937, and another two years later.

Such a flood of happy memories rushes over me in recalling those times that it is hard to enfold them in a capsule of time or space. Most of all I remember the humanity and warmth of Gertrude, the endless talk, the spriteliness of Alice Toklas, and—oddly enough—the hysterical barking of the two dogs, Basket and Pépé.

But it was the electric conversation that went on all the time that was most fascinating, so charged and vibrant and provocative that I could not but feel that the old house was a kind of inexhaustible storage battery. The chateau in which she lived was a somewhat ramshackle house, modernized with electricity and a new bathroom and hot-water system

the young Tennyson. Steward made the same comparison in his *IDJ* essay "On the Importance of Dying Young" (April 1946) when describing the world's reaction to news of A. E. Housman's death.

I wrote to her, and she answered. Steward's first letter to Stein is dated November 19, 1933, almost a year after Andrews's death. Remarkably, Stein kept these early letters of adulation from a mere graduate student, presumably because they helped to validate her own sense of her place in modern literature.

Photograph of Gertrude Stein taken by Steward during an outing to Aix-les-Bains, summer 1937. (Courtesy of the Bancroft Library, University of California, Berkeley)

of which Gertrude was very proud—as much hot water, she said, and as quickly as a hotel. Back of the house was a small garden with flower beds set within lustrous clipped edges, and beyond the low wall of the garden was a broad and beautiful valley, sloping casually down to a small river, and rising again on the other to an unforgotten circle of blue hills, under the brilliant open sky of Ain.

In the evenings we sat in the drawing room, happy after the wonderful meals that Alice supervised. In the blue paper-thin china cups, the after-dinner infusions of verveine cooled. The smoke of cigarettes drifted lazily out into the burst of rose and gold that fell upon the garden. And we talked of everything under the sun—of the ballet, of Wally Simpson and her duke, of gardens, scenery, Mussolini, politics, teaching, salads and dressings, gasoline and spiders. The timbre of Gertrude's

infusions of verveine. Tea made with leaves of the verbena plant.

Wally Simpson and her duke. Having abdicated the English throne in December 1936, Edward, Duke of Windsor (1894–1972), married Wallis Simpson (1896–1986) in June 1937 in France, just before Steward's first visit with Stein and Toklas.

Photograph taken by Steward of Gertrude Stein in her tomato garden in Bilignin, summer 1937. (Courtesy of the Bancroft Library, University of California, Berkeley)

voice was rich and deep, and her great laugh—booming out over the valley—was the throat-filling laughter of the Valkyries.

Mornings, Gertrude did not come down until late, and we generally took a walk before lunch, as well as another before dinner. Sometimes it was the "upper turn" through green and brown vineyards, heavy with purple clusters of frosted-silver grapes. At other times, it was the "lower turn," down among the cool trees, walking on a cushion of leaves and moss. And always the talk—of how the mutter of threatened summer storms frightened the farmers for their grapes, of the painting of Sir Francis Rose, of dipsomania and authors who fell into it, and of Roman roads in France.

In the afternoons there were usually excursions here and there. Gertrude and Alice delighted in showing the lovely French countryside to

laughter of the Valkyries. Another comparison used earlier in "On a Call to Paris."

Sir Francis Rose (1909–79). English painter in the circle of French avant-garde artists whom Stein met in 1931 and whose work she championed. Steward first met him at Bilignin in August 1939 when they were both guests of Stein and Toklas. Gay, hapless, and sexually indiscreet, he became a (nonsexual) friend of Steward, who drew on Rose's life as the basis of his 1984 novel *Parisian Lives* (Spring, 70–72; *Dear Sammy*, 71–80).

Steward with Stein and Toklas's dog Pépé in Bilignin, summer 1937. (Gertrude Stein and Alice B. Toklas Papers, Beinecke Library, Yale University)

their friends. Sometimes it was a flying trip to the Chambéry markets for meat and vegetables, or to Belley for rice or olive oil. Sometimes it was visiting the newest colony of surrealist artists, or a trip to the Abbey of Hautecombe for an hour with her Benedictine friends. Once it was a journey to Geneva to see the Spanish paintings from the Prado that had been sent to Switzerland for safekeeping, with a pause for luncheon in the fields, eating a delicious chicken that Alice had steamed in white wine and herbs. Again it was a lively luncheon discussion with Henry and Clare Boothe Luce at Aix-les-Bains about a proposed collaboration

Abbey of Hautecombe. Reconstructed twelfth-century Cistercian monastery in the environs of Stein and Toklas's summer home. When Steward visited with Stein and Toklas, it was occupied by the Benedictine order of monks.

Spanish paintings from the Prado. Paintings from Madrid's Prado Museum that had been shipped to Switzerland for safekeeping during the Spanish Civil War were exhibited in Geneva in the summer of 1939.

Henry and Clare Boothe Luce. Henry Robinson Luce (1898–1967) was the influential founder and publisher of *Time*, *Life*, and *Fortune* magazines. His second wife, Ann Clare Boothe (1903–87), was an author, playwright, and until 1934 managing editor of *Vanity*

on a play. Now it was a trip to Virieu-le-Grand, and a small agricultural fair, with butter in molds shaped like sheep, nine-inch mushrooms, and Gertrude shooting at the whirling tin grouse in a shooting gallery. Or it was a ride in the cool dusk, the fragrant twilight, to Artemare, to eat of duck pâté, tomatoes in oil, partridge and thin crusted potatoes, with wild small strawberries which Madame Bérrard's son had picked in the hills that afternoon.

I think I understand her place in literature, but it was hard to be conscious of it while one was near her. I remember her as a great and human woman, an intricate yet human personality, tremendously alive. I think of her on a rainy day in a small garage, down on hands and knees on the oily floor discussing the axle of her car with a mechanic. I remember how we worked together in her little garden, both bent over hoes as we weeded the tomatoes. I see her walking along the dusty roadways, switching her dog leash at the ragweed as she talked, and now and then shouting to Pépé, the little Mexican chihuahua, to stop chasing chickens. I see her turn quickly away from the sight of a helpless calf with its legs tied for market, saying "Let us not look at that." I hear her hearty laugh as she showed me how, with one quick movement, she had mastered the French trick of catching a napkin under her arms.

In the early months of 1946, Alice Toklas sent off to Yale University Library a great collection of Gertrude's correspondence, photographs, and manuscripts. In a drawer of my desk is a stack of letters from Gertrude, which I suppose should go there too. Elsewhere are the many photographs of her that I took, and in a folder is a print of her hand on a sheet of specially prepared paper. Much used—but still serviceable—is a serrated tomato knife that she and Alice bought me one day in Cham-

---

Fair magazine. As an increasingly conservative Republican in the 1940s, she was elected to the House of Representatives and later served in the Eisenhower administration as the ambassador to Italy, becoming the first American woman appointed to an ambassadorial post.

Madame Bérrard's son. Steward refers to a dinner with Stein and Toklas at the Hôtel Bérrard in Artemare during his first visit in 1937 (*Dear Sammy*, 15–16).

a stack of letters from Gertrude. Steward sold his Stein correspondence to the Beinecke Library of Yale University in the 1970s.

béry. And on a layer of cotton in a small tin box are some thorns, sentimentally plucked from the rosebushes at the house in Bilignin.

Tonight these things are scattered on the table around me. Some of them might go to Yale, but not for a while, not yet. Gertrude Stein would chuckle at her "silly, bashful boy," but she would understand. For they are all I have left, except memories, of the most wonderful woman that I have ever known.

some thorns. Steward refers to these thorns again in his *IDJ* essay "On Keepsakes, Gew-Gaws, and Baubles" (September 1948).

18

ON LITTLE WHITE RIBBONS

MARCH 1947

In his November 1944 *Illinois Dental Journal* essay on Alcoholics Anonymous, Steward presented a vivid account of the toll that alcoholism takes on an individual, cast as a story told to him by a friend. But many of the details in the essay were in fact drawn from his own life, for by that time Steward needed alcohol to negotiate every day. "Oh, when I drank, I was a prince of the world," he wrote in retrospect; "I commanded fire and flames!"[1] By early 1947, however, his world was crashing down around him. Frustrated with teaching, Steward had left Loyola University after the autumn 1945 term without any other career goals on the horizon. Seven months later, the unexpected death of Gertrude Stein had been a devastating blow that he handled with heavier-than-usual drinking.[2] One night, alone and drunk in his apartment, he hit bottom. "I remember my violent sobbing," he wrote later, "lying face down on the floor with the dust from the carpeting sharp in my nostrils. And suddenly I knew that the time had come. This was the night of my destruction; I could face life and its problems no longer." For more than two decades Steward had saved twenty-four morphine sulfate tablets that he had pocketed at age sixteen when his grandfather, a country doctor, had died; that night they would become a deadly morphine solution that he would inject with a hypodermic needle he had been using for daily shots of vitamin B_{12}. "Blinded with tears, shaken and sobbing, I pulled myself to my feet by the oven-door handle on the kitchen stove. From force of habit I took a small pan, put a little water in it, dropped the syringe and needle in, and set the water to boil to sterilize the instru-

Little White Ribbons. A ribbon bow—white, to symbolize purity—is the traditional symbol of the Women's Christian Temperance Union, founded in 1874 in Cleveland, Ohio, as a civil rights movement originally intended to protect women and families from men's abuse of alcohol.

ments." Suddenly the absurdity of sterilizing a syringe before using it to commit suicide struck him. "And so from my horrid despair, I leaped suddenly to a peak of laughter—and holding my sides, gasping for breath and with tears streaming, I roared and roared until I collapsed weakly on my bed."[3]

Within the week, Steward joined Alcoholics Anonymous. He had always been put off by the AA principle of surrendering oneself to a higher power—by which most members meant God—but found a chapter that didn't invoke divinity, a "tough-minded hard-bitten AA group in Chicago that met at the lakefront and Chicago Avenue and called itself the Water Tower Group."[4] With alcohol and his hopes of recovery on his mind, Steward returned to the subject of alcoholism with a humorous critique of the Women's Christian Temperance Union in this essay, where his forthright acknowledgment of alcohol abuse in his family and the story about his own first experience of drunkenness sound much like what one might hear from the new member of an AA group.

Soon the night of rum shall cease!

—W.C.T.U. SONGS

Ours has always been a family of boozers—one side of it, that is. The other has always been teetotalling. One of my earliest childhood memories is of a Sunday afternoon when the whole family was packed up, forcibly or otherwise, and started off to a "temprunz" meetin'. They left me behind because I was too young to know the meaning of the word.

It was a balmy day. The wind blew lightly over the wheat fields, slipped up the hill, and was cool under the huge flat-topped grape arbor, heavy with clusters of grapes and green leaves shutting out the blue sky. And there, cooling in the shade, was a barrel of apple cider, waiting patiently for its mudder to make the winter's vinegar out of it.

I ran to the barn, cut a coupla straws, and came back. I pulled a footstool out of the house, climbed up, and hammered out the bung. Then I straddled the barrel, put the straws in the hole, and drew deep. It was very good, and it stung my mouth just a little.

"Soon the night of rum shall cease!" Line from the song "White Ribbon Vibrations." Here and below, Steward quotes lyrics from *W.C.T.U. Songs* (Evanston: National Women's Christian Temperance Union Publishing House, 1928).

When the family got back from the meetin', there was little Philly lying on his back beside the barrel and gazing up at the grape leaves, burping happily and gurgling at the patches of sky.

A horrified shriek burst from a relative, as someone yanked me to my feet. "Land o' Goshen!" said a bustled aunt. "The boy's *drunk!*"

That was the first time I ever took the Daughter of the Vine to bed, as old Omar phrased it. And the sting was no longer only on my tongue when I went. But I ask you, in all honesty, would a guy my age have known enough to do that if he hadn't watched someone else do it first?

It's a sure thing that part of my frustration today is the struggle that went on during those early years between the White Ribbon and the Boozing sides of the family. My old man made fun of the White Ribbon-ers, my aunts adored them, and maybe even belonged. At any rate, there was never any booze around the house . . . to be seen.

Unquestionably Frances Willard was a sincere woman when she started the W.C.T.U. She had probably had experience with boozers in her family. Most of the band's members have likely had to put Poppa to bed at one time or another. But as the *Britannica* rather tartly and enigmatically phrases it, the cause of total abstinence "suffered in public estimation from the intemperance of some of its advocates"—evidently such gals as Carrie Nation with her little hatchet.

In the green salad days at college, we did nothing but poke fun at them. Once I went with a reporter to a convention of the ladies in

---

took the Daughter of the Vine to bed. Steward paraphrases a line from Edward FitzGerald's 1859 translation of *The Rubaiyat of Omar Khayyam*: "And took the Daughter of the Vine to Spouse" (stanza 40).

Frances Willard (1839–98). Second president of the WCTU, who ran the organization from her home in Evanston, Illinois, from 1879 to 1898. Willard did not single-handedly start the WCTU (she originally held the office of corresponding secretary), but as president she increased its political visibility and power; under her leadership, the organization effectively allied itself with the broader causes of the growing women's movement at the end of the nineteenth century.

Carrie Nation (1846–1911). Organizer of a branch of the WCTU in Medicine Lodge, Kansas, known for her practice of smashing bottles and fixtures in bars with a hatchet.

green salad days. Cf. Shakespeare, *Antony and Cleopatra*, I.v.73–74.

Columbus, Ohio. We saw a very impressive demonstration with a raw egg and alcohol, and at the end heard three thousand frayed and quavering voices raised in the W.C.T.U. pep cheer: "Down with the bootlegger. Up with the Law: We're for Prohibition—Rah, rah, rah!"

Both Alcoholics Anonymous and the W.C.T.U. have to mix their sawdust diets with a lot of religious oil to make them slip down easily. But AA is missionary only in the sense that it approaches just the drunkards who want to be dried up. The W.C.T.U., with its lopsided and shallow humanitarianism, has always dug deep into the personal freedom of everyone. Such prying and coercion is naturally resented. No wonder it has become a tradition in dry Evanston, Illinois, to break empty whisky bottles on the front lawn of the national headquarters.

My feelings on this gang of female zealots were recently stirred by a thin treasure I came across among some old papers—not my own! It is a little brochure, respectably bound in quiet brown-grey paper and

---

a very impressive demonstration. The demonstration—apparently an enduringly popular one among opponents of alcohol—was described by W. F. Pechuman in 1891: "Alcohol destroys the very life force that alone keeps the body in repair. For a more simple experiment as to the action of alcohol, take the white of an egg (which consists of albumen, and is very similar to bioplasm), put it into alcohol, and notice it turn white, coagulate and harden. The same experiment can be made with blood with the same result—killing the blood bioplasts . . . and this alone is enough to condemn its use as a medicine" (*Alcohol, Is It a Medicine?* [Detroit: Pechuman and Morrison, 1891], 7; quoted in Martha Allen, *Alcohol: A Dangerous and Unnecessary Medicine* [Marcellus: National W.C.T.U., 1900], 60).

Alcoholics Anonymous. Founded in 1935 in Akron, Ohio, AA was still quite new to Chicago when Steward wrote, the first Chicago-area meeting having been held in a private residence in Evanston in September 1939 ("History of the Chicago Group of Alcoholics Anonymous," http://www.hindsfoot.org/chicago1.pdf).

lopsided and shallow humanitarianism. Writing in his unpublished memoir about his dislike of the WCTU, Steward commented, "It is the same kind of impulse that leads me to vote against anti-smoking laws and ordinances, even though I do not myself smoke any longer. I am against anything that fetters the freedom of the human spirit in these areas" ("Autobiography," 80).

dry Evanston. The charter of Northwestern University was amended when the university opened in 1855 to ban the sale of alcohol within a four-mile radius of the campus, which effectively included the entire city of Evanston. Frances Willard's term as president of the WCTU at the end of the nineteenth century solidified Evanston's alcohol-free tradition, which remained in effect until 1972.

bearing the words *W.C.T.U. Songs* on the front. It is full of many lovely ditties. For instance, there is a gem called "It Is There to Stay." "It" refers to the Prohibition Amendment, and if there were ever a better musical example of whistling in the dark, I'd like to see it. It begins "By the life of Frances Willard, which no mortal can portray," and goes on to refer also to the similar lives of faithful women who have fallen in the fray. Then it states that the gals have woven Prohibition, warp and woof in legal way, in the Nation's Constitution, and it's there, there to stay, till the stars shall sink in silence and the sun and moon decay, till the souls of men assemble in the final Judgment Day, it is in the Constitution, and it's there, there to stay.

And do you know how it got there, by gum? By a Royal Act of Congress backed by States in strong array, by the Court's Supreme Decision, signed and sealed in legal way, by Jehovah's Ultimatum, which the people MUST obey. (Chorus)

You see, it's as simple as all that. What could the people do against Congress, the Court, and Jehovah? When such a trinity gangs up on an unsuspecting boozer, there's no hope left for him anywhere.

Yet curiously, after this nose-thumbing "Yah yah! *Now* what'll you do?" there follows a series of rather worried songs. They are on the theme that the law must be enforced. There is a task still before them. They must set the pace for other nations until they, too, see the better way. But they are dead certain there'll be no wine or beer returning to the good old U.S.A.

A decided optimistic note is sounded in one called "The World is Going Dry." Millions of hands will strike off rum's chains, and the Liberty Bell will re-echo the knell of the death of the demon of rum. Full Emancipation! Everybody singing, U.S.A. forever dry! (Bo-one dr-ry)

Still, oddly enough, with the amendment in the constitution and everything seeming settled, they must "carry on" the fight, they must

Prohibition Amendment. Steward's sarcastic treatment of the celebratory WCTU song lyrics in the following paragraphs is based on the fact that the Eighteenth Amendment (1920) survived only thirteen years before being repealed.

"The World Is Going Dry." The lyrics that Steward quotes are actually from the song "U.S.A. Forever Dry."

enforce the constitution. We see the first glimmerings of vague distrust as we leaf through the songs. They must "hold fast, without dismay." God's women must be fearless as the day, work for enforcement where they are, and above all stand loyally, just where they are in the conflict, because God placed them there for some purpose. "Our ribbon so white, emblem of right, carry it dauntless where wrong holdeth sway."

But my favorite prohibition song is from the *Prohibition Songster of South Dakota*, published at Aberdeen in the 1870s. Here it is in full, so that you can clip it for your wallets. It has a charm and quality I can't resist.

Drearily falleth the rain.
    Dark are the alleys tonight;
But the light that shines from the gay saloon
    Is mellow and warm and bright.

Fatally sweet is the snare,
    Dark are the night and the rain,
But O, beware! There is that within
    Shall blast thee in heart and brain.

        Chorus.
Sitting by peaceful fireside,
    Musing by shaded lamp;
How little we know what tempts our boys
    Away in the darkness damp.

"Our ribbon so white." The lines are from the song "Our Task."

Prohibition Songster. Steward quotes from the *Constitutional Prohibition Songster for South Dakota* (Aberdeen: Aberdeen Daily News Company, 1889).

"Drearily falleth the rain." Steward no doubt enjoyed the double meaning of lyrics about "what tempts our boys" in a "gay saloon."

19

ON BEING MUSCLEBOUND

April 1947

Bodybuilding surfaced in the United States at the turn of the twentieth century as an antidote to the perceived lack of masculinity among American men in the late 1800s, when city living and office work had largely replaced the earlier physical challenges of life on the frontier. As early as 1899, fitness enthusiast Bernarr Macfadden (1868–1955) was publishing minimally clad images of the ideal male body in his monthly magazine *Physical Culture*, which soared in popularity as muscles became the new emblem of masculinity. Gradually, what started as a solution to a social problem became sport and then competition. Much of the credit for this evolution belongs to Bob Hoffman, whose publications Steward refers to in this essay. Hoffman's foundry in York, Pennsylvania, started producing the famous York barbells in 1929, his gymnasiums attracted an ethnically diverse cadre of dedicated bodybuilders whom he nurtured and trained, and his Strength and Health publishing house produced amply illustrated magazines and books during the 1930s and 1940s that displayed the benefits of a musclebound body. In 1940, bodybuilding acquired a new level of visibility in the United States when the first official Mr. America competition was held in New York City. When Steward wrote this essay in 1947, competitive bodybuilding was thus a widely recognized cultural phenomenon, but one with still enough novelty to warrant the whimsical treatment that he gives it here.

Though he discusses bodybuilding from the perspective of a fascinated outsider, Steward's evident familiarity with the literature of physical culture is not surprising: since the time of Macfadden, bodybuilding magazines, with their copious photographs of musclebound and scantily clad men, had been popular not only with skinny kids who dreamed of having such muscles but also with gay men who dreamed of having the muscled men themselves. In an era when postal inspectors and the FBI scrutinized the mails for anything that could be considered obscene, muscle magazines escaped notice and became the legal pornography of a generation of gay men. Moreover, as Daniel Harris notes, gay publishers in the 1940s and 1950s used the bodybuilding craze as a cover to produce their own magazines with pictures of nearly naked, well-built men, which had a tongue-in-cheek but often convincing-enough similarity to the real muscle magazines to pass muster with the US Post Office.[1]

> This . . . lord of folded arms,
> Th' anointed sovereign of sighs and groans.
>
> —*LOVE'S LABOURS LOST*

Three of the most lovely chicks I ever saw sat in the row just ahead of me. From them came the perfume of Nirvana, and they were sleekly clothed in mink, fox, and beaver. Their faces were delicately yet surely put on with Max Factor's or Elizabeth Arden's help, their lashes curled up and outward, black and featherlike. Two were from the chorus line of the "Chez Paree Adorables," and the third from the Copacabana. The one on the left leaned across the middle one, and whispered to the one on the right. "My dear," she breathed, "did you ever in your life see such marvelous deltoids?"

"I don't like 'em near so well as the latissimus dorsi on that guy named Al," she said, with just a sniff in her tone. And then the middle one spoke up: "Dintcha ever see them trapezius on Clarence?"

All this may sound like double-talk to those who have not been initiated into the secret sport of weightlifting. But the devotees know the lingo, and root for their favorites in more ways than one. And who, you may say, are the weightlifters? Well, they are the great young males of the country, the physical culturists, the little sealed circle of bodybuilders. They talk in a language all their own. They spend hours a day to increase the size of their shoulders and thighs by exercise.

"*This . . . lord of folded arms.*" Shakespeare, *Love's Labour's Lost*, III.i.124–26.

"*Chez Paree Adorables.*" Celebrated dancers at the Chez Paree, a Chicago nightclub of the 1930s, 1940s, and 1950s that featured world-famous guest entertainers.

Copacabana. Famous New York nightclub that opened in 1940.

Clarence. Presumably Clarence Ross (1923–2008), winner of the Mr. America title in 1945.

And after they've done it, they can't find a suit of clothes to fit them. No coat fits around the neck, because of the enormous trapezius muscle. The seams burst out under their arms, because of the serratus magnus. All they can hope for is summer, and a chance to show up on the beach, so that they can be admired. Summer is their time, and they make a year's work out of it, what with their handstands, balancing acts, and struttings. Once a year they meet to select a Mr. America. First a contest—and the aesthetic observer finds it hard to bear the gruntings, tuggings, the sudden whistle of air through mouth as the weight goes up, the horrid veins bursting beneath the biceps. And as Mr. America poses, his muscles tremble most fearfully. He is covered with oil to make his muscles "defined," and close up he always smells a little like Mazola, olive oil, Crisco, or lard.

You may gather that my opinion of them has somewhat of the sour grape in it. Oh no, it is not that. I am completely fascinated with what they say and how they look at life. They are the male Vestal virgins. They are the Narcissus of Greek mythology, brought to the dirty sands of public beaches, to waste their godhood amongst the hot dogs and the flies.

Those three chorines, so ecstatic over the bodies of the boys, were among the nine hundred visitors at the last weightlifting contest held in Chicago. I had forgotten the strange manner of speech of the weightlifter. It took me a little while to recognize again what a "snatch" was, and how it differed from a "press," or a "clean and jerk." The deltoids and the sartorius muscle were strange terms for the moment, but gradually it all came back to me.

About seven years ago, someone sent me a subscription to a magazine called *Strength and Health*, which seems to be the daddy of them all. It was, of course, no particular joy to read. All I could do was look at the

---

Vestal virgins. Priestesses of the goddess Vesta in ancient Rome, compared to bodybuilders here because of their high social status and their isolation from the opposite sex.

Narcissus. In Greek mythology, a youth who fell in love with his own reflection in a pool.

Strength and Health. The flagship publication of Bob Hoffman's (1898–1985) bodybuilding complex in York, Pennsylvania. Originally written and edited by his cadre of bodybuilders, it appeared from 1932 to 1986.

pictures and sigh and think, "Well, I might be like that if I had started earlier." I used to feel just as inferior when I read *Esquire* with only two suits to my name. A great many men are given a body they can barely get along with, and could not at all if it did not breathe automatically and have a heartbeat inside. Yet I wonder if all these poor products have missed so much by not being Muscle Boys. College football training periods last only a few months. But the weightlifters have a lifetime of training ahead. They must eat wisely. They must spend at least one hour a day with the barbells, the foot weights, and the head lifts. They ought not to smoke and they certainly must not drink. It is almost against the rules to get married, because marriage brings a dreadful waste of energy. It is almost a terror to sleep, unless there is a towel knotted in the middle of the back. They eat carrots, greens, and raw beef; and plenty of eggs and oysters every six days.

Weightlifting is the great cure for dental caries, ulcers, corns, myopia, and almost every ailment except psychoneurosis. The "personal letter" columns of the bodybuilders' magazines are filled mostly with questions about such things. You are assured that if you press a hundred pounds eight times a day, and jerk some others, and clean a few extra, you'll be the number A-1 boy in your neighborhood. Your acne will disappear, your scalp will have no dandruff—if you just snatch, press, and clean and jerk according to the rules.

Mainly, it is the makers of barbells, steel springs, and other equipment who profit from the weightlifting racket. Tens of thousands of spindly-legged teenage boys pay out twenty to fifty bucks to develop their deltoids and be alluring to the sweater girls they know. But the takers of professional photographs of the Body Beautiful make just as much—at five bucks a set of four 8 × 10s, you don't get poor—especially when the four prints cost about eight cents each. And then there are the sleazily printed books on *Your Sane Sex Life*, containing information that you could easily get from the "Old Farmers' Almanac," which more cheaply tells you the proper time for sowing seeds. You can learn how to conquer constipation for one buck. You can have any five books for ten

---

Your Sane Sex Life. An apparent allusion to *Sane Sex Life and Sane Sex Living* by Harland William Long (1869–1943), first published in 1919 and still in print.

January 1947 issue of *Strength and Health* featuring bodybuilder Jack LaLanne (1914–2011).

bucks: *The Big Chest Book*, *Big Arms*, *Successful Happy Marriage*, *Secrets of Strength*, and so on, until your pockets are empty.

The average person believes that "Li'l Abner Yokum" is only a character in a comic strip. Yet those who know the weightlifter know also that he is a living Li'l Abner in many ways. He's big and dumb and beautiful, and he does not like the luscious Daisy Mae—he likes only the gals he can "wrassle wif." It was with a shock that I learned there are female weightlifters, handsome as "Moonbeam McSwine." The male lifters do not like to talk with them about June, moon, love, dove. Instead, they discuss their "cleans and jerks," "presses," and "snatches." The females are lovingly called "barbelles." I tell you, for once in his life, your correspondent finds himself completely speechless and flabbergasted by such fantastic and incredible goings-on.

It's a racket, but a great one, one in the grand tradition. You can say no more against it than you can against the magnificent swindles of Rockefeller and Carnegie, Pillsbury and Armour, Drew and Moody. Weightlifting appeals to the vanity of man, and it succeeds because man is vain. It catches man just a little the other side of his stage of self-love, and holds him there—physically perfect, but emotionally arrested in the limbo of the desire to keep his chassis shined and oiled. "Be admired by all!" the advertisements shriek. Yet one asks—to what end? To get a wife? Nope. Just to be admired. A woman's artifices of painting and perfuming have generally a more practical aim in view.

The Big Chest Book. This and the following three books by Bob Hoffman were published between 1939 and 1945 by his Strength and Health publishing firm.

"Li'l Abner Yokum" . . . *Daisy Mae* . . . *"Moonbeam McSwine."* Characters in Al Capp's syndicated comic strip *Li'l Abner* (1934–77), a recurring theme of which was the handsome, well-built Abner's resistance to marrying Daisy Mae.

Rockefeller and Carnegie. John D. Rockefeller (1839–1937) and Andrew Carnegie (1835–1919) made their fortunes in oil and steel, respectively; both were also notable philanthropists.

Pillsbury and Armour. Charles Alfred Pillsbury (1842–99) and Philip Danforth Armour (1832–1901) revolutionized the flour and meatpacking industries, respectively.

Drew and Moody. Daniel Drew (1797–1879) made his fortune by ruthlessly manipulating prices in the stock market; John Moody (1868–1958) developed a system of rating bonds for the financial markets.

I see by the papers that Mr. America and Miss Legionnaire are engaged to be married. It is pleasant to dally with the thought of what the children of such godlike parents might be. But somehow I think of the story about Isadora Duncan, the dancer, and George Bernard Shaw. She wrote to him, suggesting they have a child. "Think how wonderful it would be!" she cried, "if our child had my beauty and your brains!" To which he sourly replied, "Yes, but think—it might have *your* brains and *my* beauty."

Mr. America and Miss Legionnaire. In June 1947, Alan Stephan, Mr. America 1946, married fellow Chicagoan Grace Pomazal, whose beauty-pageant titles included Miss Legionnaire (awarded by the Illinois American Legion), Miss Forget-Me-Not (by the Disabled American Veterans), and Miss Quick Freeze (by the Frozen Foods Association).

the story about Isadora Duncan. Stories of this witty exchange have been ascribed to various famous pairs. Shaw flatly denied in 1926 that it ever occurred between himself and Duncan (Bernard Shaw, *Collected Letters 1926–1950*, ed. Dan H. Laurence [New York: Viking Penguin, 1988], 16–17).

20

ON TEACHING

NOVEMBER 1947

When Steward completed his PhD in English at The Ohio State University in 1934, he idealistically imagined for himself a stimulating career as an educator and writer. But in his first three teaching positions, at provincial institutions in West Virginia, Montana, and Washington state, he found neither students nor colleagues who shared his commitment to learning. In 1936, he landed a job at Loyola University in Chicago, whose English department at the time was chaired by the distinguished scholar and editor Morton Dauwen Zabel (1901–64). Steward deeply respected Zabel—he later described him as "a talented and meticulous savant with an encyclopedic mind, a giant of learning" (and as "perhaps the most closeted queen of the entire city")[1]—and for the first time, he found himself in a department where he was encouraged to teach whatever courses and works he desired. "And once again," he wrote later, "I began to like teaching."[2]

But in February 1946, after nearly ten years of work at Loyola, Steward took a leave of absence from his faculty position, and the circumstances that had driven him to that action doubtless contributed to the cynical tone of this essay about teaching. A disturbed female student in his summer 1945 graduate class on the romantic poets began covering the chalkboard with sexually explicit love messages to him every day before class began. At first, Steward passed off the delusional scrawlings as well as he could with a joke, but when they continued, he appealed to the dean to remove the student from his class. Yet the university took no action, even when the student began telephoning him at home late at night. Unable to get over his sense of betrayal by the administration, Steward left Loyola after the fall semester[3] and two years later wrote this acerbic account of "beating my feeble intellectual wings against the monumental barrier of the collective stupidity of about five thousand college students."

DePaul University yearbook photograph of Steward with students in his "Culture Corner," 1952.
(Courtesy of DePaul University Archives)

Less than a year after this essay was published, however, Steward returned to
teaching once more, this time in the English department of DePaul University in
Chicago. During his eight years at DePaul, he became one of the university's most
popular professors, described in a student publication as "witty and urbane . . .
the man who has people fighting to get in his classes, the man who presents a
cool, calm impassivity to the world."[4] In reality, his exterior demeanor concealed a
growing frustration with his meager salary, his ill-prepared students, and his colleagues, whom he considered a band of "misfits, neurotics, and drunks."[5] "During
the last years of this harrowing life things got worse," he recalled later. "I grew to
loathe the matrix which imprisoned me. On some mornings I had to take a benzedrine tablet to face the doltish students. But what else to do? All my life I had
made a living with my brain, and it had brought me little."[6]

In the middle of the spring term of 1956, the question was answered for him.
When officials at DePaul learned that Steward, using the name Phil Sparrow, was
also running a tattoo business out of a dilapidated arcade on South State Street,
at that time Chicago's sordid Skid Row, they told him that his teaching contract
would not be renewed. "I staggered back to the faculty house . . . and sat for 20
minutes staring at the wall. . . . All I could see was the appalling loss of face in
having nothing to do except be a tattooer."[7] During the remaining weeks of the

term, Steward vacillated between periods of anxiety about his future—the sense of "a new and frightening hollowness within" at the loss of his academic career—and the inescapable fact that he had come to detest teaching, "the futility of it being broken all too rarely by the reward of finding an intelligent single one whom I could watch grow." Ultimately his inherent resilience won out: "I have adjusted to many things in my life, and this is merely another," he wrote in his journal.[8] Steward proceeded to turn his tattooing into a profitable full-time business that he pursued for fourteen more years. He never taught again.

> Those who can, do; those who can't, teach.
>
> —OLD SAW

A professor is one who professes to know something. There is a great deal to be said for the teaching "profession," and a great deal to be said against it. As one who spent twelve years—the best ones—beating my feeble intellectual wings against the monumental barrier of the collective stupidity of about five thousand college students, I feel qualified to speak.

By and large, the teaching profession is filled with frustrated old maids of both sexes, incompetents who would be unable to earn a living any other way. It has been estimated that by the time a youth graduates from high school, he has passed under the hands of at least four neurotic teachers, and has accordingly suffered in varying degrees. Every psychosis is there, from Oedipus to Narcissus. A psychiatric examination of the teachers with whom I came in contact in college would provide enough material to give Freud a field day, and probably show him some things not dreamed of in his philosophy.

The gravest accusation I have to make against the academic world, however, requires the use of a medieval phrase lately restored to use. It is "climate of opinion." It means simply that there have existed from time to time certain groups—religious, artistic, or social—who have lived in an intellectual climate that is completely different from the one followed

---

Oedipus to Narcissus. Psychological complexes defined by Sigmund Freud (1856–1939): unconscious desire for the parent of the opposite sex; self-absorption that persists in an individual after puberty.

things not dreamed of. Cf. Shakespeare, *Hamlet*, I.v.185–86: "There are more things in heaven and earth, Horatio, / Than are dreamt of in your philosophy."

by most people. The academic world is quite out of the climate in which most realists live today. Conceived by the written word, bred in books, nurtured on the petty gossips of faculty teas, the teachers of today are wholly out of step with the world. No matter how well informed they may be, their reactions are unrealistic and walled in by their training and background. They are lying happily in their small routines (a word which should have the "o" and the "ine" removed to find the true meaning of it), gurgling at the sky, and kicking their heels happily at their sinking sun.

Of course, the best teachers are accomplished actors, and I will admit that it is very pleasant to have an audience. You can put on a great show once a day—although that is about all some teachers do. You use the eye, the smile, the gesture; you crack your jokes and sometimes write them in the margin of your notes so that you will remember to tell them next year at that point. One of my colleagues used to do nothing in class except tell anecdotes about World War I. It did not matter what subject he was teaching; modern drama, the novel, composition, or Shakespeare—each class got the same stories, over and over. But the audience you have is pretty terrible. Most classes are stupid, so stupid that when you walk in and say "Good morning," they will all write it down in their notebooks. They just sit there, looking as if they were painted on their seats, and stare at you with the same lively expression you might find on a potato. Once in a while there is one with a sign of talent; he grins at the right moment, asks intelligent questions, and seems to know what is going on. But in general these finds are rare joys.

One Professor Larrabee writes rather amusingly about teachers, and his general theme is they can't win. If a professor is brand new at teaching—then he lacks experience. On the other hand, if he's been teaching all his life, he's in a rut. Some will accuse him of being in love with his own voice if he does all the talking in class, but if he leaves the discussion to others, he's just too lazy for words. Get your name in the papers and you're accused of being publicity-mad, but if you never are

---

Professor Larrabee. This and the following three paragraphs are drawn with only a few changes in wording from a satirical 1947 article by Harold A. Larrabee ("Faculty Failings; Or, A Professor Can't Win," *Bulletin of the American Association of University Professors* 33 [Summer 1947]: 345–46).

seen in print, you're deadwood. Go to athletic contests, and you're a popularity-seeker, but stay away, and you're antisocial. Dress decently and you're a fashion plate—think about something besides clothes, and you're a bum. Never admit your mistakes—you're arrogant; admit 'em, and you oughta go back to bricklaying.

It could go on and on. Teach at the same college three years and you're a stick-in-the-mud; change, and you're a drifter or a rolling stone. Put an occasional joke in your lectures and you're a comedian; never crack 'em, and you're a dusty dull old fogey. Go regularly to chapel and be called a hypocrite; stay away and be a heathen. Write books and you're neglecting your teaching; don't write, and be accused of never having a thought worth printing. Hand out lots of high grades, and you have no standards; hand out low ones and you're a butcher and a stinker. Use notes, and you're unoriginal; get along without 'em and be known as an ad-libber.

If you're on good terms with the president, you're a sycophantic apple-polisher—or worse. If you don't wear a path to the administration building, you're disloyal. Get to class late? You're an oversleeper. But get there early—and "He must've lost that dollar Ingersoll he carries." Let your classes out early—you've run out of ideas. Keep them overtime—and it just shows you don't know how to plan and end a lecture. Hang around after class and it's compliments you're looking for; make a speedy exit, and you've got "studentophobia." Seldom give tests—and you're too lazy to read papers; give quizzes often, and it's "Aw, that slave-driver!" If you show your own opinions, you're a propagandist; if you mention anything Russian, you're probably getting monthly checks from Molotov. Listen to sports broadcasts and be called illiterate; but if you can't identify Fritzie Zivic and Jack Kramer, you

dollar Ingersoll. Cheap, mass-produced watches sold for one dollar at the end of the nineteenth century by the Ingersoll Watch Company, which went bankrupt after World War I. A detail added by Steward.

Molotov. Vyacheslav Molotov (1890–1986), Russian foreign minister from 1939 to 1949 under Josef Stalin.

Fritzie Zivic (1913–84). American boxer who was world welterweight champion from 1940 to 1941.

Jack Kramer (1921–2009). American tennis player who was part of the winning Davis Cup team in 1947.

ain't human. Do some outside work to amplify your meagre income, and you're greedy; do it for nothing and you're a sucker.

It seems you just can't win. Praise a book, and "He's probably getting a commission from the publisher." Pan one, and "He's just jealous." Stand up while you're teaching, and you're oratorical; sit down, and "His feet must hurt." If you're young, you need more seasoning and experience; if you're old, you're a has-been who's seen better days. Take an active part in faculty affairs and be branded a politician; stay out of them and be called a work-dodger. Stick to your specialty and you have a one-track mind; tour around through human knowledge and get a reputation for showing off. Present both sides of a question—"He's afraid to commit himself."

Thus coming and going, you get it. Most of it is well deserved, too. I resigned from the teaching profession two years ago, and wild horses couldn't drag me back into it. It makes cravens of strong men, always with the feeling that you may do something that will endanger your academic reputation, whatever that is. Teaching is supposed to make you absentminded because you have so many things on your mind. But the real truth is that you have very little *in* it if you stick to the academic life. As for the rewards of teaching, let us paraphrase Winston Churchill: "Never has so little been given to so many for such small returns."

So, you can have your noble old time-honored profession. I'll take Tallulah's any day!

---

paraphrase Winston Churchill. The British prime minister's famous line, "Never in the field of human conflict was so much owed by so many to so few," delivered in a speech to Parliament on August 20, 1940, referred to the Royal Air Force's defense of Britain against the onslaught of German bombers during the first year of World War II.

Tallulah's. In the 1944 Alfred Hitchcock film *Lifeboat*, Tallulah Bankhead (1902–68) starred as a cynical columnist—the same role Philip Sparrow adopts in this essay.

21

ON FABULOUS, FABULOUS FIELD'S

JANUARY 1948

No longer teaching at Loyola University and short of money as usual, in late 1946 Steward took a temporary holiday sales job in the book department of the grande dame of Chicago department stores, Marshall Field's. Founded as Field, Palmer, Leiter and Company in 1865 on Field's famous dictum, "Give the lady what she wants," the store in the first half of the twentieth century maintained its reputation for extraordinary customer service and fine-quality goods from around the world. Merchandise was elegantly displayed in an imposing block-long building designed by Daniel Burnham in 1907 that featured a forest of massive Corinthian columns on the main floor and the world's largest Tiffany glass dome, crowning an atrium that rose six stories above the heads of shoppers.

The third-floor book department in which Steward worked was large and famous, with annual sales of $1.5 million by the early 1950s. Book signings by celebrity authors like W. Somerset Maugham, G. K. Chesterton, Willa Cather, Aldous Huxley, Edgar Lee Masters, and Carl Sandburg were a regular event, and extravagant promotions were staged to attract customers. In 1944, for example, to feature a children's book about Eddie, "the elegant elephant," the store brought to the third floor an actual elephant who "autographed" books by swinging a rubber stamp held in its trunk.[1]

As in his essay on "balletomania," Steward's strategy in this essay is comic deflation, his early notions of working in a library-like setting of grace and decorum upset by the mundane minutiae of sales checks and Charg-a-Plates and the chaos of a department full of bewildered holiday shoppers. But the experience was memorable in one way not mentioned here: Steward's chat with a particularly handsome ex-military man named Roy Fitzgerald, whom he found working in the store's gift-wrap department, led to a fleeting sexual encounter in a freight elevator stopped between floors. Less than a year later, Roy Fitzgerald would be living in Los Angeles, where as the handsome (but closeted) actor Rock Hudson, he would be cast as the leading man in dozens of films beginning in the 1950s.[2]

> The CUSTOMER is always right.
> —MARSHALL FIELD & COMPANY

A friend of mine—or so I thought—called me up some time ago when he heard that I was temporarily "at liberty." How would you like, said he in dulcet tones, to come down to Field's to help us out in the book section during the Christmas rush? We are so very, very busy. . . . At first I demurred, remembering with a kind of agony how I had been teased into a two-year term of penal servitude with an encyclopedia, an experience which left me old and withered on the vine. "Oh, come on," he said; "it'll be a new experience for you—a real lark. You like people, you like books. I'll put you in rare books and fine bindings."

That did it, alas! I have always wanted to see myself in a fine binding, so bright one Tuesday morning I went down. I don't know exactly what I expected. I rather imagined I would go in to my friend, bow from the waist [and perhaps just *suggest* a small genuflection], be handed a sales-check book and given a cash-register drawer, step out on the "floor," and begin to sell. My gracious attitude toward the customers, my wide background in rare books, and my innate charm would all help to make me the most popular person in the department before the first day was over.

No such stuff. When I showed up, John looked up rather coolly, and said, "Oh, you're here." That was evident. "Well, you'll have to go over to the personnel department and fill out an application blank and go through the regular channels, of course." I looked dumb and founded for a moment and he saw it. "Merely a matter of routine," he explained; "everyone has to do it."

---

penal servitude with an encyclopedia. After taking a leave of absence from Loyola at the end of the fall 1945 term, Steward worked for nearly two years as a writer and editor for World Book Encyclopedia. His early work at World Book actually overlapped with his holiday stint at Marshall Field's.

see myself in a fine binding. Steward puns on his predilection for sadomasochistic sexual encounters.

So I went to the personnel office and stood in line for a long time and got some long and complicated forms to fill out, and then they gave me a number, and then I sat in a chair and waited for my interview with a Mr. Pemberton. When my number was called I watched Mr. Pemberton, and he and another guy decided to go out for a smoke, so I sat for forty-five minutes until he decided he would come back to interview me. Then there was a medical examination with all the thumpings and proddings and indignities that always accompany medical examinations, and I went back to Mr. Pemberton.

"Fine," he said, "you are accepted. And now there is a training class that lasts two days, and will you start yours on Friday next."

"T-t-training class!" I stuttered. "You mean you have to be trained before you start to work at Marshall Field's? To sell books?"

"Merely a matter of routine," he said smugly. "Everyone has to do it, not only to sell books but hairpins."

The "training class" was a fearful and wonderful thing. It consisted mainly of a series of pep talks about courtesy, the-customer-is-always-right, you'd-rather-have-a-satisfied-customer-than-make-a-sale, and lots more of the same. We saw two films, one a movie called *By Jupiter*, and the other a film that was simply a succession of still photographs with a voice behind them, and a moon face alternately grinning and frowning and leering from the middle of the big clock that hangs at Randolph and State. I began to feel somewhat nightmarish, as if this were all unreal and that soon I would waken and find myself with a pleasant hangover and nothing more. But the largest part of the training work was practicing making out sales checks.

Have you ever realized what a Field's sales check is? Many times, no doubt, you have stood fretfully beside a clerk and tapped your foot, thinking it was taking him an unconscionable long time, and wondering why Field's didn't get more efficient help. Well, I have discovered

By Jupiter. A 1946 training film produced by Marshall Field's in which veteran character actor Chick Chandler (1905–88) plays a grumpy businessman who is given the opportunity to relive the events of his day in order to learn that "courtesy is contagious." The full film is available at https://www.youtube.com/watch?v=aDHO-duygG8.

the big clock. One of two massive beaux-arts clocks, iconic Field's images, that hang from corners of the building; the other is on the corner at State and Washington Streets.

the secret. In 1881, when the original Field's partners retired from the store, Field had a long conference with Beelzebub. And the sales check in use today was its direct result. The ones we used in books had nine parts—three sheets, three carbons, and a tissue for the auditing department. Two of the sheets had perforations. I had sometimes admired the dexterity and the automatic nonchalance of Field's clerks as they unconcernedly interleaved carbons and paper, whipping them back and forth with complete and wild abandon. But that was before I "helped out" on the Christmas rush.

For two days of training we did nothing but practice making out sales checks. There were such thrilling and soul-exalting things as Cash Take, Cash Send, Charge Take [with and without a Charg-a-Plate], Charge Send [again, with and without a Charg-a-Plate], Employee Cash [with 10% or 20% discount], Employee Charge [with discount], C.O.D., Exchange Checks, and about six more—which in my few weeks I never really did learn. There was scarcely a one of the 125 in our class who was not a wild-eyed and dry-mouthed picture of befuddlement by the time the two days had come to an end.

On that first morning of *real* work we had another small class, so that we could learn where to put our coats, how to punch the time clock, and where to keep our sales books. It was scheduled for 9:00 a.m., and took place at 10:15. I looked with some amazement at my time card, and then being of a rather curious and inquiring nature, went to the great rack of cards to find my proper slot, so that I would know where it was that first evening. Lo, the poor Indian! My slot was already occupied by a Miss Jane Carver, who had the same number I did!

---

the original Field's partners. Field's early partners were Potter Palmer, who retired from the business in 1867, and Levi Leiter, who left in 1881, when the firm became known simply as Marshall Field and Company.

Charg-a-Plate. A type of metal credit card embossed with the purchaser's name, address, and account number and used to imprint this information on a sales receipt.

C.O.D. Cash on delivery.

Lo, the poor Indian! Cf. line I.99 in *An Essay on Man* (1734), by Alexander Pope (1688–1744). In the context of Pope's poem, Steward seems to be casting himself as an innocent in the baffling chaos of his job at Marshall Field's.

Well, by the time that was straightened out and I had a new number, it was noon. Clutching my red sales book in my grubby hot little paw, I ventured into the book section and out on the "floor." It was like entering a vast and noisome hell, smelly and hot and crowded. I had advanced barely five feet into the domain of culture and knowledge when the hordes saw me and descended. Do you have the new Toynbee book? Where are the books on air-conditioning? Who wrote *The Rubaiyat of Omar Khayyam?* Is *Hello, Mrs. Goose* all right for a six-year-old girl? Where is Santa Claus? Where is the men's washroom? How much is this book? Where are the indestructible linen picture books for one-year-olds? Do you sell refrigerators on this floor? Say, bud, where is the can? Have you got *The Sleepy Lion?* Where are the Lutheran religious books? Is this all the Zane Grey you have? Have you got large-print Bibles for old people? Where's the johnny? Where can I buy elastic thread? Why don't you have a stamp department anymore? Where is Santa Claus? Are these all the books you have on astrology? Can you tell me how to get to the men's washroom?

Ah, Christmas, Christmas! To me this year it was a howling madhouse, a lunatic sabbath, a frenzied nightmare of females and squalling brats, a time of aching feet and back, of muscles in the ankles and calves that shrieked with pain, of complete nervous and mental and physical exhaustion. In moments of sanity, while I pondered the state of the world over my coffee at lunch, I wondered about it all. Had the world gone mad? Or had I?

Toynbee. Arnold Joseph Toynbee (1889–1975), best-selling British historian in the 1940s. The humor here consists of Steward's juxtaposition of the erudite Toynbee with *Hello Mrs. Goose* and books on mundane subjects like air-conditioning.

Rubaiyat of Omar Khayyam. The title refers to the nineteenth-century translation by Edward FitzGerald, but the joke is of course that the author is Omar Khayyam.

Hello, Mrs. Goose. The first edition of Miriam Clark Potter's *Hello, Mrs. Goose* was published in 1947 by J. B. Lippincott.

The Sleepy Lion. Steward apparently refers to Margaret Wise's *The Sleepy Little Lion*, with illustrations by Ylla Brown, first published in 1947 by Harper and Brothers.

Zane Grey (1872–1939). Enormously popular American writer of stories and novels about American frontier life.

When I was in high school, many years ago, I thought it would be wonderful to know how a milkman felt in the early morning, to know a streetcar motorman's reactions, to experience the emotions of everyone in every kind of profession—if just for a little while. But, of course, that was when I was younger. . . .

What? No, that's all, nurse. Just loosen that right strap on my straitjacket a little before you go. Thanks a lot. Is this a cash or charge, madam?

22

ON FAIR, FANTASTIC PARIS

APRIL 1948

Steward had just turned twenty-eight when he sailed for the first time to Europe in the summer of 1937, during which he would meet Lord Alfred Douglas in London, André Gide in Paris, Thomas Mann and Thornton Wilder in Zurich, and Gertrude Stein and Alice Toklas at their summer home in eastern France. His first experience of Paris would thus always be connected in his mind to what he later termed "the magic summer." "I was young and romantic and laid open to all the city's charms," he recalled. "In the year I arrived the subtle ghosts of the great were still strolling the boulevards and drinking in the cafés. The treasures of the Louvre acted like a magnet on my art-hungry soul, and in the Golden Age of Paris no other city could compare with it."[1]

In 1939, Steward returned for a second visit to Paris followed by another stay with Stein and Toklas before the onset of World War II made such travel impossible. During the 1940s, he often thought of living in Paris permanently, and he wrote this paean to the city under the influence of those dreams. The vividness of the essay's images belies the fact that Steward had been away from Paris for nearly nine years and suggests the profound connection he continued to feel with everyday life in its streets. His imaginative power as a writer is evident in his lyrical descriptions of even the smallest events, like the onset of twilight, which "brings a soft grey-golden blueness, in which small motes of silver seem suspended."

In 1950, four years after Gertrude Stein's death, Steward sailed again for Paris to renew his friendship with Alice Toklas. But he was now over forty, and although the reunion with Toklas was warm, his journal of the trip suggests a desultory month of sexual encounters and sunbathing by the Seine, with little of the magic of his earlier visits. "That's the end of a summer in Paris, which has pretty well got me over the desire to live there," he wrote on the journal's last page.[2]

Devoted to Toklas and to the memory of Stein, Steward continued visiting Toklas in Paris until her death in 1967. But after that, he never returned.

> Oh, Paris is a woman's town,
> With flowers in her hair.
>
> —VAN DYKE

It happens to me every year when April rolls around, but somehow it is different—stronger this year. The feeling is hard to define. It is like a slight trembling of the fringe around one's soul, a vague and not unpleasant quivering of the secret marrow deep in the bones, a tickly prickling feeling in the skin that makes one restless.

For it is April in Paris, and I would like to be there once again, on a golden hazy afternoon. The first blood of spring has now come to the old city, and the trees are fair bursting their winter bondage. Tender blue and yellow flowers are springing forth from the rich soil around the bushes in the Luxembourg gardens, and the broad lawns of the Tuileries in the angle of the Louvre are misty green.

Mysteriously there has appeared from wintering quarters the old familiar army of shabby huge-mustached caretakers, and in every park in the city they are smoothing the gravel with long-fibered brooms of brush. Into even the taxicab horns has come a more youthful *beep!* A few house painters are daubing industriously here and there, and others are polishing the memorial brass plaques found on almost every house in the city ("In this house Anatole France lived while writing *Penguin*

"*Oh, Paris is a woman's town.*" Line from the poem "America for Me" (1909), by Henry Van Dyke (1852–1933), which ironically celebrates the superior virtues of the United States.

April in Paris. Steward's phrase would evoke for his contemporary readers associations with the 1932 hit song with that title, composed by Vernon Duke with lyrics by Edgar Yipsel Harburg.

Anatole France (1844–1924). Nobel Prize–winning French writer whose satirical novel *L'Île des Pingouins* was published in 1908.

Island." "Here Verlaine and Rimbaud lived for three months."). Chairs
for the café terraces are being scrubbed and brightened, a few old men
are dozing along the Champs-Élysées in the warm sunlight under the
chestnut trees, and the students are walking hand in hand. In the cemetery of Père Lachaise fresh flowers appear in the vases before the tombs
of Chopin and Oscar Wilde; and occasionally two wandering young
lovers, tittering gaily, approach to touch the magic spot on the latter's
tomb—for it is a tradition that they thereby insure themselves tranquil-
ity for the next twelvemonth. Or they wander sentimentally down the
cemetery's side hill to stand with interlocked arms and read the romantic lines written on the tomb of Héloïse and Abelard: "Here, at long last,
the ashes of Héloïse and Abelard are reunited."

New posters go up on the outsides of each little circular street-corner
building. The man at the Café de la Paix who sells merchandise and
American papers lays in a fresh stock. The clouds above the Opera are
tumbling and excited white against the bluest of skies. Even the gen-
darmes directing traffic are affected—there is a kind of lackadaisical lan-
guor in their gesture of tossing their short capes back over their shoulders. And when one breathes and looks and listens—no matter whether
you have seen one or a thousand springs in Paris—one knows that this
is the best spring that Paris ever had!

If you give way to the sweet grey spirit of the old city under its new
cloak of spring, and stay on through all of April, you can see Paris unfold
before your eyes. It was misty green when you arrived, and now it is

Verlaine and Rimbaud. Paul-Marie Verlaine (1844–96) and Arthur Rimbaud (1854–91),
French symbolist poets who had a tempestuous love affair from 1871 to 1873.

cemetery of Père Lachaise. Enormous Parisian cemetery laid out in 1804. Besides Oscar
Wilde (1854–1900) and the Polish composer Frédéric Chopin (1810–49), both Gertrude
Stein (1874–1946) and Alice Toklas (1877–1967) are buried there.

Héloïse and Abelard. Héloïse d'Argenteuil (1101–1164), a renowned classical scholar, and
Peter Abelard (1079–1142), a brilliant French theologian, whose love affair ended in
tragedy but produced a celebrated exchange of letters between the two. In 1817, their
remains were reputedly moved to a crypt in Père Lachaise that remains one of the cemetery's most famous monuments.

Café de la Paix. Famous café near the Paris Opera, opened in 1862 and designed in an
extravagant neoclassical style.

wildly green. The Bois de Boulogne is a forest of freshness and sweet odors. Old women sleepily knit in the enclosed gardens around the churches—slow in their movements as the Fates—and old men talk of their youth. Young urchins dangle their rods over the Seine, hoping some fish will take their bait. Daily the piles of fresh vegetables in the central markets of Les Halles grow higher. Melons and oranges arrive from Algeria, the cabbages are heaped in huge green and white pyramids, grapes appear—and the onion soup grows sweeter. When early twilight comes, it brings a soft grey-golden blueness, in which small motes of silver seem suspended.

These, of course, are the sensory face of Paris in springtime. What is its deeper spirit? A question like that is hard to answer—and many of her lovers who have known her better and longer than I have tried to describe her subtle charms. Was Galiani defining Paris correctly when he called it the café of Europe? For some, undoubtedly—who think of the Folies-Bergère, Montmartre, and the Latin Quarter. Was Nietzsche correct when he said that as an artist, a man has no home in Europe save Paris? Certainly it has always been the holy city of artists, writers, and composers. Its treasures in the Louvre act like a magnet on the art-drunk soul. Holmes made popular the statement that good Americans, when they die, go to Paris; and Oscar Wilde added that bad Americans, when they die, go to America.

Bois de Boulogne. Large public park designed and constructed in the mid-nineteenth century.

the Fates. In Greek and Roman mythology, three female entities who spun, measured, and cut the thread of each individual's life.

Les Halles. Produce market dating from the twelfth century and housed after 1850 in monumental iron and glass structures. It was demolished in 1971.

Galiani. Ferdinando Galiani (1728–87), Italian economic theorist who was a Neapolitan embassy official in Paris from 1759 to 1769.

Nietzsche. Friedrich Nietzsche (1844–1900), German philosopher. The quotation is from his last work, *Ecce Homo* (1888).

Holmes. Oliver Wendell Holmes (1809–94), American poet and physician. In *The Autocrat of the Breakfast-Table* (1858), he records but does not take credit for the statement Steward quotes.

Oscar Wilde. For Wilde's witty take on Holmes's comment, see *A Woman of No Importance* (1893), act 1.

Steward on the terrace of 5 rue Christine with Alice Toklas and Basket II, Paris, April 1952. (Courtesy of the Bancroft Library, University of California, Berkeley)

Pinero—probably with fashion and perfume in mind—called the city a middle-aged woman's paradise. The city of light, looking like a queen in a book, with a wreath of pearl in raven hair, and a bright brooch at her breast—this she is, and all men, and some women, must adore.

Undoubtedly, the French people themselves account for much of the spirit of Paris. It is hard for the Anglo-Saxon to understand the mercurial, unpredictable spirit of the Frenchman. The sudden storms of temperament, the equally quick forgiving and forgetting, the simplicity of the creature comforts that satisfy the average Frenchman—all these are hard for us to know. Two simple anecdotes may help.

Before World War II began, I was spending the summer in Paris. On my way to lunch I usually stopped at a small family hole-in-the-wall café for an aperitif. My clothes were a rather odd assortment—a British sport jacket, American tee-shirt, and French slacks. For many days the proprietor was wary; he could not guess my nationality. Finally he tentatively asked "You are British?" No—American. "Ah!" he exclaimed, "Touchez!" And reached to shake hands. "We are then both democrats"—and I was almost embraced. Seems that he couldn't stand the British, and for the simplest of reasons. Neither nation could stand the other's humor—and for that reason he was sure (it was August, 1939) no alliance between Britain and France could last. . . .

The other involved eating a meal with a young French friend. I had noticed that Frenchmen generally used a bit of sugar on their melons, but I used salt. "I suppose you think it strange," I said, "that I use salt instead of sugar." He put down his spoon and said: "My dear friend—it makes no difference whatsoever to me. You could put snuff on your melon if you wanted to. It is all simply *a question of taste*."

That is what Paris essentially is, I think—an immense hospitality, an overwhelming comprehension and tolerance. There were no jim-crow lines

---

Pinero. Arthur Wing Pinero (1855–1934), British actor and playwright. The line about Paris is found in *The Princess and the Butterfly* (1897), act 1.

jim-crow lines. A reference to laws enacted by southern states and municipalities in the United States beginning in the 1870s that made segregation legal by mandating separate public facilities for whites and blacks. A lifelong opponent of racism, Steward also attacks Jim Crow laws in his final *IDJ* essay, "A Modest Proposal" (July 1949).

ever drawn that I could see—and I knew persons from all paths of living. And such *receptiveness* to the quality of the city itself, and the result is not to be resisted.

What it's like now I am not sure—there are many conflicting reports about prices, discomforts, keeping warm, black markets, food, and politics. But I do have a confidence in my favorite lady. She has suffered convulsions before, been beat and kicked and trodden upon—and she has always recovered.

She is the grave yet smiling, serenely great Grey Lady of the cities of the world.

23

ON ULYSSES, GROWN OLD

May 1948

Doc Anthony, the subject of this tribute, was Dr. Stephen Anthony, whom Steward met in Chicago through his friend and frequent sexual partner Jimmy Taylor.[1] Anthony was a generation older than Steward, but both were alcoholics and were gay, and the two became friends and drinking companions as Steward sank deeper and deeper into alcoholism in the early 1940s. By that time, his classes at Loyola were scheduled only in the late afternoons and evenings, and his days were free for conversation and drinking with Anthony.[2] For Steward, who was nearing the low point of his life, the friendship with this older man was profoundly meaningful. Later he described Anthony as someone who filled the niche in his life last occupied by Claire Andrews, his professor at Ohio State; he was "another model, a father-figure, a person to admire." The only problem, Steward observed in retrospect, now sober, was that "we had lost ourselves in the bottle."[3]

> How dull it is to pause, to make an end,
> To rust unburnished, not to shine in use!
>
> —TENNYSON

It was not strange that those of us who knew Doc Anthony always thought of him as Ulysses—for he was a Greek, a wanderer over the earth, a wise

---

"How dull it is." Lines from the poem "Ulysses" (1833), by Alfred Tennyson (1809–92), a dramatic monologue spoken by the central figure in Homer's *Odyssey* at the end of his life.

man, a counsellor and friend—and like Ulysses, increasingly restless as the years crept over him. When he died two years ago, he took with him a small part of the hearts of many of us who knew him. We like to think that his spirit—freed at last from the agony and pain of a sick body—soared quickly skyward into blinding light, carrying those fragments of us with it.

You will not often hear in these days a history of such wanderings and adventures, for times have changed and such romantic sagas belong to the past. He was born in Athens, on a little hill opposite the Acropolis—a shy and sensitive youth conscious of the past glory of his homeland. As a schoolboy, on moonlit nights, he used to climb up to the ruins of the Parthenon, and there amidst the crumbling fluted columns of the great temple, declaim his favorite passages from the *Iliad* or *Odyssey*, imagining himself in turn to be Achilles, Agamemnon, Hector, Paris—and all the great and lordly ghosts whose shadows still were there.

Then came the usual period of military conscription, just when Greece was trying to annex the island of Crete—and the experiences stiffened and matured his spirit: at seventeen he was as old in the head as a twenty-five-year-old. There were brief and fearful clashes with bearded guerillas from the hills, terror and gunfire at night, and most deadly of all, the old, old boredom of waiting and wondering what it was all about.

His parents were not wealthy, but next came some years of studying chemistry at Heidelberg—almost as glamorous as life in *The Student Prince*, what with the songs in the bierstube, the drinking bouts, the pretty girls—and of course, just a faint scar on his right temple about which he never said much. Often when I was visiting him, he would

---

when Greece was trying to annex the island of Crete. Steward refers to the Greco-Turkish War of 1897, when Greece attempted to wrest the island of Crete from the Ottoman Empire.

Heidelberg. Heidelberg University, founded in 1386; its reputation for research in chemistry was established in the nineteenth century by the distinguished scientist Robert Bunsen (1811–99), who headed the program from 1852 to 1888.

The Student Prince. A 1924 operetta by Sigmund Romberg (1887–1951) about a young prince who enrolls incognito at Heidelberg University and enjoys a rowdy student life until his father dies and he must return to responsibilities at home.

bierstube. German beer hall. Steward refers to the famous "Drinking Song" ("Drink! Drink! Drink!") in *The Student Prince.*

take down a treasured memento of those days: a drinking stein in the shape of a skull on a book, inscribed at its base in Latin: "Therefore, let us enjoy ourselves, since we are young but once."

At twenty-two, speaking French, German, Latin, Italian, and Greek, but no English, he arrived in New York with a few dollars in his pocket, and a tag in his lapel directing that he be sent to a distant cousin in Minneapolis. The next years were hard, but he began to put his knowledge to use. And after a while, he was working for the government in Washington, doing chemical research and reporting on the cultivation of wild rice in Wisconsin and Minnesota. His suggestions were largely responsible for government development of the project. Then World War I came along, and America could no longer get dyestuffs from Germany. Again, largely under his inventive direction, the government chemists succeeded in developing satisfactory synthetic dyes for American use. The young Ulysses seemed to have conquered the windy plains, and to be well on the way to success.

But suddenly, in the midst of it all, he quit his government position— quit it to enter the University of Chicago as a student of medicine. "Wanted to be my own boss," he explained briefly. He was thirty-three at the time—a late age for one to start a hard profession. For the next few years he nearly starved, trying to put himself through school by washing dishes, waiting on tables, and doing any and all odd jobs that came his way. We can only imagine the thrill he got when he first hung his shingle out, and waited for his patients. But at any rate—"By golly, I was my own boss."

When I first met him professionally, his star had somewhat descended, his ambition dulled. He lived in quarters at the back of his office, and to his home trooped an unending stream of his friends for advice or counsel, to borrow money or have a drink, to talk, to be prodded into ambition or warned against folly. The habit of him grew on me, and since in those days I had little to do until late afternoons, I found myself riding down to his place almost daily to listen to his fascinating words. He was old then, and would sit rocking in his easy chair with a glass in his hand, occasionally bellowing with a hearty Rabelaisian laughter at something said or done. In

Rabelaisian. François Rabelais (1494–1553), French writer known for his raucous and sometimes coarse humor.

the mornings he generally read, and it was curious to find in him as keen an up-to-the-minute mind on current medical progress as you would find anywhere. Often I would gently prod him, ask why he did not do more with his knowledge, did not write—at which his mood would break, and he might mutter, "Wotthehell, wotthehell, it's much easier to look into the bottle and enjoy life."

What did all of us get from him? That is hard to answer, for he gave to each what each one needed. When I first met him, I was a twittering jumpy collection of the weirdest and wildest psychoses you've ever seen. And though I did not realize it until later, he expertly diagnosed me, and laughed me out of my troubles. Yes, *laughed* me out of them, until soon I found myself joining in his laughter that came rumbling straight down from Mount Olympus, filling his tiny rooms and rocking and rolling down the corridor to his office.

He loved to cook, and taught me the secrets of Greek and Italian dishes. He introduced me to the use of herbs and seasonings and foods that Americans rarely learn. From him I learned the basic sauce of onion and tomato, the use of oregano and laurel leaves; and at his house I ate strange foods that he had bought down in the Greek neighborhood of Chicago: baby octopus, squids, sparrows sautéed in garlic and olive oil, red snapper in parsley and wine, and baked goat's brain. [Ah, that was a day! I almost boggled at eating the goat's eye, but he looked at me grinning, and quoted de Sade: "The greatest pleasures are born from conquered repugnances." I ate it, but I still do not feel de Sade was altogether right.]

Doc Anthony was sensitive to the end of his days, and ever the sentimentalist. Now and then quick-tempered, he always forgave: like a

---

When I first met him. In his unpublished autobiography, Steward rewrote this sentence to express his desperate mental state at the time more clearly: "When I first met him, I was a twittering jumpy collection of wild neuroses filled with more than my share of darkness, growl, and venom" ("Autobiography," 85–86).

Mount Olympus. Home of the gods in Greek mythology.

de Sade. Donatien Alphonse François de Sade, known as Marquis de Sade (1740–1814), libertine and author of books famously banned for their obscenity. The quoted line is spoken by the character Durand in de Sade's novel *Juliette* (1797).

summer storm, there would be lightning and thunder and noise for a little while—then all was over. I have heard his phone ring: a patient many miles away was calling for him. "I will not go out there! What do they think I am? I'm getting too old," he would storm. Then, after a few moments, he would quietly get up, put on his coat, and say gruffly, "Be back soon. Take any calls that come," and disappear into the night.

Ah, Doc, Doc, you old pagan—where are you now? You might deny my words, but if the love of humankind, if charity and good works, kindliness and affection, mean anything in modern faith, you were never a pagan at all. You must be back among your friends at an endless symposium of the gods. You are back with the great Achilles whom you knew, and with a goblet of ambrosia in your hand you talk to Socrates and Agamemnon of our sad history and philosophy; Hermes hands you his caduceus, Apollo and Orpheus play for you, and Ganymede fills your cup, and there is laurel round your head.

And faintly, somewhere far, we hear your laughter once again.

Hermes. In Greek mythology, the messenger between the divine and human worlds.

caduceus. Staff carried by Hermes, adorned with two intertwined snakes.

Apollo. In Greek mythology, the god of the sun and also (in the context here) of music.

Orpheus. Poet and musician in ancient Greek legend.

Ganymede. In Greek mythology, a Trojan boy abducted by Zeus to be his lover and the cup-bearer to the gods.

24

ON THE COMIC SPIRIT

June 1948

By the summer of 1948, Steward's two years of editorial work for World Book Encyclopedia had come to an end, as had a short-lived job at Compton's Encyclopedia, and he was short of money and drinking again.[1] Yet even at this new low point in his life he could write a beguiling essay on the need to laugh at oneself—a fact suggesting that underneath the comic stories he tells here is a genuine philosophy of life: the recognition that despite our best efforts, we are never the sole "masters of our fate" and must be prepared for life's unexpected, ironic, even cruel reversals of fortune. It was a lesson Steward had learned pointedly as early as 1936, when he had every reason to believe that his career as a professional writer had been launched. For in the same month that the *New York Times* reviewer of his newly published novel, *Angels on the Bough*, compared him to Henry James and Virginia Woolf and praised the book's "architectural perfection,"[2] the president of the State College of Washington personally fired him because he had been told that the book was "a racy novel with a streetwalker in it."[3] Hilaria, Steward's impish goddess of the absurd, had struck as she usually does, "when you are getting to feel your oats too much, or being too pompous, self-inflated with your own importance, and certain of your abilities and triumphs."

The rest of Steward's career would be replete with failures and disappointments, but his life is remarkable for his seemingly inexhaustible capacity to adjust his expectations and reinvent himself as necessary, creating new identities, he once wrote, as one would pull a new leaf off an artichoke.[4] Thus Samuel Steward, the English professor at two major Catholic universities, became the *Illinois Dental Journal* essayist Philip Sparrow and then the tattoo artist Phil Sparrow, followed by Ward Stames, Thomas Cave, Donald Bishop, and others who were contributors to European gay magazines, and then Phil Andros, the author of a popular series of erotic gay novels.

In the first article he wrote for the Swiss gay magazine *Der Kreis* in 1958, and later in his published memoir, Steward implied that his resilience in the face of disappointment was grounded in what he called "detachment." In an enigmatic and unpredictable world, he wrote, mere self-preservation drives one to "settle oneself into a pattern which would permit observation—even participation—but still allow detachment . . . so that no person or thing or situation would ever have the power again to wound."[5] Phrased in the terms of this essay, not to embrace Hilaria, not to accept the comic absurdities of life, is to make oneself endlessly and pointlessly vulnerable to life's inevitable pain.

> Born with the gift of laughter and a sense that the world is mad.
>
> —SABATINI

My favorite gal is a gay little flirtatious hoyden, with a turned-up nose and lots of little flouncey curls bobbing up and down at the back of her head when she runs. Heaven knows how old she is—thousands of years at the very least—but there is not a wrinkle on her face except those laughing ones around her eyes. For she is perpetually laughing and giggling and chuckling, twinkling up at you from beneath the garland of happy herbs and gilliflowers that she wears, to see how you are taking yourself that day. In her small right hand she carries a jester's stick: at the top of it a merry-andrew's head with tinkling bells, and at the bottom a curve in the wood like a shepherd's crook. And in her left hand is a very long straw with a small bunch of red and yellow feathers tied to the end.

Who is it, this vivacious friend of mine? Lots of persons know her. She is Hilaria, the younger sister of Thalia, Muse of Comic Poetry in the days when muses lived. But my Hilaria is the real, the genuine Comic

---

"*Born with the gift of laughter.*" From the first line of the novel *Scaramouche* (1921), by prolific Italian-born English novelist Rafael Sabatini (1875–1950). (The original reads "was mad.")

hoyden. A boisterous, carefree girl or woman.

gilliflowers. Strongly scented flowers.

merry-andrew. A clown, buffoon, or jester.

Hilaria. Steward apparently names his goddess after the ancient Roman festival day of masquerades and tomfoolery usually associated with the vernal equinox.

Thalia. One of the nine muses in ancient Greek mythology.

Spirit. She's the little lady who—like a motorcycle cop hiding behind a billboard to catch a speeder—is always lurking just behind you to trip you up when you are getting to feel your oats too much, or being too pompous, self-inflated with your own importance, and certain of your abilities and triumphs. Her simpler tricks are well known to all of us. It is Hilaria who slips the banana peeling under the heel of the fat and stuffed-shirt financier who has just refused a beggar a dime for coffee; and it is she who gives the hotfoot to the elegant store's floorwalker when he is curt with the shabby woman from the west side. It is she who makes university presidents split their infinitives, gives rabble-rousing demagogues a throat ailment, and makes dentists get the toothache.

Don't get me wrong. There is nothing of the gremlin about Hilaria. She's not a mischief-maker, and she does not play tricks unless they are deserved. But if you have never learned to laugh at yourself, or if you take yourself too seriously, then look out! You are fair game for little Hilaria, and she will slyly slip that jester's crook about your ankle, or with her small silver hammer tap smartly on the bung of your ego-barrel, and let the precious stuff drain out and away. And all this, too, when you least expect it, when you most believe yourself to be your soul's only captain, your fate's only master.

Everyone knows that comedy is one of the most wholesome and effective ways of probing and purifying the ills of the world. To those who feel, the world may be a tragedy, but it is a comedy to those who think. We know, too, that men show their characters in nothing more clearly than in what they think laughable, as Goethe said; that laughter is

---

your soul's only captain. Cf. the frequently quoted final lines of the poem "Invictus" (1888), by English poet William Ernest Henley (1849–1903): "I am the master of my fate, I am the captain of my soul."

To those who feel. Deliberate inversion of a sentence by the (possibly homosexual) British politician and prolific letter writer Horace Walpole (1717–97) in a letter of August 15–16, 1776, to his friend Anne Fitzpatrick, Countess of Upper Ossory (1738–1804): "This world is a comedy to those that think, a tragedy to those that feel" ("Horace Walpole's Correspondence, Yale Edition," The Lewis Walpole Library, Yale University, http://images .library.yale.edu/hwcorrespondence/page.asp?vol=32&seq=399&type=b).

as Goethe said. This remark is found in the journal kept by a character in the novel *Die Wahlverwandtschaften* (translated as *Elective Affinities*), part 2, chapter 4 (1809), by the German writer, philosopher, and scientist Johann Wolfgang von Goethe (1749–1832).

a kind of cipher-key to unravel the whole secret of a man's personality. These things, however, all belong to Thalia, the Muse of Comedy. To Hilaria, the little sister, the Comic Spirit, belong those things that are loved best.

The man is not laughed at who can laugh at himself first. How many of us have not been the victim of one of Little Sister's pranks? The examples are too many even to begin to list; they happen every day; the papers are full of them. There is the young minister delivering a sermon, and flattered to pieces by the continued nods of approval from the charming young lady in the front row. Afterwards, she approaches with a companion. The companion flatters the young man even more by asking for a copy of the sermon, "because, you see, my friend"—the one who had nodded—"is completely deaf." There is the very proper lady walking along the street, quite unaware that one stocking is down. At the airport one Sunday was a most officious dark-jowled little gnome, ready to meet a learned judge who was to arrive at noon. Behind the fellow was a motorcycle escort, and behind that, photographers. He ranted, he raved, because the plane was announced as twenty minutes late. "Whaddya want me to do?" asked a clerk; "send up a sky-hook and pull 'em down?" To which the little fatty announced he'd see the clerk got sacked. Then Hilaria stepped in. She spread her dress around a little, reached for a convenient grey cloud, and drew it down low, until it touched the top of the airport building, and left it there all the rest of the day! No planes landed, and at six in the evening—hearing the judge had landed at South Bend and would stay there—the little man, the escort, and the photographers all went home. The clerk still has his job.

By now you have probably seen Walter Huston in the movie called *The Treasure of the Sierra Madre*. It is a great pleasure to see Hollywood do an occasional good thing. But I loved the movie because the last ten minutes of it belong to Hilaria herself. When the precious gold dust— earned by ten months of hard work—blows away in a wind storm, Walter Huston as the old coot of a miner begins to laugh. It is Hilaria

Walter Huston (1883–1950). American actor who won an Academy Award for his role in the 1948 film *The Treasure of the Sierra Madre*, written and directed by his son John Huston (1906–87).

at work—it is Hilaria's laugh. It rolls from the screen, it fills the theater, it washes and cleanses the ears and minds of the audience. Few regret the fact that two miners have lost a hundred thousand bucks, for they have seen Hilaria at her best, and know the end could not be otherwise.

The saddest man I ever knew was one who could not learn his lesson from Hilaria—he was a colleague of mine many years ago. Time after time she tripped him, her pranks getting more severe with each repeat. As an undergraduate in college, he was an insufferable conceited boor— very intelligent in a plodding way, but not reticent in letting the world know it, nor in gloating over his fellow students. Once a woman pianist came to the campus to give a concert. From the stage she explained her companion was ill—would someone volunteer to turn the music for her? Little Bright-Eyes Karl, sitting in the front row, popped onto the stage. All went well for the first few moments. Then he turned a page, and she as quickly flipped it back. He fainted, had to be carried off, and for weeks avoided everyone on the campus. But he didn't learn. Ten years later he was reading for his doctoral thesis on Landor, and was still the same boorish conceited bore. Kept his voluminous notes on cards in twenty shoeboxes, and read and read and talked and talked Landor until even his most charitable and forgiving friends wished him on Bikini. He was out playing bridge one night, babbling about his love, when Hilaria got really mad. She took a match and dropped it in a bird's nest under the eaves of his apartment. And when he got home—Landor was gone up in smoke.

Oh, yes—Hilaria can be grim if you do not learn to laugh at yourself. But she treats her friends well, if you can beat her to the draw. For instance, tonight I'm going out to lecture on my new theory about

---

Little Bright-Eyes Karl. Steward apparently refers to Karl G. Pfeiffer, who was a faculty member in English at the State College of Washington when Steward taught there in 1935–36, completed a PhD dissertation on the nineteenth-century essayist Walter Savage Landor in 1939, and went on to write a widely panned biography of the novelist W. Somerset Maugham. For Steward's readers, his disparaging moniker would have recalled Shirley Temple's 1934 film *Bright Eyes.*

Bikini. Bikini Atoll in the Marshall Islands, which by 1948 had already been rendered uninhabitable by American nuclear testing.

Othello—a spankingly original idea I'm sure no one ever has had before. It's so startling I think I'll do a paper on it. Almost dressed, I'm hurrying to add the last lines to this article. . . .

Hey! what gives here? Oof—tugh—tugh! Now can you imagine such a thing! Caught right in the middle and won't budge either way—up or down! Pliers! Help! These confounded zip—

Do I hear someone laughing somewhere?

25

ON KEEPSAKES, GEW-GAWS, AND BAUBLES

September 1948

When Steward wrote this essay, he was living in the fourth apartment he had occupied since moving to Chicago twelve years earlier, but as he observes at the beginning, these various moves had not prevented him from accumulating "appalling piles of junk." The situation would only get worse later in his life: after moving to Berkeley, California, in 1964, Steward lived in the same six-hundred-square-foot bungalow until his death in 1993, and his hoarding tendencies during these nearly thirty years—combined with his dachshunds' fouling of the house and its contents when he became too ill to take them outdoors—made the house "a stinking, densely packed mess."[1] Michael Williams, his friend and literary executor, described the interior in Steward's final years: "There were files and pigeon-holes and boxes and shelves everywhere and all were overflowing with supplies, letters to answer, manuscripts, photographs and books. I [later] found chairs buried under the mass of things. . . . It would have been impossible to cook in the kitchen. . . . There was [only] a very narrow path [through it] to the back door. . . . There were tins of coins, boxes of can openers, bottle openers, and salt dispensers, piles of papers and lots of rinsed, empty dog-food cans which hadn't made it to the garbage pail . . . clutter everywhere."[2]

Writing this poignant essay at the young age of thirty-nine, Steward seems not fully to have perceived in himself the hoarding impulse that would immobilize him late in life. Yet he forthrightly calls himself a "keepsaker"—one who saves things that might appear worthless to others but that to the possessor are permeated with meaning and value because of the people and places they evoke. The example

of John Henry Newman's cloak, borrowed here from Steward's doctoral dissertation, is telling, for in his description of Newman's life as "unhappy, broken, with
lost friends, wrecked ambitions—cut up and disorganized," one readily senses
Steward's own sense of unfulfillment as he approached middle age. He had failed
to find in teaching the satisfaction he expected, had left the profession, and at
this writing was unemployed; he had not published anything since his novel in
1936 except these essays; he had spent more than a decade sunk in debilitating
alcoholism; he had had thousands of sexual encounters with hundreds of men
but had formed no lasting personal relationships; he had been crushed two years
earlier by the death of the person who seems to have mattered most in the world
to him—Gertrude Stein. Yet out of the incompleteness of Steward's life comes
this remarkable sentence about the value of keepsakes: "We fasten ourselves to
happiness with thousands of these little anchors. Our pleasant or sad or gay memories revive when we touch these magic things, and for a little while we escape
from the present into the golden past, where we lie bound, gagged, and deliriously
drugged among our souvenirs."

> 'Tis strange that I should care so much,
> And bring away with me today
> A water-glass your lips had touched.

André Gide once said that everyone ought to make at least one sharp
break in his life—be it with his home, his thought, his environment,
or even the room in which he lives. But I believe that Gide didn't go
far enough and was not sufficiently explicit. I would be in favor of a
pint-sized amendment to our constitution that would force every person
alive to move from his house or rooms at least once every five years.

I have been looking around my apartment, and am moved to this
dreary and bitter conclusion by the appalling piles of junk I see everywhere. This accumulation (plus the fact that the day is sloppy outside

---

André Gide (1869–1951). Gay French author and winner of the Nobel Prize for literature
in 1947. The passage Steward cites is found in Gide's *Les norritures terrestres* (1897):
"When your surroundings have taken on your likeness, or you yourself have grown like
your surroundings, they have ceased to profit you. You must leave them. There is no
greater danger for you than *your own* family, *your own* room, *your own* past" (Dorothy
Bussy, trans., *The Fruits of the Earth* [New York: Knopf, 1949], 40).

force every person alive to move. In fact, at the time he was writing, Steward had not stayed
in any of his Chicago apartments more than four years.

and the meatloaf for lunch did not agree with me) has put me into a mood of bleak hopelessness and frustration. I think I know now what William Blake must have felt when in 1819 he made one single-line entry in his diary: "Tuesday, May 18th. From two in the afternoon until nine of the evening—Despair."

This melancholy thought, and the unending rain in its dull whisper outside the venetian blinds, set me to pondering the question: Why do we keep things?

Certain groups don't count as "keepsakers." We must discount those people that keep things through laziness, or through being a little potty in the head. String, for instance. To some persons a long piece of thick white cotton string is better than fine gold, and more to be prized than rubies. Some like to wind it hit-or-miss into a huge ball, tying green string to white and whipcord to hemp. Others have separate balls for white, green, or red; thick, medium, or thin. And in this same group are those who save old wrappings and corrugated paper, against the day when they may have to do up a package to send through the mails.

Of course, these people think they are being thrifty—they belong to the "useful" school made popular by radio's Fibber McGee. Who has not heard Fibber open his closet door, forgetting the stuff piled up behind? Everything tumbles out over him, in one of the most nerve-shattering, ear-splitting rackets on the airwaves. Here also are the magpie and pack-rat people—those who can't bear to part with useless old golf clubs, old shoes and trousers, broken-stemmed pipes, old neckties, and tennis rackets. Either they are planning to get 'em repaired or cleaned, or give 'em to Cousin Willie, or "find some use for 'em someday." Two of the most insidious clutterers-up of the house are the magazines *Time* and

---

William Blake (1757–1827). English poet and printmaker considered eccentric during his lifetime but now regarded as a central figure in British romanticism. Steward apparently cites from memory; the entry, found in the so-called Rossetti Manuscript of Blake's notebook, reads "Tuesday, January 20, 1807, between Two and Seven in the Evening, Despair!" The edition Steward would have known is *The Note Book of William Blake Called the Rossetti Manuscript*, ed. Geoffrey Keynes (London: Nonesuch, 1935).

Fibber McGee. The comically inept husband in the radio show *Fibber McGee and Molly*, which ran from 1935 to 1959 and starred long-time radio performers Jim and Marian Jordan. The overstuffed closet was a recurring joke in the series.

Life. One rarely reads them through the moment they come, but one always sees an article that looks promising enough to read a little later. Before you get around to it, the next week's copies arrive; they are added to the growing pile—and so it goes. One hates to throw 'em away, donchaknow.

"Keepsakers" do not include, either, the real collectors of things—vases, or stamps, or matchcovers. These may collect books because they know first editions are valuable, and someday plan to sell them, or give them to a library which will name a wing after the donor. Similarly with those who collect coins, phonograph records, etchings, or butterflies—such are not keepsakers. Thomas Mann called such collecting activities "sinking back into the great dullness"—after one loses one's inner excitement, in boredom one turns outside to find an interest. With the collectors go the aesthetes, who like the rose glass or the shape of just one antique vase, one perfect medallion, one flawless amethyst. Still another group must be discounted as keepsakers—the persons who gather up things merely to satisfy their sense of possession, whether they "collect" real estate, stocks, bonds, the coins of a miser, diamonds, a wife, a car, or a house in the country. They own these things, and the ownership makes them proud and gives them a sense of importance.

Thus we are down to the genuine keepsakers at last. Oh, yes, you are one! Look around at your own collection—the souvenir programs, the framed diplomas, the photographs, the pressed flowers, the letters, ring, and locket, the samurai sword you got from a dead soldier on Saipan, the first dollar you ever earned, the lock of hair, your father's heavy hunting-case watch. There is the ornate old wine glass out of which *She* sipped some Madeira one night, with the dried wine still in the bottom, through all these years untouched, unwashed. There is the ancient key

---

Thomas Mann (1875–1955). German novelist and essayist and winner of the Nobel Prize for literature in 1929, whom Steward met in Switzerland during his first trip to Europe in 1937. Steward refers to the chapter "The Great Stupor" ("Der grosse Stumpfsinn") in Mann's novel *The Magic Mountain* (*Der Zauberberg*, 1924).

Saipan. Pacific island that was the site of a World War II battle between American and Japanese forces in July 1944.

to a room in the Chateau de Chillon that you picked up in Switzerland. There is a sterling butter dish from the Café de la Paix in Paris, a dagger from Algiers, a huge and lovely stein from Bavaria, and some thorns from a well-loved rosebush in a garden set among an unforgotten circle of blue hills. There are the treasured letters from old loves long forgotten, and friends who died, and names from youth and the past, dim and misty as dreams half-remembered at noon. All of these things touch the little chords of memory; they are the visible and tangible talismans that call occasions back to us, acquaintances and friends. They are the things that do not change, although friendships ripen and die, and people fade.

Cardinal Newman was such a one. He had a keen clear mind, and a heart of such tenderness and romanticism that had he not been a churchman he would have been a Byron. Making the Grand Tour through the Mediterranean to Italy and Greece, he fell ill of a fever in Malta. Gennaro, a little Sicilian boy, nursed him through the sickness, and Newman asked him what he wanted in payment. Gennaro asked for Newman's old blue cloak. But Newman would not give him that, for "I had such an attachment for it—it had covered me when cold, had ever

key to a room in the Chateau de Chillon. Castle on the shore of Lake Geneva dating from the twelfth century. In his unpublished memoir, Steward describes this item less grandly as "the key to the *Latrinenhaus*" ("Autobiography," 338).

Café de la Paix. Famous café near the Paris Opera, opened in 1862 and designed in an extravagant neoclassical style.

a dagger from Algiers. See Steward's *IDJ* essay "[On Mohammed Zenouhin]" (October 1948).

some thorns. The rosebush was in Stein and Toklas's Bilignin garden ("Autobiography," 145).

Cardinal Newman. John Henry Newman (1801–90) was a well-known Anglican priest and theologian and a leading figure in the Oxford Movement, which sought to restore elements of pre-Reformation Christianity to the Church of England. A prolific writer on doctrinal and educational issues, Newman converted to Catholicism in 1845, was ordained a Catholic priest in 1846, and became a cardinal in 1879. Steward's source for the story of Gennaro and Newman's cloak, which he also included in his 1934 PhD dissertation on romanticism and the Oxford Movement, was Newman's diary entry of March 25, 1840, describing his illness in Malta in May 1833 (Anne Mozley, ed., *Letters and Correspondence of John Henry Newman* [London: Longmans, 1898], 1:377). Here Steward again seems to repeat the story from memory, since the quotation is a rough paraphrase of the original text.

been with me since school, had wrapped me against the chill wind." In Newman's private chapel at St. Mary's, there were twenty-four portraits of his friends upon the walls, instead of saints. When he visited Oxford for the last time, he pulled a handful of black willow leaves, which he thrust into his bosom to remind him of happier days. In death, he asked to be buried in the same grave with Ambrose St. John.

And why—why all these things? Well, the answer is a profound and subtle one. Newman's life had been unhappy, broken, with lost friends, wrecked ambitions—cut up and disorganized. Only the tangible things remained to be sure of—his cloak, the willow leaves, the portraits. These things could not be taken from him by death, disaster, or destiny.

So it is with all of us. We fasten ourselves to happiness with thousands of these little anchors. Our pleasant or sad or gay memories revive when we touch these magic things, and for a little while we escape from the present into the golden past, where we lie bound, gagged, and deliriously drugged among our souvenirs.

Rainy afternoons are good days to clean out drawers and throw away keepsakes. There's quite a stack of old magazines there on the floor, and soon I'll begin on the drawers. But boyohboy! you sure turn up a lot of valuable things just cleaning out magazines! I found those slippers I bought in Morocco, that shiny little gendarme's whistle I picked up one afternoon in Paris, and all those lottery tickets I wasted my money on in France! Am I glad to see them again! They sure mean a lot to a guy.

Ambrose St. John (1815–75). Lifelong friend of John Henry Newman, who like him converted from Anglicanism and was ordained a Catholic priest.

bound, gagged. Steward's metaphorical description of the pleasure afforded by keepsakes is characteristically masochistic.

26

[ON MOHAMMED ZENOUHIN]

OCTOBER 1948

Long before his first trip to France in the summer of 1937, Steward had written to André Gide (1869–1951), as he had written earlier to Stein and many other literary celebrities, and had received an invitation to visit if he were ever in Paris.[1] It would be ten years before Gide's work would be recognized with the Nobel Prize in literature, but for a gay man like Steward, living in a homophobic country like the United States in the 1930s, Gide's open discussion of his homosexuality in *Corydon* (1923) and in *Si le grain ne meurt* (1924), which described his first sexual encounters with Arab boys in North Africa, had made him "a lighthouse in those dark and stormy days."[2] Steward called on Gide that summer, and they talked about books and authors. His fascination with North Africa was sealed ten days later when Gide arranged a sexual encounter for him with his eighteen-year-old Arab houseboy, whose beauty had struck Steward from the moment he had first opened the door of the apartment in the rue Vaneau and who, smiling now as he lay on Gide's huge, pink, circular bed, "sensually stretched his naked limbs . . . and held out his arms in invitation. 'I am Ali,' he said."[3]

Back in France in 1939 for a second stay with Stein and Toklas, Steward excused himself in advance of the arrival of other guests at Bilignin and set off on his first trip to Algiers, where an enterprising young man named Mohammed Zenouhin offered his services as Steward's guide for a small daily fee. Like his *Illinois Dental Journal* essays on Gertrude Stein and Doc Anthony, this one, published without a title, is what Steward called a "tribute" essay. Suffused with nostalgia, it demonstrates his skill at weaving bits of description, narrative, and dialogue into a touching portrait of Mohammed and at the same time recreating a memorable experience in what was to him the exotic setting of Algiers.

Because of the imperfect English in the message that Steward received nine years later about Mohammed's death, the specific reason why his father poisoned him is conveniently ambiguous: it may be taken as Mohammed's unaccountable delay in marrying, as custom demanded of the oldest son, or as his father's suspicion of his sexual orientation in a society where homosexuality was flatly unacceptable. Given the grisly nature of his father's act, the latter reading seems more likely, though it may not have occurred to many of Steward's dentist readers in 1948. In any case, the fact that Mohammed's last thought was of Steward closes the essay with a poignancy very much in keeping with its overall tone.

> More precisely, I was attracted to them by what remained of the sun on their brown skins.
>
> —ANDRÉ GIDE

The two African fleas that the Arab tailor sewed into the seams of my Algerian costume bit me behind the knee again last night. Over the years I have tried to kill the beasties by every means of dry cleaning known, but still they go on living, eating heaven knows what, for I do not willingly feed them.

The costume is a handsome thing, of a kind of soft, dark blue twill. The trousers are characteristically baggy, and fasten tight at the ankle; the jacket is like a long-sleeved vest, and both trousers and top are decorated with intricate Arabian designs sewed on in white. Just the thing for lounging, I decided when I saw them in Algiers, and brought them home with me. That was nearly ten years ago, and though the pants have split a little unmentionably here and there, they are still the most comfortable clothes I have.

I do not know what it was that drew me to northern Africa in the summer before the last war started, but it was powerful. In each of us there is a certain "call," an attraction or a feeling of spiritual kinship with one or two spots in the world. We feel that we must go there, that perhaps we lived there in some former time, and that we must

---

"More precisely, I was attracted to them." English translation (apparently by Steward) of a line from Gide's autobiography, *Si le grain ne meurt*. The passage is given a curiously poetic rendering in the standard English translation by Gide's friend and translator Dorothy Bussy (*If It Die . . .* [New York: Modern Library, 1935], 273).

somehow get back before we die. Perhaps I had been reading too much of the strange and exotic travels of André Gide in Algeria and Tunisia, accounts filled with descriptions of tawny, long-limbed people, of a culture different from any I had ever known. Or perhaps it was just that I had recently seen the movie *Algiers*, and was half-hoping to find Hedy Lamarr or Charles Boyer still lurking in the dark wet twisting alleys of the Casbah.

At any rate, I went. The city of Algiers, seen from the cobalt-blue sea, is breathtaking. It is built on a high hill, with buildings a rich cream in color; under the morning sun it explodes in a dazzling burst of white radiance that sends reflected golden spikes of light into the purple sky. My hotel was halfway up the hill, and looked down over the switchback streets that climbed up to it among the creamy buildings; the bay of Algiers glittered in the distance.

In a new place one always feels a little lost at first; in the climate of Algiers in August, one is also bound to feel a little lazy. I wandered over to the pleasant small park with a fountain, and sat on a bench to watch the people—the men in burnoose and scarlet fez, the veiled women with curious blue jewels of tattoos upon their foreheads or heels, the porters carrying bundles—even a sofa—on their heads.

It was there Mohammed Zenouhin found me, and picked me to be his employer during my stay in Algiers. I had absolutely nothing to say about it—he saw me and I was his thereafter. How he did it I will never know, but those children of the East have a psychological know-how that makes the most sophisticated Western expert in human relationships look and feel like a two-year-old. By this kindness, that suggestion, this wish for my amusement or comfort, he had woven me into his subtle silken web before the evening was over. He was

strange and exotic travels. Steward seems to refer to Part II of *Si le grain ne meurt*, in which Gide describes his awakening homosexuality during his travels in Tunisia and Algeria in his early twenties.

tawny, long-limbed people. In his unpublished memoir, Steward rewrote this line more honestly as "tawny long-limbed young men, darkly handsome" ("Autobiography," 221).

Algiers. 1938 film starring Charles Boyer and Hedy Lamarr and directed by John Cromwell.

burnoose. A long hooded cloak worn by Arabs and Berbers of North Africa.

an attractive sixteen-year-old, wearing a European coat and trousers with an open shirt; his only Arabian article was an old red chéchia with a black tassel, worn cockily angled on his sleek black hair. His handsome skin had the sun in it beneath the surface, and his black eyes were keen and laughing.

Looking back on that visit now, I do not know how I would ever have got along without Mohammed. I had planned to stay only a few days, but under his gay and teasing guidance the stay stretched to two weeks, then three. The twenty francs, about sixty cents, that I gave him every evening when we said good night, seemed little enough, but it was evidently a huge and satisfying sum to him.

Mohammed's French was not very good, but we understood each other. His Arabic, of course, was evidently superb, judging from the rows he could stir up with it. Before Mohammed came one day, I made the hideous mistake of giving the great gift of five francs to a gamin bootblack for shining my shoes at the sidewalk café. By the time Mohammed got there I was surrounded by half the little Arabs of Algiers, all clamoring for money. With a few excellently chosen words, Mohammed chased them off: what he told them I'll never know, but they used to run from me after that when they recognized me. It was Mohammed who first guided me down the Rue N'Fissa in the Casbah, protecting me from beggars and helping me dodge the slop thrown out of the upper windows, keeping me out of the way of the panniered donkeys that plodded slowly up the stairway streets. With him I went to the huge church of Notre Dame d'Afrique, high on

---

an attractive sixteen-year-old. In his unpublished memoir, Steward describes Mohammed as eighteen years old ("Autobiography," 222). The age he gives here may have been intended to desexualize Mohammed for *IDJ* readers, though Steward's Stud File card for Mohammed indicates that they in fact had two sexual encounters (see also Spring, 69).

chéchia. A fez.

gamin. A street urchin.

Rue N'Fissa in the Casbah. Famously narrow, hilly, and picturesque street in the old city of Algiers.

panniered. Laden with baskets.

Notre Dame d'Afrique. Our Lady of Africa, a Catholic basilica dedicated in 1872 on a cliff overlooking the Bay of Algiers.

a bluff overlooking the Mediterranean, to see the famous black Virgin's statue, whom sailors in danger implore—but he, a good Moslem, tactfully excused himself from going inside. Together we went to see a park wherein were many rare and monstrous blooms of Africa, and curious animals I had never even heard of. With him I smoked my first tiny pipeful of "kif," a by-product of hashish, which he seemed to enjoy very much but which left me with a dreadful headache and a dry, brackish mouth. And one day, putting our shoes back on after leaving a mosque, he gave me something to think about the rest of my life. He looked thoughtful, and at last came out with his philosophy: "The beggar who lies in the street, the worker, the tired woman—all those who believe in the bon Dieu receive force from Him, force which makes them live when they have nothing to eat and nowhere to go except the gutter. I myself believe in this force."

"Do you go regularly to the mosque?" I asked.

"Yes," he said. "Yes. We and the bon Dieu are all comrades here."

It was a tug to leave, but at last I had to. Then the war came, and there were only two letters for several years, written for him by a professional scribe whom I pictured sitting crosslegged in one of the narrow streets. Mohammed was well and happy. Then silence, until only two weeks ago when I got a letter in not-very-good English from an unknown Frenchman, a law student and friend of Mohammed. Here it is in part:

> It was some time ago he comes to me one day and said he feel very sad and fed-up because his father ask him to come home spend the holiday with family. He crys! So, what happen? I told him. You go and you will be back in few days in Algiers (his family was near Constantine in Djidjelli). "I suppose," he said, "I will never see you again nor anybody in the world . . . I will never be able to come here. My father want I get married with Arabian girl. I can't. I will refuse. . . ."
>
> In family he was the oldest. As you know, it is habit with Arab people, the oldest son must be married first if he wish to keep his father's fortune

---

an unknown Frenchman. In his unpublished memoir, Steward identifies the correspondent as "a Polish law student who was later to become my best friend in Paris—Pick, who had been attached to Mohammed Zenouhin the way I had been" ("Autobiography," 224). Steward eventually met Witold Pick during his trip to Paris in 1950 (Spring, 124).

and to take that of his future wife. He doesn't like the girls at all. He refuse to his father's proposals. One evening his father gave him during the supper a poison in the meal.

The next day Mohammed died. . . .

In his latest minutes before death—his mouth and face have turn blue—he gasp to cousin to write tell me what happen, and to tell you also goodbye.

27

ON THE DREAM, THE ILLUSION

DECEMBER 1948

In his sardonic November 1947 essay, "On Teaching," Steward wrote that after his eleven years of college-level teaching, "wild horses couldn't drag me back into it." But in 1948, unemployed and so short of money that he could not afford to attend his father's funeral, he applied for a faculty position in the English department of DePaul University in Chicago and was hired.[1] At that time, DePaul was dominated by its downtown professional schools, and the liberal arts campus in the Lincoln Park neighborhood of Chicago consisted of just a few undistinguished buildings huddled near the elevated train tracks. From the start, Steward found his new job disheartening. He considered his colleagues "mediocrities," resented the university's emphasis on basketball, and was annoyed to discover that unmarried faculty were paid less than their married colleagues. Surveying a typical class, he discovered that three-quarters of his first-year students knew how to change a spark plug, but none of them had heard of Homer.[2]

As he neared the end of his first term of teaching at DePaul, Steward wrote this somber essay about the need to protect one's cherished memories, to keep them "green in the baked bright desert of today." The first five years after he completed his PhD in 1934 had been full of such memorable events: he had published a novel praised by the *New York Times*, landed a challenging job at Loyola University, met Thornton Wilder, Thomas Mann, and André Gide, and developed a life-altering friendship with Gertrude Stein and Alice Toklas. But Stein's death in 1946 had created a painful vacuum in his life, teaching had failed to offer the fulfillment he had expected, and fifteen years of heavy drinking and hundreds of sexual encounters had left him little energy to continue his writing career beyond these obscurely published essays. With its warning that life's illusions are "filled with nothing but dust and ashes," this essay—unread and unknown at the time by anyone except dentists in Illinois—is both a comment on and an emblem of the fragility of human dreams.

> Whence comes solace? In cleaving to the Dream,
> And in gazing at the Gleam
> Whereby grey things golden seem.

The world of a child is bright and various and new. It is a world of shining color and sound, filled with the mystery of stars whereon loved ones live, of rain falling like the tears of God, of snowflakes floating earthwards from a plucked white bird, and rainbows ending in pots of gold in far-off fields. It is a magic world peopled with brownies living in the root-caves of trees, with a sun-god driving his chariot daily across the sky, and a man-in-the-moon solemnly smiling at night. Then, as age comes with its explanations and reasons, the silken veil slips gradually down; the shimmer of the fairy tale is replaced by a cold hard white light, and the world appears in all its wrinkled ugliness.

The first half of the twentieth century will doubtless be remembered for many things—two world wars and the beginning of a third, nuclear fission, radio, television, and the thousand devices to make people comfortable and lazy. Among these things, the future historian will also remark a certain tendency: the rapid growth of the delight in debunking. No other century has debunked the past so thoroughly and happily. We have been gleefully told that Washington never chopped down a cherry tree, that President Grant was a fearful drunkard, that Queen Elizabeth was bald and Socrates a corrupter of the youth of Athens, and that—in fact—you could familiarly call any of your idols "Old Clayfoot" if you had a mind. They are all toppled over, and with them beliefs and faiths and old ideas. But the "scientific method" goes doggedly on, its rays dissolving the statues down the line, and with each crash the glare of "enlightenment" becomes brighter and hotter and drier, until it is well-nigh impossible to live under it.

"*Whence comes solace?*" Lines 1, 5, 6, and 7 from the poem "On a Fine Morning" (1899), by Thomas Hardy (1840–1928).

"*Old Clayfoot.*" That is, a person of note with a hidden weakness ("feet of clay"); see Daniel 2:31–33.

This state of affairs is very bad, and there is little to be done. Perhaps, however, we can still remember enough of the formulas of the old magic to draw a circle around some of the parts of our own past that we cherish. So set off and protected, these moments or things will stay green in the baked bright desert of today. Or perhaps we can deliberately create a new illusion for ourselves. One of the most charming essays about a created illusion is Stephen Leacock's on his fishpond. It was a wondrous still little lake, hidden among brown protecting hills, quietly isolated, and perfect for fishing. The only trouble was that there was not a fish in it. Yet Leacock created an illusion for the friends who visited him, and made them happy. His stage props were a small rowboat, a fishing shack with tackle tangled on the walls, old hats, a bottle with a wee drap in it, and all the rest so dear to a fisherman's heart. Then with whispered talk about trout biting before a rain [or after], with rowing hither and thither on the still water, and with skillful remarks and questions, he enchanted them all with an afternoon's "fishing." And later, back in the city, they would reminisce about the big ones that got away, the bites they had, the perfection of that private hidden lake, and the good fortune of owning such an anglers' retreat.

In some measure we have all created within our hearts a few illusions and dreams which we love. Let us leave them alone, for they are fragile things, and will crumble at any second touch or exploration. Who has not, like Miniver Cheevy, sighed for the "good old days"? As we remember them, they were golden and perfect, for we have forgotten all except the pleasant parts. This is fine, and we should leave it so. I have never had the slightest desire to return to the campus of my college years, for I know that I would find the buildings shrunken, the glass brown, and the pleasant lake no longer enchanted in its surrounding greenery. Perhaps I

Stephen Leacock (1869–1944). British-born Canadian who earned a PhD in political science at the University of Chicago and taught at McGill University in Montreal but owed his worldwide celebrity to his humorous fiction and essays. "My Fishpond" was first published in the *Atlantic Monthly* in December 1936.

Miniver Cheevy. Character in the 1910 poem of the same name by Edwin Arlington Robinson (1869–1935) who spends his life lamenting that he had not been born earlier in history.

the pleasant lake. Mirror Lake on the campus of The Ohio State University.

was fortunate to be cautioned by a wise professor: "Remember," he said when I was a freshman, "remember that you are now living in the very middle of what you will later call the 'good old days.' Live each day fully; squeeze from each one every drop of pleasure in it. Then you will never want to haunt the campus at homecoming-game time, looking forlornly for the vanished glamor by the light of your gin bottle." And oh, how right he was!

Another fragile crystal best left hanging untouched in the cave of the past is the memory of the first kiss from your first love. Certainly, certainly, before you found your dream girl and married her and settled down, there was one other, was there not? How shy she was, that first one, and how adorable! How prettily she blushed when you looked at her! Maybe it was on the school picnic, and the two of you had gone exploring a little way into the woods, looking for daisies or hazelnuts. Perhaps it was sitting on the side porch of her house in the gliding swing, or walking home from a movie and pausing in the leaf-checkered shadows beyond a street light. You remember in that breathless moment the small dark curl that lay along her cheek, the glint of light on the silver pin at her throat. . . .

Well, leave her lay there, Mac. She's old and fat and forty by now.

Last summer in New York I saw one of the strangest movies of this generation. It was called *Dreams That Money Can Buy*—and I, who rarely see a movie twice, took my money and bought two afternoons' worth of the dreams which that picture sold. It was very "modern," very surrealistic, in rich technicolor reminding you of jewel tones and heavy oil paints from artists' tubes and dark red roses at midnight. Its theme was compelling and hypnotic, the story of a young poet who discovered he could interpret people's inmost dreams, and who opened an office to sell to his clients the dreams he molded from their subconscious. The film records the sequences of six dreams the poet sold his customers, and the seventh is the poet's own. At its end, a bust of Zeus which represents

Dreams That Money Can Buy. Influential surrealist film directed in 1947 by avant-garde artist and filmmaker Hans Richter (1888–1976), with individual segments written and/ or directed by artists such Alexander Calder (1898–1976), Marcel Duchamp (1887–1968), and Man Ray (1890–1976).

the poet's dearest memories is shattered to bits, and he as a person dissolves. All that remains of him are his works, bright color compositions flowing through space. The point of the whole picture is clear: when the last dream is shattered and the last illusion destroyed, there is little left to live for.

Literature is full of novels, stories, and poems on cherishing the gleam of one's illusions and dreams: the theme has constantly kept its appeal. The range is all the way from Shakespeare and Shelley down to Thurber, whose "Secret Life of Walter Mitty," done into a zany movie by Hollywood, gave a silly and extreme expression to the idea. Obviously, anyone who lives only for his dreams and illusions is on dangerous ground—the illusions easily become delusions, and you waken to find yourself strapped in a paranoiac's straitjacket with yesterday's paper dolls cluttering the floor around you.

We are fairly wild free colts when we start out, but life is not long in saddling and bridling us, and we are ridden pretty hard towards our final destination. Let us see if we cannot carry along with us a few of the bright red apples of illusion. But remember—they are only for looks; if we try to bite into them, we will probably discover that—like the apples of Sodom—they are filled with nothing but dust and ashes.

"Secret Life of Walter Mitty." Short story by American humorist James Thurber (1894–1961) about a mild-mannered character who imagines himself in a series of larger-than-life roles involving danger or heroism. First published in the *New Yorker* in 1939, it was made into a film in 1947 directed by Norman Z. McLeod and starring Danny Kaye.

apples of Sodom. Fruit that turned to ashes when picked, as first described by the Jewish-Roman historian Josephus (b. 37 CE).

28

ON TIME-SAVING DEVICES

February 1949

Though inspired by a characteristically macabre Charles Addams cartoon that humorously illustrates the unsavory uses to which time-saving devices may be put, this essay is actually less about modern appliances than about modern conceptions of time. As Steward approached his fortieth birthday in July 1949, he became increasingly sensitive to the unstoppable passing of time, and so it is perhaps not surprising that Addams's cartoon leads him here to a witty but telling critique of the metaphor of "saving" time and to thoughts about the relation between time and "our knowledge of how to live." Steward's discussion of the potentially destructive effects of time-saving devices on the quality of life—starting, unexpectedly, with the Tower of Babel—is surprisingly relevant nearly seventy years after he wrote. His complaint, for example, that the benefits of the telephone are offset by its intrusion into "our hard-won solitude, or our relaxing companionship" is easy to translate into terms that apply to a world where people walk, converse, eat, and even drive cars while keeping one eye on a smartphone and readily interrupt whatever they are doing to answer its often loud and jarring ringtone.

The poem by S. Weir Mitchell from which the essay's epigraph derives is particularly appropriate, for as a poem about idleness—about doing literally nothing—it is a celebration of living free from the insistent demands of time that Steward laments: "And I can be / Stiller than some gray stone / That hath no motion known. / It seems to me / That my still idleness doth make my own / All magic gifts of joy's simplicity."

There is no dearer lover of lost hours
Than I.

— S. WEIR MITCHELL

Some months ago readers of the *New Yorker* shuddered with delight over one of Charles Addams's macabre cartoons. A slatternly woman sat in a chair in a police station with four stolid cops around her, and a fifth taking down her confession. The caption read: ". . . and then I disconnected the booster from the Electro-Snuggie blanket and put him in the deep-freeze. In the morning, I defrosted him and ran him through the Handi-Home Slicer and then the Jiffy Burger Grind, and after that I fed him down the Dispose-All. Then I washed my clothes in the Bendix, tidied up the kitchen, and went to a movie."

Certainly, if you are pressed to dispose of a corpse that is unhandily cluttering up the house, there is no better way to set about it than by using these various time-saving devices. If minutes are precious, no time should be wasted with the old hacksaw and cleaver, or in laboriously washing the blood stains out by hand. The time so saved can then with profit be spent at the nickelodeon, establishing the necessary alibi.

What curious paradoxes we all are! There are few men living who would not fight to the death for their freedom—and yet it was man himself who invented the idea of time, the great enslaver, the most merciless and tireless tyrant-master of all. The ancients did not worship time as much as we do, or at any rate they were not able to pay so much attention to its small divisions as we are. The Indians measured months by

---

"There is no dearer lover." Opening lines of the poem "Idleness" (1892), by S. Weir Mitchell (1829–1914), American physician and writer known for his pioneering work in the field of neurology and less favorably for his development of the rest cure as a treatment for postpartum depression and other nervous disorders.

Charles Addams (1912–88). American cartoonist whose work frequently appeared in the *New Yorker* starting in the 1930s and was the basis of the film and television productions *The Addams Family.* The cartoon Steward refers to was published on page 20 of the October 30, 1948, issue. With the exception of Bendix (from Bendix Home Appliances, a leading marketer of automatic washing machines in the 1940s), the brand names are apparently fictitious.

nickelodeon. Small neighborhood movie theaters popular in the early twentieth century.

moons, and would undoubtedly have found it a little hard to boil their eggs exactly three minutes by the moon. Medieval wives, using sundials in the daytime, must have found it difficult to determine exactly what hour their husbands came home after dark. The hourglass and the water clock kept track of no smaller units of time than the hour, and would be of little help to a traffic cop timing a speeder.

Have you ever followed the second hand on your watch around two full minutes? I find it one of the most irritating things I know. There it goes, busily tripping and jerking its way from second to second, unheeding the figures it reaches and passes over, leaves behind, leaves far behind, approaches, and comes on to again. It has no feeling, takes no notice of division lines or numbers. Should it not give some small sign when it passes sixty—hesitate just a little to show this is the end of one thing and the beginning of the next? It does not—all the figures and divisions are simply beneath its notice, and it hurries on, and on.

Perhaps man at first enjoyed his invention of the concept of time. It was only as the years slipped by that he began to realize what a Frankenstein's monster he had created, and then it was too late, for he was in its power. Time grew to be precious to him and he came to think of it as money, measurable in dollars and cents. To save time, then, was to save money, and to save money was to grow rich. "This device is a great time saver," the salesman says, and you buy it because you are greedy for greater wealth. Actually, it is impossible to "save time" at all—there is no little bank or box in which you can store time up, to be enjoyed at the end of the day. A new means of transportation gets you to the office in eighteen minutes instead of thirty—so what? Your first appointment is at 8:30 anyway, and you twiddle your thumbs for twelve minutes until the patient arrives. We continually rush to "save time" to get some place, and have nothing to do when we get there—except take time to catch our breath.

Science has made us very comfortable and lazy, indeed, but it is doubtful that it has improved our knowledge of how to live. The telephone is a useful gadget at times, but for me it is one of the most annoying of all time-saving devices. People lived on the earth for thousands of

Your first appointment. A rare allusion to Steward's dentist readers.

years without it; certainly they did not make much more of a failure of living without the telephone than we are making of living with it. We are today the ragged, nerve-bitten slaves of its noisy, imperious jangling—day and night, in our hard-won solitude, or our relaxing companionship. At the loud summons of its bell we run to it, forsaking the visitor who has traveled miles to call on us. It ruins our meals and interrupts our love-making. Of course, one recognizes and admits its usefulness, and it *is* possible to free oneself from its tyranny. Years ago I learned to control my telephone reflexes that sent me bounding to my feet and racing toward the ringing bell. Now, if I am doing something else, I let it ring—assuring myself that if it's important, it'll ring again. This, naturally, is one of the best ways known to miss out on the invitation you especially wanted—but you keep your soul free.

Airplanes are another time-saving device the world could have well done without. Undoubtedly, the Wright brothers thought of their achievement with noble sentiments—it would be a quicker means of transportation and thus help draw the world together, increase the unity and brotherhood of man, be a potent force for good, etc. Instead—well, it would be silly and pointless to remind ourselves of all the death and tragedy for which the airplane has been responsible. One of the Wright brothers on his deathbed regretted the evil uses to which the airplane had been put. Looking thus, as we are, wholly on the darkened side of the account book, we are almost forced to admit that it would be better *not* to be brought into closer communication with the rest of the world, since contact only means that there are more chances for trouble to arise.

When the sons of Noah reached the plains of Shinar, they said, Go to, let us build a temple to reach heaven—because they wanted to find out

racing toward the ringing bell. An allusion to the famous experiments in conditioning devised by Russian physiologist Ivan Petrovich Pavlov (1849–1936).

all the death and tragedy. Writing in the shadow of World War II, Steward likely has military rather than commercial aircraft in mind.

One of the Wright brothers. At the end of August 1945, after the bombing of Hiroshima and Nagasaki, Orville Wright wrote to his friend Lester Gardner, "I once thought the aeroplane would end wars. Now I wonder if the aeroplane and the atomic bomb can do it." He died two years later, on January 30, 1948 (Tom D. Crouch, *The Bishop's Boys: A Life of Wilbur and Orville Wright* [1989; New York: Norton, 2003], 521).

about heaven quickly—and the tower of Babel was their wondrous time-saving device. What happened to those boys who got too big for their britches is pretty well known. And today, reading of possible atomic fuels that may produce a shocking time-saving 25,000 mph, enabling a rocket to take off for the moon—well, is there anyone in the audience who is beginning to feel a bit chilly about the shape of things to come? Is it about time for us to be slapped down?

Laboriously, using a quill feather and berry juice, I have copied this manuscript by candlelight in longhand. I made the candle myself, rendering the beeswax from my own hive over a small fire of twigs in my cave. These words will be winged off to press by one of my flock of carrier pigeons, and I will watch the horizon for a smoke signal announcing a safe arrival. Boy, this really is the life! What on earth would we do without it?

tower of Babel. See Genesis 11:4–9.

29

ON GETTING TO BE FORTY

MAY 1949

In his unpublished autobiography, written when he was nearly seventy, Steward looked back philosophically at his gradual aging: "I grew older and passed into the land where Everyman must eventually go, that of the older human being. The carefree life of one's prime, and the ease with which romantic encounters had been so carelessly and happily made—those things vanished so slowly that one was scarcely aware they were diminishing. But go they did, leaving a kind of bittersweet afterglow, a flickering tapestry of golden memories, from which one now and again arose with nostalgia and a barren pleasure."[1] At thirty-nine, however, the future looked significantly less benign, and neither the humor nor the witty literary allusions in this essay disguise the anxiety Steward felt as he approached his next birthday. For a gay man whose physical attractiveness had been essential to securing the sexual encounters that played such a large role in his life, turning forty was a depressing portent of declining allure. As he puts it obliquely in this essay, "Old maids and bachelors, of whom I am one, look on forty as the finish line for their conquests and adventures."

Steward's sensitivity to turning forty was heightened by what seemed to be the meager accomplishments of his life so far, exemplified by the teaching job he had begun in the previous year at DePaul University, where he felt overqualified and underpaid and had no chance of appointment to a permanent position. In the same month that he published this essay, Alice Toklas wrote him with encouragement that nonetheless must have only intensified his sense of having failed professionally: "It will be the deepest satisfaction to me if you [write] something of your real quality—you know Gertrude expected it of you and in all your fancy there is evidence of a direction."[2] Whether because of Toklas's prodding or Steward's own need for change as he reached a milestone in his life, he would publish only two more essays in the *Illinois Dental Journal*—a conventional essay on television in June 1949 and a most unconventional essay in July, which would force an end to the series.

> Ho, pretty page with the dimpled chin,
> All your wish is women to win—
> Wait till you come to Forty Year.

Some years ago Thornton Wilder called my attention to a passage that Gertrude Stein had once written in *A Long Gay Book* about getting old. "Do you know," he said intensely, for he had just passed forty, "I have read this passage aloud to many people, and have seen them actually grow pale as Gertrude approached the description that fitted them."

I read it idly, saw its remarkable aptness, but worried little about it, for I was then but twenty-nine. A year later, in France, I passed my thirtieth birthday, and had an *awful* time! Gertrude Stein said to me: "Of course Philly you had a bad time getting to be thirty, the decade years are always bad, but just wait until you have to be forty, then you will really have a bad time and that is the truth."

So it is that sometime this summer, in the dread and hateful month of July, in the wretched and loathsome year of 1949, I am going to have to face my Bad Time, and come to be forty. There is, after all, nothing whatever I can do about it. Time runs, and we slide along in its shadow—and eventually everyone still above ground has to be forty.

"Ho, pretty page." Lines 1, 3, and 5 from the poem "The Age of Wisdom" (1849), by William Makepeace Thackeray (1811–63).

A Long Gay Book. One of three pieces of early prose self-published by Stein in 1933 in a collection titled *Matisse Picasso and Gertrude Stein.*

I was then but twenty-nine. Steward met the playwright Thornton Wilder (1897–1975) for the first time in Zurich in September 1937 after visiting Gertrude Stein and Alice Toklas at their summer home in Bilignin, France. The two men promptly fell into a casual sexual relationship that continued into the mid-1940s, usually in room 1000 of the Stevens Hotel (now the Hilton Chicago) whenever Wilder was in Chicago (*Chapters,* 70–77). Steward's second and last visit with Stein and Toklas, during which he turned thirty, occurred in summer 1939.

Philly. Stein's actual nickname for Steward was "Sammy."

In the past, and in these pages, I have shown myself that I can be fairly expert at rationalizing troublesome things away. And many years ago I took for my own the motto of Socrates: "Know thyself." Yet for once it is impossible to rationalize, and impossible to get at the cause of my upsetting confusion. My dreams are full of large figure 40s, and the other day I snapped viciously at a kind old lady who remarked that I looked as if I needed forty winks. Just last month, rereading the *Arabian Nights*, I felt a sudden revulsion for one story, and skipped it. Yeah, you're right. It was "Ali Baba and the Forty Thieves."

That other persons have felt the same way about forty, there is plenty indication. Literature has abundant references to the "foolish age." "Fair, fat, and forty" was an expression used by Dryden and Scott. Walter Pitkin wrote a self-help book called *Life Begins at Forty*—but I have scorned it so far; for me, life ends at forty. Browning wrote: "Grow old along with me; the best is yet to be." But that's all poppycock. It's whistling in the dark to keep up a courageous front. You're frightened and you're trapped, and you know it. Others have passed the Awful Age; one can see that by looking around. The question is: How in hell did they do it?

In a way I have been extremely fortunate. It is not self-delusion when I say that I must look lots younger. People are invariably astonished when they learn my real age—although I will say that fewer and fewer persons are hearing what it is these days. My mom and pop passed on to me an average, fairly solid body, and when I was fifteen I learned to

---

"*Fair, fat, and forty.*" The phrase originated with the novelist Sir Walter Scott (1771–1832) in *Saint Ronan's Well* (1824), chapter VII: "For the love of Heaven," said her ladyship, "who can that comely dame be, on whom our excellent and learned Doctor looks with such uncommon regard?" "Fat, fair, and forty," said Mr. Winterblossom; "that is all I know of her—a mercantile person." A similar phrase by the poet and dramatist John Dryden (1631–1700) occurs in *Secret Love, or The Maiden Queen* (1667): "I am resolved to grow fat, and look young till forty, and then slip out of the world with the first wrinkle, and the reputation of five-and-twenty" (III.i).

Walter Pitkin. The self-help book *Life Begins at Forty* (1932), by Walter B. Pitkin (1878–1953), established the catchphrase in twentieth-century popular culture.

"*Grow old along with me.*" The first two lines of the poem "Rabbi Ben Ezra" (1864), by Robert Browning (1812–1889).

keep my belly muscles taut, so that the tension today is a mere conditioned reflex all the time, save when I am asleep, perhaps. Little laugh lines appeared at the corners of my eyes, and character "thought" lines in my forehead when I was seventeen. I still have all my hair, and only seventeen grey ones (a furious knocking on wood here), and enough teeth to chew with, if I am careful of that front cap and don't eat rye bread or corn on the cob. My skin has lost some of its elasticity, but it does not yet look crepey nor hang in folds. These phenomena of preservation I always used to explain laughingly, during my drinking days, as the result of my being completely pickled all the time. Now that the joys of the grape are no more, I am continually thinking that my fate will certainly be the same as that of the wonderful one-hoss shay of Oliver Wendell Holmes. On the morning of My Terrible Day I shall probably wake up and find my hair and teeth on my pillow, with my face looking as ravaged as the portrait of Dorian Gray just before Dorian plunged the dagger into his own heart.

Said Gertrude Stein in that passage: "When they are a little older they are commencing mentioning ageing to prepare any one for some such thing being something that will be showing in them." That's me, bub. I've been howling my head off and crying my eyes out for the past six months to everyone who knows how old I really am, complaining and referring to myself as already forty—just to accustom myself to the frightful reverberation of the two syllables in my own ear. I remember that Thornton, that year he was forty, was doing a lot of hollering about

---

one-hoss shay. "The Deacon's Masterpiece or, the Wonderful 'One-hoss Shay'" (1858), a poem by Oliver Wendell Holmes (1809–94), tells the story of a deacon intent on building a carriage with no weak components that could fail as it aged; he succeeds, but eventually the entire carriage falls to pieces at once.

Said Gertrude Stein. A few sentences of context: "When they are a little older they are certain that they can be older and that being older will sometime be coming. When they are a little older they are commencing mentioning ageing to prepare any one for some such thing being something that will be showing in them. When they are a little older they are commencing mentioning that they are expecting anything. When they are a little older they are commencing mentioning any such thing quite often. When they are a little older they are not mentioning being an older one, they are then mentioning that many are existing who are being young ones" (Matisse Picasso and Gertrude Stein, with Two Shorter Stories [1933; Mineola: Dover, 2000], 26).

how old he was and about his wasted years, until Gertrude finally made a rather sharp observation about how there was nobody younger than a young man hollering about being old. After that Thornton sort of quieted down in his moaning to a muted *obbligato* which you sensed rather than heard.

Edward Young once wrote that all men think all men mortal but themselves, and I suspect he was right. More than half of the sorrow of living lies in the obscure consciousness that we are slowly dying. It's like getting cancer—which always happens to the other fellow, not to oneself. Hence the utter and complete astonishment of the cancer victim, or the man on his deathbed, or the one approaching forty—and his voiced incredulous amazement: "But this *can't* be happening to *me!*" And yet it always is.

Actually, I suppose the deep-hidden Don Juan complex has a lot to do with the fear of forty. Old maids and bachelors, of whom I am one, look on forty as the finish line for their conquests and adventures. The whole weight seems to fall so suddenly and irrevocably—Serutan, dentures, toupees, girdles, transformations, wimpuses, bifocals, testosterone propionate, Calmitol, and Lydia Pinkham's Compound. It's hard to be a glamour girl or a dashing fellow under the weight of all those.

If any of you good people reading this have any Practical Hints or Useful Suggestions to help your poor old bedraggled droopy-tailed bird-brained friend over this hurdle, please send 'em along. Meanwhile, I'm

---

Edward Young (1683–1765). English poet from whose long poem *The Complaint: or Night Thoughts on Life, Death, and Immortality* (1742–45) Steward quotes line I.424.

Serutan. Fiber laxative first marketed in the 1930s with the slogan reminding shoppers that Serutan spelled backwards is "nature's."

testosterone propionate. Anabolic steroid developed in the 1930s to treat male hormone deficiencies and still marketed to promote muscle development.

Calmitol. Anti-itch medication marketed in the 1930s and 1940s by Thomas Leeming and Company.

Lydia Pinkham's Compound. Tonic created in 1873 by Lydia Estes Pinkham (1819–83) and marketed as a remedy for menstrual cramps ("Lydia Estes Pinkham," Harvard University Library Open Collections Program: Women Working, 1800–1930, http://ocp.hul.harvard .edu/ww/pinkham.html).

going to go out to look for a man I've never met. I'll touch up my temples just a weeny bit with moustache wax, and use some of that wonderful new temporary wrinkle remover currently on the market, put on a pair of those effective "Belly-in" shorts, and set forth on my quest.

The name of the man I'm looking for? Oh, yes. It's Ponce de León.

Ponce de León. Juan Ponce de León (1474–1521), Spanish explorer of the New World who is traditionally linked with the search for the Fountain of Youth.

30

A MODEST PROPOSAL

JULY 1949

By the spring of 1949, Steward was unhappily teaching at DePaul University in Chicago and had begun to weary of writing his monthly column for the *Illinois Dental Journal*. In the preceding five years, he had published more than fifty essays as Philip Sparrow (as well as six book-review columns that had appeared under his own name), and he was beginning to feel that he had exhausted the opportunities that the column had given him to "air my loves and prejudices, likes and dislikes, foibles and fripperies, reminiscences and tributes."[1] Alice Toklas had read most of the essays published since Stein's death in July 1946 and had enjoyed their "whimsy" and "Sammish impishness,"[2] but in a letter on May 27, 1949, she agreed that it was perhaps time for him to move on. "The dental journal articles are gay and personal," she wrote, "but if you're going to really get to work on something really your own you're right about giving them up—they'd be getting in your way."[3] Still, Steward seems to have been reluctant to disappoint William Schoen by resigning from the position that the dentist had generously offered him five years earlier and that he had enjoyed and taken some pride in.

But perhaps he could get himself fired?

Steward later described his July 1949 column as a "calculated gesture" to accomplish just that.[4] Borrowing his title from Jonathan Swift's familiar 1729 ironic proposal for eating children, he called for the states of the American South to secede and "let us alone to try to make a cleaner world to live in for ourselves!" But unlike the cool aloofness of Swift's narrator, who seems not to comprehend the horror of what he proposes, Philip Sparrow's outrage over what he called "the dirty infected evil-smelling yellow-dripping ulcerated sore of prejudice" in the South left no room for irony and robbed the essay of whatever humor the proposal for southern secession might have had. Through a standing exchange agreement among state dental journals, moreover, the essay also made its way to a number of southern states, which "exploded in anger and dismay at such insults," as Steward noted later. "As usual, I was in trouble again . . . and enjoyed every minute of it."[5]

For the next regular issue, under the headline "Sparrow Brings Mail," Dr. Schoen responded to the firestorm of protest that had broken out over the essay by calmly observing that "we are particularly happy that our Journal is so well read" and reminding readers that "printed opinions are those of the author and not of the journal."[6] But despite Schoen's seeming support, the Illinois State Dental Society passed a resolution publicly apologizing for Sparrow's "unwarranted and unjustifiable attack upon the traditions and customs of the Southern States of this country" and demanding an end to his column in the pages of the *Illinois Dental Journal*.[7] Schoen had to act quickly to comply. With the September issue already set in type, it was too late to remove his defense of Sparrow or even to drop Philip Sparrow from the table of contents, but readers looking for his column on page 378 found instead an article on socialized dentistry reprinted from the previous month's *British Dental Journal* that was conveniently the same length as the Philip Sparrow column it had replaced, apparently at the last minute before publication. Steward was free—and as someone who had valued black culture and opposed racism throughout his life, he no doubt took some additional pleasure in having elicited from the Illinois State Dental Society a defense of Jim Crow laws in the South as legitimate "traditions and customs" that his essay had unfairly maligned.

> Since there's no help, come let us kiss and part,
> Shake hands for ever, cancel all our vows . . .
>
> —MICHAEL DRAYTON

When I was six years old, my family moved to Richmond, Virginia, and about life in Richmond I retain two vivid memories. One was that I was immediately branded a "damyankee" by my playmates, and subjected to all manner of animal cruelties by my little fellow savages. Their main sport was to get the neighborhood bully, a big guy, to lift me up by the ears—a painful procedure, but not without the happy result of stretching my flappers to a good keyhole-cover size, most useful to me today. The other memory is of some sort of a celebration or carnival to which

---

"Since there's no help." Lines 1 and 5 from Sonnet LXI in the sonnet sequence *Idea* (1619), by Michael Drayton (1563–1631).

my father took me. On a building with a peak-angled roof were all the flags of the world lined up in a row, with the Confederate flag fluttering from the central point of honor. "But where," I asked the old man, "is the United States flag?" Pop looked unhappy. "It isn't there," he said, and that was all.

A civil war leaves many scars on the mind and emotions, and history has shown that some of them never fade. The simple truth of the matter is that the South, in our civil war, was a Poor Loser. This in itself is very odd, for the South prides itself on its sportsmanship, and sportsmen are supposed to be good losers. But the South was a Poor Loser, and one of the very worst kind—the Grudge-Bearing type. There is even a little southern town which proudly claims that it has never surrendered at all, and still lives under the Confederation. The feeling of the average Southerner for the North is still one of hot, smoldering resentment and hate, the cheap kind of resentment you find in the thwarted villains of Horatio Alger novels.

When you open up the dirty infected evil-smelling yellow-dripping ulcerated sore of prejudice and go probing around for the cause, you bring to light many foul things. It is not proposed to catalogue them here. But in the case of the South, they all circle around the Negro and the issue of slavery. Why was the South, until very recently, always considered solidly Democratic? Because Abraham Lincoln freed the slaves, and Lincoln was a Republican—and the South, grudge-bearing and spiteful as a spoiled child, voted Democratic thereafter, or until Truman started to reemphasize a program of civil rights. These rights are listed plainly in the Constitution of the United States, under which all sections of the country live—theoretically. But with what evasions in the South!

Horatio Alger (1832–99). American novelist known for his stories of impoverished but instinctively virtuous boys, often beset by villains, who through hard work and good fortune become financially prosperous members of society.

Truman started to reemphasize a program of civil rights. In December 1946, Harry Truman appointed the President's Committee on Civil Rights to investigate civil rights in the United Sates and make recommendations ending discrimination. In June 1947, Truman became the first president to address the annual convention of the NAACP, and in July 1948 he acted by executive order to implement two of his committee's recommendations by desegregating the armed forces and the federal work force.

With what winkings at the Bill of Rights, what shoulder-shruggings over black burned bodies turning slowly at the ends of ropes, what blind spots in the prejudice-infected brains of southern gentlemen! How dare they claim the Constitution of the United States as their governing code? How dare they live under it so brazenly and hypocritically as they do?

Clean up the sore of prejudice, you piously say? A little course of education-penicillin will cure it? Bosh! Stuff and nonsense. The prejudice is too deeply rooted by now, and legislation won't remove it. The chancre on the body of the South has been passed on like a congenital disease from father to son to the fourth generation: the spirochetes have invaded the secret centers of the brain, and are there to stay. Let's face it realistically. Jim Crow is a permanent guest in the south wing of our hotel.

With these melancholy conclusions in mind, permit me to make my modest proposal:

On April 9th next, anniversary of the ending of the Civil War, let the South quietly secede from the United States. Let it be done peacefully, without unnecessary fanfare, but with a kind of silence that will mask the feeling of jubilation in the hearts of Southerners, and equally conceal the great sigh of relief that will rustle windily through the North. On that day let customs and border stations begin to function on the

---

black burned bodies. Steward refers to lynching—the abduction, torture, and murder, often by hanging or burning alive or both, of African Americans by white vigilante groups in the South from the end of the nineteenth century through the first half of the twentieth. Typically pursued as mob punishment for alleged crimes, lynching was a weapon of terror intended to maintain black subservience. Though Steward here writes only of blacks in the South, many victims of lynching were white, and the practice was not confined to the South.

from father to son to the fourth generation. Cf. Numbers 14:18: "Yahweh, slow to anger and rich in faithful love, forgiving faults and transgression, and yet letting nothing go unchecked, punishing the parents' guilt in the children to the third and fourth generation."

Jim Crow. Jim Crow laws, enacted by southern states and municipalities beginning in the 1870s, made segregation legal by mandating separate public facilities—from schools and streetcar seats to restrooms and drinking fountains—for whites and blacks. Facilities for blacks were invariably greatly inferior. Many of these laws remained in force until the passage of the Civil Rights Act of 1964—fifteen years after Steward wrote—which was vigorously opposed by southern legislators, most of them Democrats.

Mason and Dixon line separating Maryland from Pennsylvania. Let this imaginary line be extended westward down the Ohio River and across the Mississippi to include those uncertain states which by a vote this fall will make their own decision to go with the new nation or stay with the old. Then let the line turn south, and by all means run along the west border of Texas, for in freeing the United States of Texas, not only does the North lose a large hunk of prejudiced land but a great deal of braggart b.s. besides.

Let the South, after this move, at once draw up its new constitution, legalizing the Ku Klux Klan, jim crowism, segregated education and religion, lynchings, torture and mayhem of Negroes, and anything else its little heart desires. Let it have a relaxed immigration law that will admit any Negro-hating Northerner who will take an oath of allegiance to the principles of St. Huey Long, and swear to abide by the newly written Articles of Prejudice against the Negroes, Catholics, and Jews. Let a new system of high export duties be devised, the profits from which will be used to finance free transportation out of the South to all Northern-bound freedom-loving Negroes and sharecroppers, or idealistic souls who want to unkennel themselves from the envenomed quadrant of our Great Commonwealth. Finally, let the new nation be called by an appropriate name, such as *Prejudicia*, or *Bigotria*, or if those be too difficult to pronounce, perhaps *Biassia* [from "bias"].

Personally, I shall not be sorry to see the mean little states depart. The South has contributed little to the American scene except the mint julep and the southern drawl. The South is actually a frame of mind—infantile, grudge-bearing, spiteful, petty, quarrelsome, waspish, peevish, and resentful—like that of any bad-tempered brat bested in a free-for-all.

Here at last, O you sweet lil Southland, is your chance to get even with the damyankees. Secede! Take away from us all youah cute lil

Mason and Dixon line. Line surveyed in the 1760s by Charles Mason and Jeremiah Dixon to establish the boundaries between the British colonies of Pennsylvania, Maryland, Virginia, and Delaware. The phrase is often used (inexactly) as shorthand for the boundary between the North and the South.

Huey Long (1893–1935). Populist governor of Louisiana (1928–32), notorious for his political control of the state even after being elected US senator in 1932. He was assassinated in Baton Rouge in 1935.

southun gals, youah cohen-pone an' chitlins, youah mimosa and bour-bon, youah Kaintucky cuhnels and Huey Longs, youah racehorses and lynchin' trees, youah faiah women and fine southun gennelmen. Take 'em away—and allow me to make a suggestion as to their ultimate disposition . . .

Secede, I say! Citizens of Biassia, arise! Throw off the galling hated Yankee yoke! The hour is now. Secede! And then for God's sake, let us alone to try to make a cleaner world to live in for ourselves!

APPENDIX 1

ESSAYS IN THE *ILLINOIS DENTAL JOURNAL* BY PHILIP SPARROW

In addition to the fifty-six essays below that appeared under Philip Sparrow's name, Steward as Sparrow published two other pieces: a humorous letter to the editor, occasioned by a printers' strike in October 1945 that forced the combination of the journal's October and November issues, in which he recounts the fifteenth-century legal dispute between Johann Gutenberg and his financier Johann Fust ("Philip Sparrow Writes a Letter," *Illinois Dental Journal* 14 [October–November 1945]: 435); and a column in which, posing as Schoen, he praises the essays of Philip Sparrow that have been published to date ("About Philip Sparrow," *Illinois Dental Journal* 16 [June 1947]: 247–48). The style and tone of the latter piece clearly indicate that it is Steward's writing, and he includes it in his personally typed list of contributions to the journal (*Illinois Dental Journal* Articles—Black Binding, Yale Steward Papers, Box 6).

"The Victim's Viewpoint: On Sublimated Sadism; or, the Dentist as Iago." *Illinois Dental Journal* 13 (January 1944): 22–23.
"The Victim's Viewpoint: On Getting an Appointment in Wartime." *Illinois Dental Journal* 13 (February 1944): 78.
"The Victim's Viewpoint: On the Prospect of Confinement by Porcelain Arms." *Illinois Dental Journal* 13 (March 1944): 120.
"The Victim's Viewpoint: On the Survival of the Medieval." *Illinois Dental Journal* 13 (April 1944): 173.

"The Victim's Viewpoint: On Logorrhea." *Illinois Dental Journal* 13 (May 1944): 214–15.

"The Victim's Viewpoint: On Psychic Somersaulting." *Illinois Dental Journal* 13 (June 1944): 248–49.

"The Victim's Viewpoint: On Bread and Butter." *Illinois Dental Journal* 13 (July 1944): 312–13.

"One Man's Viewpoint: On the Songs of War." *Illinois Dental Journal* 13 (September 1944): 419.

[Beginning with the next issue, the name of the column changes to "Philip Sparrow."]

"On Cryptography." *Illinois Dental Journal* 13 (October 1944): 452–53.

"On Alcoholics Anonymous." *Illinois Dental Journal* 13 (November 1944): 498–99.

"On Christmas." *Illinois Dental Journal* 13 (December 1944): 540–41.

"On Fifteen Years of Lent." *Illinois Dental Journal* 14 (January 1945): 34–35.

"On Soldiers and Civilians." *Illinois Dental Journal* 14 (February 1945): 74–75.

"On How to Cook a Wolf." *Illinois Dental Journal* 14 (March 1945): 128–29.

"On How to Be a Spy." *Illinois Dental Journal* 14 (April 1945): 156–57.

"On Psychiatry." *Illinois Dental Journal* 14 (May 1945): 214–15.

"On Balletomania." *Illinois Dental Journal* 14 (June 1945): 248–49.

"On the Dilettanti." *Illinois Dental Journal* 14 (July 1945): 302–3.

"On Books from Prison." *Illinois Dental Journal* 14 (September 1945): 398–99.

"On Cemeteries." *Illinois Dental Journal* 14 (October–November 1945): 438–39.

"On Basic English." *Illinois Dental Journal* 14 (December 1945): 472–73.

"On the Laws of War." *Illinois Dental Journal* 15 (February 1946): 68–69.

"On a Call to Paris." *Illinois Dental Journal* 15 (March 1946): 124–25.

"On the Importance of Dying Young." *Illinois Dental Journal* 15 (April 1946): 152–53.

"On Witch-Doctoring." *Illinois Dental Journal* 15 (May 1946): 196–97.

"On Reading Experiences." *Illinois Dental Journal* 15 (July 1946): 290–91.

"On Chicago." *Illinois Dental Journal* 15 (August 1946): 338–39.

"On How to Write an Encyclopedia." *Illinois Dental Journal* 15 (October 1946): 436–37.

"On Aviating." *Illinois Dental Journal* 15 (November 1946): 478–79.

"On Operas and Operating." *Illinois Dental Journal* 15 (December 1946): 520–21.

"On Men and Their Feathers." *Illinois Dental Journal* 16 (January 1947): 18–19.

"On Gertrude Stein." *Illinois Dental Journal* 16 (February 1947): 64–65.

"On Little White Ribbons." *Illinois Dental Journal* 16 (March 1947): 108–9.

"On Being Musclebound." *Illinois Dental Journal* 16 (April 1947): 152–53.

"On Life Insurance Agents." *Illinois Dental Journal* 16 (May 1947): 188–89.

"On My Poor Old Radio." *Illinois Dental Journal* 16 (August 1947): 342–43.

"On the Beach and Me." *Illinois Dental Journal* 16 (September 1947): 388–89.

"An Open Letter to My Landlord." *Illinois Dental Journal* 16 (October 1947): 426–27.

"On Teaching." *Illinois Dental Journal* 16 (November 1947): 476–77.

"To a Chance Acquaintance." *Illinois Dental Journal* 16 (December 1947): 512–13.

"On Fabulous, Fabulous Field's." *Illinois Dental Journal* 17 (January 1948): 22–23.

"On Rooshia." *Illinois Dental Journal* 17 (February 1948): 76–77.

"On Fair, Fantastic Paris." *Illinois Dental Journal* 17 (April 1948): 164–65.

"On Ulysses, Grown Old." *Illinois Dental Journal* 17 (May 1948): 202–3.

"On the Comic Spirit." *Illinois Dental Journal* 17 (June 1948): 240–41.

"On Those Precious Two Weeks." *Illinois Dental Journal* 17 (July 1948): 294–95.

"On Keepsakes, Gew-Gaws, and Baubles." *Illinois Dental Journal* 17 (September 1948): 392–93.

[On Mohammed Zenouhin]. *Illinois Dental Journal* 17 (October 1948): 438–39.

"On Tipping." *Illinois Dental Journal* 17 (November 1948): 480–81.

"On the Dream, the Illusion." *Illinois Dental Journal* 17 (December 1948): 516–17.

"On Misplaced Eyebrows." *Illinois Dental Journal* 18 (January 1949): 32–33.

"On Time-Saving Devices." *Illinois Dental Journal* 18 (February 1949): 72–73.

"On Table Manners." *Illinois Dental Journal* 18 (April 1949): 126–27.

"On Getting to Be Forty." *Illinois Dental Journal* 18 (May 1949): 182–83.

"On TV." *Illinois Dental Journal* 18 (June 1949): 228–29.

"A Modest Proposal." *Illinois Dental Journal* 18 (July 1949): 276–77.

APPENDIX 2

BOOK-REVIEW ARTICLES IN THE *ILLINOIS DENTAL JOURNAL* BY SAMUEL STEWARD

William P. Schoen became the editor of the *Illinois Dental Journal* in December 1942 and the next year introduced the innovation of an annual issue devoted to book reviews, enlisting his dental patient, Samuel Steward, as one of the regular reviewers. In issues that featured reviews of titles like *Fractures of the Jaws and Other Facial Bones*, *The Impacted Lower Third Molar*, and *Fundamentals of Occlusion*, Steward's literary-themed columns were delightful misfits. "A Miscellany about Books" offers a history of the book from papyrus to the present, with diverting digressions on bookworms and book bindings and a concluding thought from Thomas Carlyle: "Of all the momentous and magnificent gifts to man, the book is the greatest." "How to Read" is an accessible discussion of elements in a text that a careful reader needs to note, including the writer's purpose, diction, and tone, and concludes with a detailed analysis of logical fallacies illustrated with timely examples from Nazi propaganda. "The Power of Books" discusses books that have changed the world, from Harriet Beecher Stowe's *Uncle Tom's Cabin* to John Milton's *Areopagitica* to William Godwin's *Political Justice* (described dishearteningly as "the sort of thing through which professors have to plow so that their students will not"). "The Literature of Prophecy" includes the Bible, Nostradamus, and H. G. Wells, as well as a warning against reading too much of such literature "unless one has something strong to hold on to, something to act as a balance wheel to the voice of doom." In "The Dentist's General Library," Steward presents a bibliography that might be mistaken for a PhD-exam reading list in Western civilization, starting with "the rip-roaring comedies of Aristophanes" and ending with *Bartlett's Familiar Quotations* and *The Oxford Companion to English Literature*. Steward's final review essay, whose title recalls the 1932 novel *Little Man, What Now?* by the German writer Hans Fallada, is an astute and lucid review of the historical events and intellectual currents that affected American and European literature in the first half of the twentieth century.

What becomes clear in reading these essays is that Steward's goal was not to create a new demand for copies of *Areopagitica* but rather to enlarge the intellectual horizons of his readers by suggesting how books and reading have shaped the world we live in. The volumes that Steward discusses are sometimes weighty, but his tone is never dry; instead, he becomes in these essays an engaging embodiment of the breadth of knowledge and facility with language that reading offers—the same kind of model that inspired his students during twenty years of teaching. Despite the oddity of Steward's approach to the genre of the book review, Schoen, to his credit, seems to have liked it well enough not only to invite him back year after year but also to offer him the monthly column as Philip Sparrow that began in January 1944.

"A Miscellany about Books." *Illinois Dental Journal* 12 (September 1943): 382–84.

"How to Read." *Illinois Dental Journal* 13 (September 1944): 386–89.

"The Power of Books." *Illinois Dental Journal* 14 (September 1945): 370–72, 374.

"The Literature of Prophecy." *Illinois Dental Journal* 15 (June 1946): 222–24.

"The Dentist's General Library." *Illinois Dental Journal* 16 (June 1947): 218–20.

"Modern Literature: Little Author, What Now?" *Illinois Dental Journal* 18 (January 1949): 4–7.

NOTES

Introduction

1. "Editor's Note," *Illinois Dental Journal* 13 (January 1944): 22.
2. Philip Sparrow, "On Sublimated Sadism; or, the Dentist as Iago," *Illinois Dental Journal* 13 (January 1944): 22.
3. A complete bibliography of Steward's publications may be found in Spring, 442–50.
4. Spring quotes Steward writing in 1977, at age 68, that he had documented 4,541 separate encounters with 801 men (380). Steward described his boyhood visit to Valentino's Columbus, Ohio, hotel room in a 1989 interview with Carl Maves ("Valentino's Pubic Hair and Me," *The Advocate*, June 6, 1989, 72–74). In *Chapters*, Steward noted that in high school he had sex with "four members of the football team, all of the basketball, three of the track" (12) and described his 1937 meeting with Lord Alfred Douglas (44–51). His encounter with Roy Fitzgerald (Rock Hudson), when the two of them were working in Marshall Field's department store in December 1946, is documented in Steward's Stud File; see also Spring, 94n. Steward observed that during his years at DePaul "there were a half-dozen contacts between certain handsome male students and their beloved teacher" ("Autobiography," 251), two of which are also documented in the Stud File. He later estimated that over the years in Chicago he had had sex with "a coupla hundred" sailors (quoted in Spring, 85).
5. Steward's original Stud File card index is in the Yale Steward Papers.
6. "Autobiography," 310.
7. Ibid.
8. Ibid., 264.
9. The September 1944 column was titled "One Man's Viewpoint," but all subsequent columns were simply titled "Philip Sparrow."
10. Sparrow, "On Sublimated Sadism," 23.

11.   The opening sentences of Bacon's essays "Of Great Place" and "Of Studies."

12.   Philip Sparrow, "On Cryptography," *Illinois Dental Journal* 13 (October 1944): 452; "On Alcoholics Anonymous," *Illinois Dental Journal* 13 (November 1944): 498.

13.   "Autobiography," 310.

14.   Philip Sparrow, "On Teaching," *Illinois Dental Journal* 16 (November 1947): 476.

15.   Philip Sparrow, "On Soldiers and Civilians," *Illinois Dental Journal* 14 (February 1945): 75.

16.   Philip Sparrow, "On Balletomania," *Illinois Dental Journal* 14 (June 1945): 249.

17.   Philip Sparrow, "On Fabulous, Fabulous Field's," *Illinois Dental Journal* 17 (January 1948): 23.

18.   Philip Sparrow, "On the Beach and Me," *Illinois Dental Journal* 16 (September 1947): 389.

19.   Philip Sparrow, "On Keepsakes, Gew-Gaws, and Baubles," *Illinois Dental Journal* 17 (September 1948): 393.

20.   Philip Sparrow, "On the Dream, the Illusion," *Illinois Dental Journal* 17 (December 1948): 517.

21.   Philip Sparrow, "On Getting to Be Forty," *Illinois Dental Journal* 18 (May 1949): 182.

22.   Philip Sparrow, "On Gertrude Stein," *Illinois Dental Journal* 16 (February 1947): 64–65.

23.   "About Philip Sparrow," *Illinois Dental Journal* 16 (June 1947): 247–48.

24.   Steward's essays in the journal's annual book-review issues began in 1943, before the creation of Philip Sparrow, and ended in 1949.

25.   Philip Sparrow, "On Basic English," *Illinois Dental Journal* 14 (December 1945): 472.

26.   Samuel Steward, "A Journal of a Tattoo Artist," 325 (March 19, 1956), Kinsey Steward Collection, Box 1, Series 2.

27.   Philip Sparrow, "On Men and Their Feathers," *Illinois Dental Journal* 16 (January 1947): 18.

28.   Sparrow, "On Basic English," 472.

29.   Philip Sparrow, "On How Cook a Wolf," *Illinois Dental Journal* 14 (March 1945): 129.

30.   Philip Sparrow, "On Chicago," *Illinois Dental Journal* 15 (August 1946): 338.

31.   The phrases are from Sandburg's well-known poem "Chicago" (1916).

32.   "Alfred Kinsey and Homosexuality in the '50s," interview with Samuel Steward by Len Evans, ed. Terence Kissack, *Journal of the History of Sexuality* 9 (2000): 482.

33.   Spring, 411.

34.   *Dear Sammy*, 157.

35.   Steward to Alfred Kinsey, TLS, February 20, 1950, Kinsey Steward Collection, Box 1, Series 1.

Chapter 1

1.   "Editor's Note," *Illinois Dental Journal* 13 (January 1944): 22.

Chapter 2

1.   "Autobiography," 131.
2.   Ibid., 132.
3.   Ibid.

Chapter 3

1.   "Autobiography," 82.
2.   *Chapters*, 34.
3.   "Autobiography," 83.
4.   Ibid., 83–84.
5.   *Dear Sammy*, 17.
6.   "Autobiography," 88.

Chapter 4

1.   Paul Metzger, "Jonathan Forman, MD: A Visionary of the Last Century," *House Call* [Medical Heritage Center of The Ohio State University] 5.2 (Winter 2002): 1, 3.
2.   "Autobiography," 126.
3.   Ibid., 129.
4.   Ibid., 133.
5.   Steward's illusions about a navy career had been shattered almost immediately after he enlisted by the discovery that neither his PhD nor his cryptography expertise was of interest to anyone and that the rigors of basic training with much younger recruits were clearly beyond his abilities. He was only too happy to receive a medical discharge (ibid., 133–36).
6.   Ibid., 131.

Chapter 5

1.   A haunting contemporaneous account of the mental disorientation, depression, and hallucinations that shell shock might entail—and of the failure of

the medical profession to understand and deal with it effectively—is Virginia Woolf's depiction of the fictional character Septimus Smith in her 1925 novel, *Mrs. Dalloway*.

Chapter 6

1. M. F. K. Fisher, *How to Cook a Wolf* (1942; New York: North Point Press, 1988), 24-5.

Chapter 7

1. Perry R. Duis, "Great Lakes Naval Training Station," in *The Encyclopedia of Chicago*, ed. James R. Grossman, et al. (Chicago: University of Chicago Press, 2004), 362.
2. Quoted in Spring, 85.
3. On the date of Steward's purchase of his Polaroid Land Camera, see Steward to Alfred Kinsey, TLS, February 21, 1951 (Kinsey Steward Collection, Box 1, Series 1). Steward's Polaroids are reproduced in Justin Spring, *An Obscene Diary: The Visual World of Sam Steward* (n.p.: Antinous Press/Elysium Press, 2010); the originals are in the Yale Steward Papers.

Chapter 8

1. Philip Manning, *Freud and American Sociology* (Cambridge: Polity Press, 2005), 11. See also "The Sigmund Freud and Carl Jung lectures at Clark University," *Clark University Archives and Special Collections*, http://www.clarku .edu/research/archives/archives/FreudandJung.cfm.
2. Sigmund Freud, "An Autobiographical Study," in *The Standard Edition of the Complete Psychological Works of Sigmund Freud*, ed. James Strachey (London: Hogarth Press, 1959), 20:52.
3. Richard Skues, "Clark Revisited: Reappraising Freud in America," in *After Freud Left: A Century of Psychoanalysis in America*, ed. John Burnham (Chicago: University of Chicago Press, 2012), 76.

Chapter 9

1. "Autobiography," 11.
2. *Bad Boys*, 9.
3. "Autobiography," 15.

Chapter 10

1. "Autobiography," 309.
2. *Dear Sammy*, 56.
3. "Autobiography," 308.
4. Ibid., 190.

Chapter 11

1. "Hartsdale Pet Cemetery," http://www.petcem.com/.
2. "Autobiography," 355.
3. "Cranford" [typescript], Yale Steward Papers, Box 2.

Chapter 12

1. Stein to Steward, ALS, June 16, 1936, Stein Letters.
2. The 1933 publication of *The Autobiography of Alice B. Toklas* had "transformed Stein from an obscure, parodied literary experimentalist to a central modernist public figure and cultural critic" (Sarah Wilson, *Melting-Pot Modernism* [Ithaca: Cornell University Press, 2010], 184).
3. Samuel M. Steward, *Dear Sammy: Letters from Gertrude Stein and Alice B. Toklas* (Boston: Houghton Mifflin, 1977).
4. Ibid., 97.

Chapter 13

1. C. M. Bowra, "The Scholarship of A. E. Housman," *Spectator*, June 19, 1936, 1137.
2. John Carter, ed., *A. E. Housman: Selected Prose* (New York: Cambridge University Press, 1961), 150.
3. Michael Irwin puts it this way: "He had double, or triple, reason to be in a forlorn state of mind. The man he worshipped to the point of obsession had rejected his love, had married, and had quitted the country, leaving him bereft. The newspapers were reminding him that such love as he had to offer was in any case 'unnatural' and illegal. It is hardly surprising that he turned in upon himself" (Introduction to *The Collected Poems of A. E. Housman* [Ware: Wordsworth Editions, 1994], 10–11).
4. Ibid., 7.
5. *Chapters*, 37.
6. Ibid., 46.

Chapter 14

1. *Chapters*, 39. Steward had also made himself unpopular with the administration at Washington State by taking the students' side in a strike over the publication of a puritanical new code of student conduct (ibid., 38).
2. Ibid., 40.

Chapter 15

1. Robert C. Marsh and Norman Pellegrini, *150 Years of Opera in Chicago* (DeKalb: Northern Illinois University Press, 2006), 121–26.
2. "Autobiography," 15.
3. Richard S. Davis, "Flagstad Sets Opera on Fire: Triumphs as Isolde," *Milwaukee Journal*, November 17, 1947, 22.
4. Giorgio di Corfu, "Flagstad, Uncut Act II Tristan," *Opera-L Archives* (October 7, 2013), http://listserv.bccls.org/cgi-bin/wa?A2=ind1310A&L=OPERA-L&D =0&P=173521.
5. "Autobiography," 16.

Chapter 16

1. "Autobiography," 115.
2. Ibid., 132.
3. *Bad Boys*, 8–9.

Chapter 17

1. Steward to Stein, ALS, November 19, 1933, Steward Letters.
2. *Chapters*, 20.
3. "Autobiography," 139-41.
4. Steward to Stein, ALS, January 21, 1934, Steward Letters.

Chapter 18

1. "Autobiography," 88.
2. Steward to Alice Toklas, TLS, May 15, 1947, Steward Letters, Box 137.
3. "Autobiography," 89.
4. *Dear Sammy*, 93. In 1978, Steward wrote in his unpublished memoir that he attended AA meetings twice weekly for three years and that "though it took

me some time before I stopped 'slipping,' on August 10, 1947 I had my last drink—and have had none since" ("Autobiography," 90, 91). But see Spring, 103–4, on Steward's relapse in 1948.

Chapter 19

1. Daniel Harris, "A Psychohistory of the Homosexual Body," *Salmagundi*, no. 109–110 (Winter–Spring 1996): 105–7.

Chapter 20

1. "Autobiography," 190, 186.
2. Ibid., 186.
3. Ibid., 230–33.
4. "Portraits: Samuel Steward," *Trajectories-VII: Literary Supplement to the DePaulia*, April 1953, 1.
5. "Autobiography," 246. Steward doubtless recognized his own membership in all three of these groups.
6. *Bad Boys*, 8.
7. Samuel Steward, "A Journal of a Tattoo Artist," 326 (March 29, 1956), Kinsey Steward Collection, Box 1, Series 2.
8. Ibid., 359 (June 8, 1956); 327, 326 (March 29, 1956).

Chapter 21

1. Lloyd Wendt and Herman Kogan, *Give the Lady What She Wants!* (Chicago: Rand McNally, 1952), 362–63.
2. Spring, 94.

Chapter 22

1. *Chapters*, 52
2. "Holograph Travel Diary, 1950," Yale Steward Papers, Box 9.

Chapter 23

1. "Autobiography," 84. In this final typescript of Steward's unpublished autobiography, the name is changed with correction fluid and pen from "Taylor" to "Taylick." See Spring, 60.

2. "Autobiography," 85.
3. Ibid., 87.

Chapter 24

1. "Autobiography," 244; Spring, 103–4.
2. Stanley Young, "Trouble in Academe," review of *Angels on the Bough*, by S. M. Steward, *New York Times Book Review*, May 31, 1936, 7, 15.
3. *Chapters*, 39.
4. "Autobiography," 321.
5. *Chapters*, 140. An earlier formulation of this idea is found in Steward's "Journal of a Tattoo Artist" as he contemplated life after his dismissal from DePaul University. There he writes that he must now follow what he has been "saying to classes for the past twenty years, such things as how happy and excited the possession of inner resources makes the thinking man, or the man able to think; . . . how a man can be happy anywhere; how the individual can scorn conformity and the opinion of others (350 [June 8, 1956], Kinsey Steward Collection, Box 1, Series 2).

Chapter 25

1. Spring, 407.
2. Quoted in Spring, 400.

Chapter 26

1. *Chapters*, 44, 52.
2. Ibid., 53.
3. Ibid., 58.

Chapter 27

1. "Autobiography," 244.
2. *Bad Boys*, 7–8.

Chapter 29

1. "Autobiography," 321.
2. *Dear Sammy*, 172.

Chapter 30

1.   "Autobiography," 310.
2.   *Dear Sammy*, 157, 163.
3.   Ibid., 172.
4.   "Autobiography," 310.
5.   Ibid., 311.
6.   William P. Schoen, "Sparrow Brings Mail," *Illinois Dental Journal* 18 (September 1949): 374.
7.   "A Resolution," *Illinois Dental Journal* 18 (October 1949): 423.

INDEX

Page numbers in italics refer to illustrations.

Abelard, Peter, tomb of, in Père Lachaise, 163

Achilles, 170, 173

Adams, James Eli, "The Dandy," 126n

Addams, Charles, 199, 200; *The Addams Family*, 200

Admiral Togo (horse), 81, *84*, 86

Advocate, 2

Agamemnon, 170, 173

aging: Gertrude Stein on, 208; *IDJ* essay on, 205–10

Ain, 92, 130

Aix-les-Bains, *130*, 132

alcohol: egg whites, demonstration of effect on, 138; Evanston, Illinois, banned in, 138; as medicine (*see* Allen, Martha; Pechuman, W. F.); prohibition of, 27, 29, 138–40; Steward's first experience with, 136; use of, among Steward's family members, 136–37. *See also* Alcoholics Anonymous; alcoholism

Alcoholics Anonymous, 29, 81, 135, 138; belief in a greater power required by, 31, 136; first Chicago-area meeting of, 138; founding of, in 1930s, 30; *IDJ* essay on, 27–32; Steward as member of, x, 27, 136, 228–29n4 (chap. 18)

alcoholism: and Dr. Stephen Anthony, 169; and John Barrymore, 102; effects of, 29; *IDJ* essays on, 27–32, 135–40; treatment of, 29, 62. *See also* Alcoholics Anonymous; Jackson, Charles; Steward, Samuel: alcoholism of; Women's Christian Temperance Union

Alger, Horatio, 213

Algiers, 185; Steward's 1939 visit to, 187–91. *See also* Zenouhin, Mohammed

"Ali Baba and the Forty Thieves," 207

Allen, Martha, *Alcohol*, 138n

allergy, 7; Dr. Jonathan Forman, early research by, 33; Francis Hare, food and illness studied by, 34; *IDJ* essay on, 33–38; Clemens von Pirquet, term coined by, 34. *See also* Steward, Samuel: allergies of

American Medico-Psychological Association, 59

American Psychiatric Association, 39, 59; *Diagnostic and Statistical Manual of Mental Disorders*, 39. *See also* posttraumatic stress disorder

Amigo, 2

Anderson, Sherwood, 128

Andrews, Clarence ("Claire") E.: death of, 89, 127, 129; and Steward, 89, 127, 169; as teacher of Stein's work, 89, 127

Andros, Phil (pornographer). *See* Steward, Samuel: as Phil Andros

Angers, 75

Anthony, Dr. Stephen, 109; alcoholism of, 169; compared to Ulysses, 169–70; effect of on Steward's life, 172; *IDJ* essay on, 169–73; Steward's friendship with, 169

Aphrodisia (cologne), 126

Apollo, 173

Arabian Nights, 207

Archimedes of Syracuse, 60

Argentina. *See* World War II

Aristagoras, 22

Aristophanes, 222

Armour, Philip Danforth, 146

Augeas, King, 64

Austin, Thomas, ed., *Two Fifteenth-Century Cookery-Books*, 48n

Babel, Tower of, 199, 203

Bach, Johann Sebastian, 1, 18

bachelor, gay implications of term, 63

Bacon, Francis: ciphers, alleged use of, 22–23, 25; model for Steward's early *IDJ* essays, 7

ballet, 100, 130; *IDJ* essay on, 65–71. *See also* Nault, Fernand; Steward, Samuel: and ballet; Steward, Samuel: sexual encounters of

Ballet Russe de Monte Carlo, 8, 65–68, 70; Steward's first encounter with, 65

Ballets Russes, 66, 67, 68, 70

Bankhead, Tallulah, 154

Barrymore, John, 102

Bartlett's Familiar Quotations, 222

Bell, Alexander Graham, 95

Bellini, Vincenzo, *Norma*, 114

Bell Telephone Company, 90, 93

Bendix Home Appliances, 200

Berkeley, California. *See* Steward, Samuel: Berkeley, California, residence in

Berlin, 55, 78, 126

Bible, 221; Daniel 2:31–33, 194n; Genesis 3:19, 98n; Genesis 11:4–9, 203n; Numbers 14:18, 36n, 214n

Bikini Atoll (Marshall Islands), 179

Bilignin: summer home of Gertrude Stein and Alice Toklas, 89, 91, 92, 128, 131, 132; Steward meets Sir Francis Rose in, 131; Steward visits Stein and Toklas in, 89, 91, 127, 128, 129–34, 187, 206; thorns from rosebushes in, 134, 185

Bizet, Georges, *Carmen*, 114, 116–17, 119

Blake, William, 183. *See also* Keynes, Geoffrey

bodybuilding, 4, 8, 60, 81; books about, 146; culture of, 142–44; and Bob Hoffman, 141, 143, 146; *IDJ* essay on, 141–47; and Li'l Abner Yokum, 146; and Bernarr Macfadden, 141; magazines about, popularity with gay men, 141–42; Miss Forget-Me-Not, 147; Miss Legionnaire, 147; Miss Quick Freeze, 147; Mr. America (1946), 147; Mr. America competition, 141, 143; origins

of, in the United States, 141; *Strength and Health*, 143, 145

Boethius, *Consolation of Philosophy*, 74

Boswell Club, 94

Bowra, C. M., 97; "The Scholarship of A. E. Housman," 227n1 (chap. 13)

Boyarski, Bill, *Big Daddy*, 40n

Boyer, Charles, 189

Bradley, A. C., *Shakespearean Tragedy*, 19n

Breneman, Tom, 119, 122; *Breakfast in Hollywood*, 122

Bridewell, 79

British Dental Journal, 212

Brown, Ylla, 159

Browning, Robert, "Rabbi Ben Ezra," 207

Brunnhilde, 91, 95, 114, 116

Bunsen, Robert, 170

Bunyan, John, 75–76; *Pilgrim's Progress*, 76

Burke, Patrick, *Come In and Hear the Truth*, 50n

Burnham, Daniel, 106, 111, 155

Burnham, John, ed., *After Freud Left*, 226n3 (chap. 8)

Burns, Robert, "A Winter Night," 28

By Jupiter. See Marshall Field's

Byron, George Gordon, 99, 129, 185

Caesar, Julius, 22, 24, 26, 46, 49

Café de la Paix, 163, 185

Calder, Alexander, 196

Callas, Maria, 114

Calmitol, 209

Cambronne, Pierre, 87

Capp, Al, *Li'l Abner Yokum*, 146. *See also* bodybuilding

Carlyle, Thomas, 221; *Life of John Sterling*, 91

Carnegie, Andrew, 146

Carroll College, 27, 65, 68

Carter, John, ed., *A. E. Housman*, 227n2 (chap. 13)

cemeteries: for animals (*see* pet cemeteries); *IDJ* essay on, 81–87. *See also* Père Lachaise

Chandler, Chick, 157

Charles VII, 102

Chauncey, George, *Gender, Urban Culture, and the Making of the Gay World, 1890–1940*, 50n

Cheevy, Miniver. *See* Robinson, Edwin Arlington

Chez Paree, 142

Chicago, Illinois, xi, 2, 4, 5, 7, 15, 23, 27, 41,
73, 81, 83, 92, 94, 112, 113, 129, 169, 181,
223; Alcoholics Anonymous in, 31, 136,
138; Art Institute of, 111; Ballet Russe
performances in, 8, 65, 68; black-and-tan
bars, 109; Bridewell (prison), 79; Carson
Pirie Scott (department store), 106; Chez
Paree (nightclub), 142; Chicago Symphony
Orchestra, 111, 113; Civic Opera House,
113, 115; elevated train, 106–7; Field
Museum of Natural History, 111; Foster
Beach, 9, 108; as Gargantua, 112; Gold
Coast, 107; homosexuals in (1930s and
1940s), 13, 105, 108; *IDJ* essay on, 105–12;
Jackson Park, 112; Lake Shore Drive
("Outer Drive"), 109; Lincoln Park, 112,
193; Loop, 53, 105–6, 108; Lyric Opera of
Chicago, 113–14; as "man-city, healthy,
sweaty," 13, 112; Michigan Avenue, 106;
neighborhoods in, 107, 172; Oak Street
Beach, 105, 108; opera productions in,
113–18; Petrillo Bandshell, 111; Pure Oil
Building (Jewelers Building), 110; sailors
on leave in (1940s), 51; Carl Sandburg's
poems about, 105, 106, 107; John G. Shedd
Aquarium, 111; Skid-Row, 2, 11, 107, 150;
State Street, 106; Stevens Hotel (*see*
Hilton Chicago); Stratosphere Club, 110;
Tribune Tower, 107; University of Chicago,
171, 195; weightlifting competition in, 143;
Wrigley Building, 106. *See also* DePaul
University; Great Lakes Naval Training
Station; Loyola University Chicago;
Marshall Field's; Steward, Samuel: and
Chicago, Illinois
Chicago Daily News, 109
Chicago River, 106
Chillon, Chateau de, 185
Chopin, Frédéric, tomb of, in Père Lachaise,
101, 163
Churchill, Winston, 154
cipher, 7, 22–26, 56–57, 178; vs. code, 24; letter
frequency in, 24, 57; "rail-fence," 25; types
of, 24–25. *See also* code; cryptography
Clark University, 59
Clark University Archives and Special Collec-
tions, "The Sigmund Freud and Carl Jung
Lectures at Clark University," 226n1 (chap. 8)
clothing, men's: drabness of, 119–21; on Hal-
lowe'en, 119, 122, 125; history of, 121; in
Hollywood, 121; *IDJ* essay on, 119–26; and

jewelry, 126; military uniforms, 125; on
New Year's Eve, 119, 122; and role playing,
119–20, 123, 124. *See also* drag
Cocteau, Jean, *Le Grand Écart*, 74
code, 7, 23–24; vs. cipher, 24. *See also* cipher;
cryptography
Coleridge, Samuel Taylor, 91, 128; "motiveless
malignity," 19; "willing suspension of
disbelief," 114
cologne, 126
Columbus, Ohio, 27, 35, 77, 105; Benjamin
Musser, Steward meets, in, 108; Rudolph
Valentino, Steward visits hotel room of, 101,
223n4; WCTU rally, Steward attends, in,
137–38. *See also* Ohio State University, The
cooking: American, 47; history of, 45; medi-
eval, *IDJ* essay on, 45–50; wolf, instruc-
tions for cooking, 12, 49. *See also* Austin,
Thomas; Fisher, M. F. K.
Copacabana, 142
Cortesi, Arnaldo, "Argentines View Italy with
Calm," 23n
Coué, Émile, 60; Couéism, 60
"Cranford" (dachshund obituary), 82, 227n3
(chap. 11)
Cricket, Jiminy, 62
Cromwell, John, dir., *Algiers*, 189
Crouch, Tom D., *The Bishop's Boys*, 202n
cryptography, 4; in the ancient world, 22; ban
on books about, during wartime, 23–24;
definition of, 23; *IDJ* essay on, 21–26;
Steward's study of, 21, 225n5 (chap. 4);
Steward's teaching of, at Loyola University,
x, 21–22. *See also* Bacon, Francis; cipher;
code; Pratt, Fletcher
Culoz, 91
curfew. *See* World War II

dandy, gay implications of term, 121, 126
Daniel, Thomas M., *Pioneers of Medicine and
Their Impact on Tuberculosis*, 34n
Danilova, Alexandra, 70–71
d'Argenteuil, Héloïse, tomb of, in Père
Lachaise, 163
da Vinci, Leonardo, 121
Davis, Richard S., "Flagstad Sets Opera on
Fire," 228n3 (chap. 15)
Davis and Elkins College, 73
death, premature, *IDJ* essay on, 97–103
Defoe, Daniel, 76; *The Review*, 76; *The Shortest
Way with Dissenters*, 76

de León, Juan Ponce, 210

dentists: and Alcoholics Anonymous, 30; book recommendations for, by Steward, 222; as Iago, 18–19; *IDJ* essay about, 17–20; instruments used by, 1, 18, 20; as sadists, 1, 17, 19–20, 62; as Philip Sparrow's readers, ix, 1, 4, 8, 12, 13, 45, 90, 188, 194, 201; as subject of Steward's first seven *IDJ* essays, 1, 5, 17, 40

DePaulia, article about Steward in, 150, 229n4 (chap. 20)

DePaul University, ix, 2, 106; Steward fired by, 150–51, 230n5; Steward hired by, x, 150, 193; Steward's "Culture Corner" at, 150; Steward's sexual encounters with students at, 2, 223n4; Steward's unhappiness at, 150, 193, 205, 211; students at, 193. *See also* teaching

de Sade, Marquis, *Juliette*, 172

Diaghilev, Sergai, 67

di Corfu, Giorgio, "Flagstad, Uncut Act II Tristan," 228n4

Dietrich, Marlene, 25

Diogenes of Sinope, 82. *See also* Laertius, Diogenes

Doctor of Frustration, 94

dogs: burial of, in pet cemeteries, 84–86; Fala, 49. *See also* Stein, Gertrude: Basket; Stein, Gertrude: Pépé; Steward, Samuel: and dogs

Don Juan, 209

Douglas, Lord Alfred, 2, 161, 223n4

Dowson, Ernest, "Non Sum Qualis Eram Bonae Sub Regno Cynarae," 37

drag, 119

Drayton, Michael, *Idea*, 212

dreams, fragility of, *IDJ* essay on, 193–97

Drew, Daniel, 146

Dryden, John, *Secret Love, or The Maiden Queen*, 207

Duchamp, Marcel, 196

Duis, Perry: *Challenging Chicago*, 79n; "Great Lakes Naval Training Station," 226n1 (chap. 7)

Duke, Vernon, 162

Duncan, Isadora: death of, 100; and George Bernard Shaw, 147

Dunning, John, *On the Air*, 62n, 122n

Edward, Duke of Windsor, 130

Edwards, Cliff, 62

Elizabeth I, 75, 194

Ellis, Havelock: discovered by Steward as teenager, 110; *Studies in the Psychology of Sex*, 110

entrechat, 67

Eos, 2

espionage. *See* World War II

Evan, Taylor, "Sunbeam Mixmaster," 92n

Evanston, Illinois, 13, 112; alcohol ban in, 138; Alcoholics Anonymous, first Chicago-area meeting of, 138; WCTU headquarters in, 137

ex cathedra, 91

Fala. *See* dogs

Fallada, Hans, *Little Man, What Now?*, 222

FBI (Federal Bureau of Investigation), 52, 53, 55, 142

feather in hat, homosexual implications of, 121

Fibber McGee and Molly, 183

Fields, W. C. (William Claude Dukenfield), 83

Fisher, M. F. K.: *How to Cook a Wolf*, 12, 45, 226n1 (chap. 6); *Serve It Forth*, 45

FitzGerald, Edward, *The Rubaiyat of Omar Khayyam*, 99, 137, 159

Fitzgerald, Roy. *See* Hudson, Rock

Flagstad, Kirsten, 113

Flood, Michael, ed., *International Encyclopedia of Men and Masculinities*, 126n

Fokine, Michel, 67

food. *See* allergy; cooking; Fisher, M. F. K.; Toklas, Alice

Forman, Dr. Jonathan, 33, 35; Steward's allergies diagnosed by, 36–37

France, Anatole, *Penguin Island*, 162–63

Franks, Wilbur R., 56; Franks Flying Suit, 56

Freemasons. *See* Masons

Freud, Sigmund, 61, 110, 151; Clark University lectures by, 59; psychological complexes defined by, 151; on sadism, 19–20. *See also* Burnham, John; Clark University Archives and Special Collections; Manning, Philip; Skues, Richard

—works by: "An Autobiographical Study," 226n2 (chap. 8); *Five Lectures upon Psycho-Analysis*, 59; *Three Essays on the Theory of Sexuality*, 19

Fust, Johann, 217

Gaîté Parisienne (Massine), 65

Galiani, Ferdinando, 164

Galilei, Galileo, 60
Ganymede, 173
Gargantua, Chicago as, 13, 112
George IV, 76
Gestapo, 17, 20
GI Bill, 41
Gide, André, 161, 188, 193; open homosexu-
    ality of, 187; travels of in North Africa,
    187, 189; visited in Paris by Steward, 187.
    See also Steward, Samuel: sexual encoun-
    ters of
—works by: *Corydon*, 187; *Immoralist*, 12; *Les
    norritures terrestres* (*The Fruits of the Earth*),
    182; *Si le grain ne meurt* (*If It Die . . .*), 187,
    188, 189
glissade, 67
Godwin, William, *Political Justice*, 221
Goethe, Johann Wolfgang von, *Die Wahlver-
    wandtschaften* (*Elective Affinities*), 177–78
Gounod, Charles, *Faust*, 188
Graham, Anderson, Probst, and White, 113
Grant, Ulysses, 194
Gray, Thomas, "Elegy Written in a Country
    Churchyard," 38
Great Lakes Naval Training Station, 2, 21,
    51, 57
Greco-Turkish War of 1897, 170
Grey, Zane, 159
Grossman, James R., ed., *The Encyclopedia of
    Chicago*, 108n, 226n1 (chap. 7)
Gubbins, Nat, 63
Gutenberg, Johann, 217

Hagelin, Boris, 56. *See also* Type M-209
    Converter
Hamelin, Pied Piper of, 61
Harburg, Edgar Yipsel, 162
Hardy, Thomas, "On a Fine Morning," 194
Harleian: *MS. 279*, 45, 48; *MS. 4016*, 48
Harris, Daniel, 142; "A Psychohistory of the
    Homosexual Body," 229n1 (chap. 19)
Hartsdale Pet Cemetery, 81, 227n1 (chap. 11)
Hautecombe, Abbey of, 132
Heap, Chad, "Gays and Lesbians," 108n
Hecht, Ben: *Fantazius Mallare*, 110; *1001
    Afternoons in Chicago*, 109. *See also* Smith,
    Wallace
Hector, 170
Heidelberg University, 170
Heifetz, Jascha, 1, 18
Hells Angels, 2

Hemingway, Ernest, 128
Henley, William Ernest, "Invictus," 177
Henry, O. (William Sidney Porter), 77
Hercules, 64
Herman, Barbara, *Scent and Subversion*, 126n
Hermes, 173
Herodotus, *Histories*, 22
Hilaria: *IDJ* essay on, 175–80; Steward's god-
    dess of the absurd, 175
Hilton Chicago, 206
Hinsdale Animal Cemetery, 81, 83–87, *84*
Hiroshima, 202
Histiaeus, 22
Hitchcock, Alfred, 25
Hitler, Adolf, 52, 78
hoarding, and Steward, 181–82. *See also*
    keepsakes
Hoffman, Bob. *See* bodybuilding
Hoffman, Malvina, 111
Holmes, Oliver Wendell: *The Autocrat of
    the Breakfast-Table*, 164; "The Deacon's
    Masterpiece or, the Wonderful 'One-hoss
    Shay,'" 208
homosexuality. *See* Chicago, Illinois; Hous-
    man, A. E.; *Illinois Dental Journal* essays;
    navy; Steward, Samuel: sexual encoun-
    ters of
Housman, A. E.: Cambridge professorship of,
    97–99; death of, 97, 98, 99, 129; homo-
    sexuality of, 97–98; *IDJ* essay on, 97–103;
    influence of on Steward, 98; Moses
    Jackson, love for, 97; poetic themes of,
    97–99; Steward visits former Cambridge
    residence of, 98; as textual critic, 97, 99.
    See also Bowra, C. M.; Carter, John; Irwin,
    Michael
—works of: "The Application of Thought to
    Textual Criticism," 97; *Last Poems*, 99;
    More Poems, 99; "Poem 54," 98; *A Shrop-
    shire Lad*, 28, 97–98, 99; "Terrence, This
    Is Stupid Stuff," 28; "To an Athlete Dying
    Young," 98–103
Housman, Laurence, 99
Hudson, Rock (Roy Fitzgerald), 2, 156, 223n4
Hull, Cordell, 23
Hunt, Josephine P., 26
Hunt, Leigh, 76–77; *Autobiography*, 76; *The
    Examiner*, 76
Hurd, Clement, 90
Huston, John, dir., *The Treasure of the Sierra
    Madre*, 178

Huston, Walter, 178

Huxley, Aldous, *Brave New World*, 40, 46

Huysmans, Joris-Karl: *Against the Grain*, 119; *Là-Bas (Down There)*, 47

Iago (*Othello*), 1, 17–19

Ides (of March), 49

Iliad, 170

Illinois Dental Journal essays, Samuel Steward's: allusiveness of, 4; autobiographical elements of, 4, 7, 13; and essay tradition, 4, 13; homosexuality coded in, 4, 12–13, 45, 50, 63, 119, 121, 126, 140, 141–42, 188, 205; list of, 217–19; manuscripts of, xvii; page of, illustrated, 6; place of, in Steward's career, x, 15; plan of, 5; publication, obscurity of, ix, xi, 14–15; spoof of readers in, 10–11; Steward's personality revealed in, 14; Steward's satisfaction with, 14; style of, 4, 13–14; and Alice Toklas, 14, 211. *See also* Steward, Samuel: as Philip Sparrow

Illinois State Dental Society, ix; apologizes for Steward's final *IDJ* essay, 212; "A Resolution," 231n7; terminates Steward's *IDJ* essays, 212. *See also* racism

inferiority complex, 61, 62

Ingersoll Watch Company, 153

Irwin, Michael, introduction to *The Collected Poems of A. E. Housman*, 227n3 (chap. 13)

Jackson, Charles, description of alcoholism in *The Lost Weekend* by, 29, 32

James, Henry, Steward compared with, by *New York Times*, 175

James I, 75

Jim Crow, 166–67, 212, 214, 215

Joan of Arc, 102

Jordan, Jim and Marian, 183

Josephus, 197

Kaye, Danny, 197

Keats, John: death of, 100; *Endymion*, 86; "On First Looking into Chapman's Homer," 48

keepsakes, 4, 9, 134; *IDJ* essay on, 181–86; value of, 186. *See also* hoarding; Newman, John Henry

Kershaw, Ian, *Hitler*, 78n

Keynes, Geoffrey, ed., *The Note Book of William Blake Called the Rossetti Manuscript*, 183n. *See also* Blake, William

Kinsey, Alfred, 224n32, 224n35; Steward as contributor to research of, 15; Steward meets, x, 2; Steward sends *IDJ* essays to, 14; Steward writes about new Polaroid Land Camera to, 226n3 (chap. 7)

Kinsey Institute for Research in Sex, Gender, and Reproduction, x–xi

Kissack, Terence, ed., "Alfred Kinsey and Homosexuality in the '50s," 224n32

Kramer, Jack, 153

Kreis, Der, xi, 2; first article by Steward in, 176

Kreisler, Friedrich "Fritz," 1, 18

Ku Klux Klan, 122, 215

Laertius, Diogenes, *Lives of Eminent Philosophers*, 82. *See also* Diogenes of Sinope

Lamarr, Hedy, 189

Lamb, Charles, 76–77

Landor, Walter Savage, 179

Landsberg am Lech, 78

Larrabee, Harold A., "Faculty Failings; Or, A Professor Can't Win," 152n

Laurence, Dan H., ed., *Bernard Shaw*, 147n

Leacock, Stephen, "My Fishpond," 195

Le Dandy (cologne), 126

Leiter, Levi, 155, 158

Lewis, Sinclair, *Babbitt*, 52, 122

Lichine, David, 70

Lincoln, Abraham, 213

Locker-Lampson, Frederick, 99

Long, Harland William, *Sane Sex Life and Sane Sex Living*, 144

Long, Huey, 215, 216

Lovelace, Richard, "To Althea, from Prison," 74

Loyola University Chicago, 2, 34, 106; Steward hired by, 105, 149, 193; Steward's alcoholism while teaching at, 27; Steward's class schedule at, 196; Steward's cryptography course at, 21–22; Steward's leave of absence from, x, 135, 149, 155, 156; Steward's teaching load at, 73. *See also* teaching; Zabel, Morton Dauwen

Luce, Clare Boothe, 132–33

Luce, Henry Robinson, 132–33

Lydia Pinkham's Compound, 209

Lyly, John, *Euphues*, 120

lynching, 214, 215, 216

Lyric Opera of Chicago. *See* Chicago, Illinois

Lysander of Sparta, 22

macaroni, homosexual implications of term, 121

Mann, Thomas, 12, 161, 193; *Der Zauberberg* (*The Magic Mountain*), 184

Manning, Philip, 59; *Freud and American Sociology*, 226n1 (chap. 8)

Manteno State Hospital, 29

Marquis, Donald Robert Perry, 66

Marsh, Robert C., and Norman Pellegrini, *150 Years of Opera in Chicago*, 228n1 (chap. 15)

Marshall Field's (department store), x, 106; book department of, 155, 159; *IDJ* essay on, 155–60; Steward's holiday employment at, 8, 9, 155–60; Steward's sexual encounter with Roy Fitzgerald (Rock Hudson) in, 155–56, 223n4; training film (*By Jupiter*) produced by, 157

Martin, William H., and Sandra Mason, *The Art of Omar Khayyam*, 99n

Mason and Dixon line, 215

Masons, 119, 122

Massine, Léonide, 68

Mata Hari (Margaretha Geertruida Zelle), 25, 52

Maves, Carl, "Valentino's Pubic Hair and Me," 101n, 223n4

McLeod, Norman Z., dir., *The Secret Life of Walter Mitty*, 197

mental illness, pharmacological treatment of, in 1940s, 62–63

Metzger, Paul, "Jonathan Forman, MD," 225n1 (chap. 4)

Meung, 75

Meynell, Alice, 119, 125; *The Rhythm of Life and Other Essays*, 125

Michigan, Lake, 9, 105, 107, 108, 112

Miller, Henry, 73

Milton, John, *Areopagitica*, 221, 222

Minsky brothers, 68

Mitchell, S. Weir, 199, 200; "Idleness," 200

mixmaster. *See* Sunbeam Mixmaster

Molotov, Vyacheslav, 153

Moody, John, 146

moon, travel to, 203

Mozley, Anne, ed., *Letters and Correspondence of John Henry Newman*, 185n

Mr. America. *See* bodybuilding

muscles. *See* bodybuilding

Musser, Benjamin, 108

Mussolini, Benito, 130

Nagasaki, 202

Narcissus, 151; bodybuilders as, 143. *See also* bodybuilding

Nation, Carrie, 137

Nault, Fernand, 69, 70

navy, homosocial mythology of, 21. *See also* Steward, Samuel: navy career of; Steward, Samuel: sailors, sexual appeal of

neurasthenia, 62

Newman, John Henry: blue cloak of, 9, 182, 185–86; friends of, 186; as keepsaker, 185–86; Oxford, last visit to, 186; and Oxford Movement, 185; in Steward's PhD dissertation, 185; unhappy life of, 9, 182, 186. *See also* Mozley, Anne; St. John, Ambrose

Newton, Sir Isaac, 60

New Yorker, 90, 197, 200

New York Times, review of *Angels on the Bough* (Steward), 105, 175, 193

Nietzsche, Friedrich, *Ecce Homo*, 164

Nijinski, Vaslav, 67

Noah, 202

Nostradamus, 221

Nutcracker, The (Tchaikovsky), 65, 119

O'Connor, Richard, *O. Henry*, 77n

Odyssey, 169, 170

Oedipus complex, 61, 151

Ohio State University, The, 10, 33, 47, 169; Mirror Lake at, 195; Steward's PhD at, 2, 65, 149, 182, 185. *See also* Andrews, Clarence

Olympus, 95, 172

opera, 4, 62; *IDJ* essay on, 113–18; Metropolitan Opera (New York), productions in Chicago, 1946–54, 113; New York City Opera, productions in Chicago, 1946–54, 113. *See also* Chicago, Illinois: Civic Opera House; Chicago, Illinois: Lyric Opera of Chicago; Steward, Samuel: and opera

Orpheus, 173

Orson Welles Theater. See Welles, Orson

Oxford Companion to English Literature, 222

Paderewski, Ignacy Jan, 1, 18

Palmer, Potter, 155, 158

Paris (city), xi, 4, 25, 52, 75, 89–95, 101, 111, 127, 128, 185, 186; *IDJ* essay on, 161–67; spirit of, 164–66; spring in, 162–64; Steward meets Witold Pick in, 191; Steward's first trip to, 161; Steward visits Alice Toklas in, 120, 161–62, 165; studio photographs of Steward in, 120, 123; temperament of residents, 166–67

Paris (literary character), 170

Parran, Thomas, Jr., 71

Paul, Saint, 90

Pavlov, Ivan Petrovich, 202

Pechuman, W. F., *Alcohol, Is It a Medicine?*, 138n

Peck, Gregory, ix

Père Lachaise (cemetery), 101, 163

pet cemeteries, 4, 60, 81; *IDJ* essay on, 81–87.
    See also Hartsdale Pet Cemetery; Hinsdale
    Animal Cemetery

Pfeiffer, Karl G., 179

Pick, Witold, 191

Pillsbury, Charles Alfred, 146

Pinero, Arthur Wing, *The Princess and the
    Butterfly*, 166

Pinocchio, 62

Pitkin, Walter B., *Life Begins at Forty*, 207

Pliny the Elder (Gaius Plinius Secundus), 56

Plutarch, *Lysander*, 22

Polaroid Land Camera, 51, *54*, *55*, *124*, 226n3
    (chap. 7)

Pomazal, Grace. *See* bodybuilding: Miss
    Legionnaire

Pope, Alexander, *An Essay on Man*, 158

Porter, William Sidney. *See* Henry, O.

posttraumatic stress disorder (PTSD), 39. *See
    also* war, effects on soldiers

Potter, Miriam Clark, *Hello, Mrs. Goose*, 159

Prado Museum, 132

Pratt, Fletcher, *Secret and Urgent*, 22, 24, 26

prison, authors who wrote in, *IDJ* essay on, 73–79

Prohibition. *See* alcohol

Proust, Marcel, *Swann's Way*, 125

psychiatry, 4, 81; development of, 59–60; *IDJ*
    essay on, 59–64. *See also* American Medico-
    Psychological Association; American
    Psychiatric Association; Freud, Sigmund;
    mental illness

psychoanalysis, 59, 63, 110

psychology, 55, 59, 61

PTSD. *See* posttraumatic stress disorder

pussy, homosexual implications of term, 87

Pyle, Ernie, "The Death of Captain Waskow,"
    102. *See also* Waskow, Henry T.

Queensbury, Marquis of, 77

Rabelais, François, 5, 112, 171

Rachmaninoff, Sergei, 1, 18

racism: American South, in the, 211–16; *IDJ*
    essay on, 211–16; Steward as lifelong oppo-
nent of, 122, 166, 212; Steward's *IDJ* essay
    on, readers' objections to, 212; Steward's
    IDJ essays terminated because of essay on,
    212. *See also* Illinois State Dental Society;
    Jim Crow; lynching; South, American

radar, 53, 56

Raleigh, Sir Walter, *The History of the World*, 75

rationing. *See* World War II

Ray, Man, 196

Richmond, Virginia, 212

Richter, Hans, dir., *Dreams That Money Can
    Buy*, 196

Rimbaud, Arthur, 12, 163

Robert the Bruce, 43

Robinson, Edwin Arlington, "Miniver Cheevy,"
    195

Rockefeller, John D., 146

Rockne, Knute, 103

Rogers, Will, 103

Romberg, Sigmund, *The Student Prince*, 170

Roosevelt, Eleanor, 49

Roosevelt, Franklin, 103

Rose, Sir Francis, 2, 131

Ross, Clarence, 142

Rossetti, Dante Gabriel, 71

Rubaiyat of Omar Khayyam, The. *See* FitzGer-
    ald, Edward; Martin, William H.

Sabatini, Rafael, *Scaramouche*, 176

sabotage. *See* World War II

sailors. *See* Steward, Samuel: sailors, sexual
    appeal of

Saint-Saëns, Camille, *Samson and Delilah*, 117

Salve Regina, 86

Sandburg, Carl, *Chicago Poems*, 105–7

Scheherazade (Fokine), 65, 68, 118, 119

schizophrenia, 62

Schoen, William P., ix, 17, 211, 222; defends
    Steward's *IDJ* essay on racism, 212; initi-
    ates annual book-review issue of *IDJ*, 221;
    recruits Steward to write monthly essay,
    5; "Sparrow Brings Mail," 231n6; Steward
    writes *IDJ* notice posing as, 11, 217

Scott, Walter, *Saint Ronan's Well*, 207

Selective Service, 41, 53

Serutan, 209

Shakespeare, William, 1, 18, 19, 84, 121, 152,
    197; authorship of plays, 23

—works of: *Antony and Cleopatra*, 137; *Hamlet*,
    36, 151; *1 Henry IV*, 66; *King Lear*, 105;
    Love's Labours Lost, 142; *Macbeth*, 93; *The*

Merry Wives of Windsor, 60; *Othello*, 1, 18–19, 61, 180; *Romeo and Juliet*, 34; *The Tempest*, 40, 46; *Venus and Adonis*, 128
Shaw, George Bernard, and Isadora Duncan, 147
Shelley, Percy Bysshe, 197
"shell shock." *See* war, effects on soldiers
Simpson, Wallis, 130
Skelton, John, "The Book of Phillip Sparrow," 5
Skues, Richard, 59; "Clark Revisited," 226n3 (chap. 8)
Smith, Wallace, 110
Socrates, 173, 194, 207
Sodom, apples of, 197
soldiers. *See* war: effects on soldiers
South, American: *IDJ* essay on, 211–16; post–Civil War attitudes of, 212–16. *See also* racism
Spanish Civil War, 132
Sparrow, Phil (tattoo artist). *See* Steward, Samuel: as Phil Sparrow
Sparrow, Philip (essayist). *See* Steward, Samuel: as Philip Sparrow
Spengler, Oswald, *The Decline of the West*, 46–47, 78
Spring, Justin, xiii, 13
—works by: *An Obscene Diary*, 226n3 (chap. 7); *Secret Historian*, ix–xi, 2
Stalin, Joseph, 78
Stars and Stripes, 41
State College of Washington (Pullman), 179, 228n1 (chap. 14); Steward fired from, 105, 175
Stein, Gertrude, 3, 4, 8; on aging, 206, 208–9; on alcoholism among writers, 27, 131; *Angels on the Bough* (Steward), opinion of, 89; Basket (dog), 129, 165; as Brunnhilde, 91, 95; children's books by, rugs with illustrations from, 90; conversation of, 129; death of, x, 10, 14, 89, 128–29, 135, 161, 182, 193, 211; *IDJ* essays on, 89–95, 127–34; letters to Steward from, 2, 133; memoir of, by Steward, 89; as "modernist public figure," 227n2 (chap. 12); papers of, donated to Yale, 133; Pépé (dog), 10, 129, *132*, 133; Père Lachaise, buried in, 163; photographs of, by Steward, *130*, *131*; "Pigeons on the grass, alas!," 128; "Rose is a rose is a rose is a rose," 128; Steward's alcoholism recognized by, 27; Steward's correspondence with, 10, 89, 127–28, 129;

Steward sends Sunbeam Mixmaster to, 92, 94; Steward's friendship with, x, 2, 8, 14, 89–90, 182, 193; as Steward's mentor, 73; Steward studies works of at Ohio State, 89, 127; Steward telephones, in France, 93–95; Steward visits, in France, 33, 89, 91, 127–28, 161, 187, 206; as Valkyrie, 91, 95, 131. *See also* Bilignin; Sunbeam Mixmaster; Toklas, Alice
—works by: "As a Wife Has a Cow," 127; *The Autobiography of Alice B. Toklas*, 90, 227n2 (chap. 12); *A Long Gay Book*, 206; *Matisse Picasso and Gertrude Stein*, 206, 208; *The World Is Round*, 90
Stephan, Alan. *See* bodybuilding: Mr. America (1946)
Sternberg, Josef von, dir., *Dishonored*, 25
Steward, Samuel: *Advocate*, contributor to, 2; *Amigo*, contributor to, 2; Berkeley, California, residence in, 2, 81, 106, 181; book-review columns in *IDJ* by, 5, 11, 211, 224n24; Compton's Encyclopedia, employed at, 175; cryptographic study by (*see* cryptography); DePaul University, professor at (*see* DePaul University); "detachment" as life philosophy of, 176; disappointments in life, 175, 182, 193–94; *Eos*, contributor to, 2; first tattoo of, 65; fortieth birthday of, 199, 205–10; and André Gide (*see* Gide, André); hoarding tendencies of, 181–82, 184–85, 186; identities of, multiple, 15, 53, 175; and Alfred Kinsey (*see* Kinsey, Alfred); *Der Kreis*, contributor to, xi, 2, 176; Loyola University, professor at (*see* Loyola University Chicago); masochism, predilection for, 5, 14, 156, 186; navy career of, x, 21, 33–34, 51, 53, 119, 225n5 (chap. 4); photographs of Gertrude Stein by, *130*, *131*; pseudonyms of, 15, 175; resilience of, 151, 175, 230n5; risk-taking, delight in, 11–12; sailors, sexual appeal of, 21, 51 (*see also* Steward, Samuel: sexual encounters of); and Gertrude Stein (*see* Stein, Gertrude); Stud File (*see* Steward, Samuel: sexual encounters of); suicide attempt, 135–36; teacher, popularity as, 22, 150, 222 (*see also* teaching); and Alice Toklas (*see* Toklas, Alice); and Thornton Wilder (*see* Wilder, Thornton); World Book Encyclopedia, employed as writer/editor at, x, 156, 175. *See also*

Steward, Samuel (*continued*)
Andrews, Clarence; Anthony, Dr. Stephen; Bilignin; Ellis, Havelock; Housman, A. E.; Marshall Field's; Newman, John Henry; Ohio State University, The; Paris; racism; Schoen, William P.; State College of Washington; Women's Christian Temperance Union; Zenouhin, Mohammed
—alcoholism of, x, 27–28, 29, 74, 135, 169, 182, 193, 208; recognized by Gertrude Stein, 27; relapse in 1948, 175. *See also* alcohol; Alcoholics Anonymous
—allergies of: diagnosed, 36–37; *IDJ* essay on, 33–38; Steward discharged from navy because of, x, 21, 33–34, 51, 53; Steward outgrows, 34; Steward's diet because of, 34, 37
—as Phil Andros (pornographer), xi, 2, 14, 15, 175; *The Boys in Blue*, 108
—and ballet: Steward's "balletomania," 12, 65–71, 118, 155; Steward's love of, 65–68; Steward's roles as super in performances of, 65, 68–71, 119
—and Chicago, Illinois: initially repelled by, 105–6; love of, 111–12; mugged in, 111; opportunities for sexual encounters in, 11, 105, 108; Steward's apartments in, 51, 54, 55, 108, 181, 182. *See also* Chicago, Illinois
—and clothing: appeal of, in Catholic liturgy, 119; navy uniform, 21, 51, 119; and role playing, 119–20; studio portraits of Steward in costume, 120, *123*, *124*; as super in ballet and opera productions, 119. *See also* clothing, men's
—and dogs: with Stein and Toklas's dog Basket II, *165*; with Stein and Toklas's dog Pépé, *132*; Steward's, 81–82, *85*, 181
—and opera: attitude toward, 114; "curtain boy" in Chicago productions, 114; "super" in Chicago productions, x, 113, 116–18
—photographs of: with dachshund, *85*; as DePaul University professor, *150*; in late 1940s, *3*; as sailor, *124*; with Stein and Toklas's dog Pépé, *132*; as street tough, *123*; with Toklas, *165*
—sexual encounters of, x, 74, 182, 193, 223n4; with ballet dancers, 65–66, 70; card-file record of ("Stud File"), xi, 2, 4, 14, 51, 70, 223n5; in Chicago, 105, 108; with DePaul students, 2; with dominant men, 50; with Lord Alfred Douglas, 2; with André

Gide's houseboy, 187; with his high-school basketball team, 2; with Rock Hudson, 2, 155–56; with Benjamin Musser, 108; with Fernand Nault, 70; with sailors, x, 2, 51, 54–55; with Jimmy Taylor, 169; total number of, 2; with Rudolph Valentino, 2, 101; with Thornton Wilder, ix, 206; with Mohammed Zenouhin, 190
—as Phil Sparrow (tattoo artist), x, 2, 175; Chicago tattoo business of, 107, 150–51; Hells Angels, tattoo artist for, 2
—as Philip Sparrow (essayist), 1, 2, 5, 211; debut in *IDJ*, 1, 17; as dental patient, 5, 17–18; and essay tradition, 4, 13; homosexuality of, suggested, 4, 12–13, 15, 50; personality of Steward reflected in, 14; persona of, xi, 4, 10–11, 17, 21, 60; readers, relationship with, 8, 10–11, 13, 40; roles of, in *IDJ* essays, 7–8, 10–11; voices of, 7–10, 13. See also *Illinois Dental Journal* essays: homosexuality coded in
—works by: *Angels on the Bough*, ix, 5, 73, 89, 105, 175; *The Boys in Blue*, 108; *Chapters from an Autobiography*, 14; "Holograph Travel Diary, 1950," 229n2 (chap. 22); "A Journal of a Tattoo Artist," 224n26, 229n7, 230n5; list of, 2–3; *Pan and the Firebird*, 108; *Parisian Lives*, 14, 131; "Toilet Correspondence," x; unfinished novels, 73. See also *Illinois Dental Journal* essays
St. John, Ambrose, and John Henry Newman, 186
Storni, Segundo, 23
Stowe, Harrriet Beecher, *Uncle Tom's Cabin*, 221
Strachey, James, ed., *The Standard Edition of the Complete Psychological Works of Sigmund Freud*, 226n2 (chap. 8)
Strategic Services, Office of, 55
Strauss, Johann, Jr., *Blue Danube*, 67
Strength and Health. See bodybuilding
"Stud File." *See* Steward, Samuel: sexual encounters of
Suetonius, *The Life of Julius Caesar*, 22
Sullivan, Louis, 106
Sunbeam Mixmaster, 92, 94
Svanholm, Set, 113
Swift, Jonathan, 211

Taylor, Jimmy, 169, 229n1 (chap. 23)
Taylor, Robert, 63

Tchaikovsky, Pyotr Ilyich, *Swan Lake*, 70
teaching: as acting, 152; *IDJ* essay on, 149–54; stupidity of most students, 151–52. *See also* Larrabee, Harold A.
—Steward's attitudes toward: at Carroll College, 27; at DePaul University, 150–51, 193; at Loyola University, 149
telephone, 83, 90, 199, 201–2; Steward telephones Stein in Paris, 93–95
Tennyson, Alfred, 99, 129; "Ulysses," 169
Tennyson, Hallam, *Alfred Lord Tennyson*, 99n
testosterone propionate, 75, 209
Thackeray, William Makepeace, "The Age of Wisdom," 206
Thalia, 176
Thomas, Theodore, 111
Thurber, James, "The Secret Life of Walter Mitty," 197
time: conceptions of, *IDJ* essay on, 199–203; invention of, 200–201; as money, 201; "saving" of, 199, 201–2; as tyrant, 200
Time (magazine), 39, 40–41
Toklas, Alice: death of, 162; food prepared by, 33, 130, 132; Père Lachaise, buried in, 163; photograph of, with Steward, *165*; "spriteliness" of, 129; Stein's papers donated to Yale University by, 133; Steward encouraged to write by, 205, 211; and Steward's alcoholism, 27, 34; Steward's friendship with, 89–90, 127–28, 161–62; Steward's *IDJ* essays read by, 14, 211; Steward's memoir of, 2, 89; Sunbeam Mixmaster bowl dropped by, 92. *See also* Stein, Gertrude
Toynbee, Arnold Joseph, 159
Trovets, 40
Truman, Harry: addresses NAACP, 213; civil rights initiatives of, 213; desegregation orders of, 213
Type M-209 Converter, 56. *See also* Hagelin, Boris

Valentino, Rudolph, 2; death of, 101–2; films by, 102; pubic hair of, saved by Steward, 11, 101. *See also* Maves, Carl
Valhallah, 78
Valkyrie. *See* Stein, Gertrude
Van Dyke, Henry, "America for Me," 162
Verdi, Giuseppe: *Aida*, 115; *La Traviata*, 117
Verlaine, Paul-Marie, 163
Verulam, Lord. *See* Bacon, Francis

Vestal virgins, bodybuilders as, 143. *See also* bodybuilding
Veterans' Administration, 41
Villon, François, 71, 74–75, 79
—works by: "Ballade des dames du temps jadis," 71; "Ballade of the Hanged Ones," 75; "Song for My Mother," 75; "Where are the snows of yesteryear?," 75

Wagner, Richard, 78, 91, 113, 114, 115
—works by: *Lohengrin*, 115; *Tristan and Isolde*, 113; *Der Ring des Nibelungen*, 78, 91, 114
Walpole, Horace, 177
war, effects on soldiers: camaraderie created by, 42; history of, 39; *IDJ* essay on, 39–44; and posttraumatic stress disorder, 39; and "shell shock," 39, 225–26n1 (chap. 5); veterans vs. civilians, 39–44. *See also* Woolf, Virginia: *Mrs. Dalloway*
War Department, 53, 57
War Information, Office of, 52, 53
War Manpower Commission, 41
Washington, DC, 55, 65, 66
Washington, George, 194
Washington, State College of. *See* State College of Washington
Washington Naval Conference, 26
Waskow, Henry T., 102
weightlifting. *See* bodybuilding
Welles, Orson, 25, 62; *Orson Welles Theater*, 62
Wells, H. G., 221
Wendt, Lloyd, and Herman Kogan, *Give the Lady What She Wants!*, 229n1 (chap. 21)
Wheatstone, Charles, 57; Wheatstone principle, 57
Wilde, Oscar, 12, 62, 79, 164; as "dandy," 126; tomb of, in Père Lachaise, 163; trial and imprisonment of, 77, 97
—works by: "Ballad of Reading Gaol," 77; *De Profundis*, 77; *Picture of Dorian Gray*, 62, 208; *A Woman of No Importance*, 164
Wilder, Billy, 25, 29
Wilder, Thornton, ix, 193, 206, 208–9; Gertrude Stein, friendship with, 128; Steward, friendship with, x, 2; Steward meets, 161, 206. *See also* Steward, Samuel: sexual encounters of
Willard, Frances, 137, 138, 139
Williams, Michael, xiii, 181
Wilson, Sarah, *Melting-Pot Modernism*, 227n2 (chap. 12)

Winchell, Walter, 22

Wise, Margaret, *The Sleepy Little Lion*, 159

wolf: gay implications of term, 50; instructions for cooking, 49

Wolfe, Thomas, *Look Homeward, Angel*, 71

Women's Christian Temperance Union, 4, 60; founding of, in 1874, 135; *IDJ* essay on, 135–40; songs of, 136, 138–40; Steward's attitude toward, 138. *See also* Nation, Carrie; Willard, Frances

Woodsfield, Ohio, 109, 110, 122

Woolf, Virginia: *Mrs. Dalloway*, 225–26n1 (chap. 5); Steward compared with, by *New York Times*, 175

Wordsworth, William, 100; "Three Years She Grew in Sun and Shower," 51

World War II, 202; Argentina's neutrality in, 23; curfew during, 50; death toll in, 78; espionage during, *IDJ* essay on, 51–57; rationing during, 45–47; sabotage during, 52, 57; soldiers returning from, psychological state of, 39–44

Wotan, 78, 91

Wright brothers, 202; Orville Wright, 202

Yankee Doodle, 121. *See also* feather in hat; macaroni

Yardley, Herbert Osborne, 26

Yon, Pietro, 1, 18

Young, Edward, *The Complaint*, 209n

Young, Stanley, "Trouble in Academe" (review of *Angels on the Bough*), 230n2 (chap. 24)

Zabel, Morton Dauwen, 149

Zenouhin, Mohammed: *IDJ* essay on, 187–92; philosophy of, 191; poisoned by father, 191–92; sexuality of, 188, 191–92; as Steward's guide in Algiers, 189–91. *See also* Steward, Samuel: sexual encounters of

Zivic, Fritzie, 153